MASCULINITY AND ITALIAN CINEMA

To Martin and Bjarne

MASCULINITY AND ITALIAN CINEMA

Sexual Politics, Social Conflict and Male Crisis in the 1970s

Sergio Rigoletto

EDINBURGH
University Press

© Sergio Rigoletto, 2014

Edinburgh University Press Ltd
The Tun – Holyrood Road
12(2f) Jackson's Entry
Edinburgh EH8 8PJ
www.euppublishing.com

Typeset in 10/12.5 pt Sabon by
Servis Filmsetting Ltd, Stockport, Cheshire,
and printed and bound in Great Britain by
CPI Group (UK) Ltd, Croydon CR0 4YY

A CIP record for this book is available from the British Library

ISBN 978 0 7486 5454 3 (hardback)
ISBN 978 0 7486 5455 0 (webready PDF)

The right of Sergio Rigoletto to be identified as
Author of this work has been asserted in accordance
with the Copyright, Designs and Patents Act 1988,
and the Copyright and Related Rights Regulations
2003 (SI No. 2498).

CONTENTS

ACKNOWLEDGEMENTS

I owe Massimo Sturiale and Lynne Segal a big thank you for believing in me and for supporting me so generously and enthusiastically when I expressed my desire to embark on a PhD. As a graduate student at the University of Reading, I was extremely lucky to work under the supervision of Christopher Wagstaff. I am particularly grateful to him for his persistence in pushing me for 'more'. His criticism has always been challenging and provides a constant source of intellectual nourishment. At Reading, Daniela La Penna and Paola Nasti were two amazing intellectual interlocutors. During these years, they also became two real friends. At the University of Oregon, I found the ideal conditions to complete this book, and a circle of wonderful colleagues who have made me feel at home since the very first day. I wish in particular to thank Kathleen Karlyn, Katharina Loew, Roger Grant and Amanda Doxtater for their friendship and for the occasions on which they have shown interest in this project. Many thanks also to Amalia Gladhart and Michael Aronson for granting some time off teaching when it was most needed. During my time at the University of Oregon, I have encountered a number of colleagues whose integrity, intellectual rigour and sense of collegiality have been a constant source of inspiration to me. I would especially like to thank my colleagues in Romance Languages and in particular Nathalie Hester, Massimo Lollini, Gina Psaki, Fabienne Moore and Robert Davis. Thanks also to Michael Allan and Rocio Zambrana for their friendship. My London-based friends were there for me from the very beginning. During the last few years, Marcella De Marco has been a selfless, generous friend. Her love and support kept me going when I was feeling most uncertain about my ability to complete this project. Thanks to Piero Toto for being such a great listener and for having been a dear friend during the last few years. Tiziana Mancinelli has changed my life in ways that I cannot possibly describe. With her courage and passion for life, she has taught me many important lessons. Special thanks go to Silvia Nutini and Serena Giudice for their love and encouragement, and for being constantly present in my life despite the physical distance that has separated us over the last ten years. Thank you also to my family for their support and love.

As well as funding my doctoral studies, the Arts and Humanities Research Council provided a bursary to undertake archival work in Italy. A Junior Professorship Development Award granted by the University of Oregon enabled me to complete this project.

I would like to thank the following people for suggesting and providing material, for offering their expertise and for giving invaluable advice: Sandro Davanzo, Ernaldo Data, Christopher Duggan, John David Rhodes, Michael Lawrence, Richard Dyer, Alex Marlow-Mann, Alan O'Leary, Sofia Serenelli and staff at the British Film Institute Library in London, the Cineteca di Bologna, the Museo del Cinema di Torino, Milan Arcigay archive and the Cassero Lesbian, Gay, Bisexual and Transgender Centre in Bologna. I am particularly indebted to Christopher Wagstaff, Alex Marlow-Mann and Giovanni Rigoletto for allowing me to access films from their collections. A number of people read drafts of my work and gave useful feedback at various stages: Louis Bayman, Danielle Hipkins, Dominic Holdaway, Daniela La Penna, Tiziana Mancinelli, Paola Nasti and Marc Schachter. Their comments have proved invaluable for the development of the project and have helped me shape and better articulate many of the ideas expressed herein. I owe a big thank you too to my editor at Edinburgh University Press, Gillian Leslie, who has been extremely helpful, supportive and understanding since the early stages of the project.

Finally, my deepest thanks are owed to Martin, who has read parts of this manuscript, provided excellent feedback and offered his editing talents. During the last few years, he has enriched my life in many ways. Without his patience, encouragement and love, this would have been a much less enjoyable journey.

Chapter 3 was published, in revised form, in *Italian Studies*, 67:1, 2012, pp. 124–46. A section of Chapter 4 appeared in *Popular Italian Cinema*, Louis Bayman and Sergio Rigoletto (eds) (Basingstoke: Palgrave, 2013). I thank the editors for granting permission to reprint these materials here.

LIST OF FIGURES

1. INTRODUCTION

This book is about a particular moment in the history of Italian cinema when the understanding of what it is to be a man undergoes a radical redefinition. Much has been written about experiences of male disempowerment and vulnerability in film, the emphasis of this scholarship invariably being either on representations of scarred, damaged male bodies or on accounts of male suffering and loss. Less has been written about the opportunities that cinema provides for considering masculinity in relation to an experience of transformation. It is not just that change, with its complexities and contradictions, is difficult to locate and observe.[1] The problem is how the idea of change itself seems to raise immediate suspicion, if not blatant pessimism. Paul Powrie, Ann Davies and Bruce Babington, for example, have argued that the image of a new, transformed cinematic man, beyond the oppressive constraints of patriarchy, may merely represent 'a repositioning or realignment with patriarchal power structures'.[2] Accepting the meaning of change as 'the process of becoming something different', one could argue that in studies of masculinity in film too much attention has been paid to considerations about the expected end result (a fully formed new masculinity), rather than to the intricacies of the very *process of becoming* something different. To consider change does not necessarily mean looking at where this change has already run its course. It also makes sense to pay attention to the points where the change appears less than smooth and where walls hampering the possibility for further transformation spring up. Equally, it may be worth considering the spaces of desire where change has not yet occurred. This is where unfulfilled possibilities for transformation appear most visible and where the potential for *becoming something different* may be most promising.

Masculinity and Italian Cinema examines one of the most complex and, oddly, under-examined periods in the history of Italian cinema. The 1970s were a decade of innovation and challenging work for Italian filmmakers, one that was marked by radicalism and heated debates about the function of cinema as a political medium and as a mass cultural phenomenon.[3] During these years, Italian cinema experienced a proliferation of sexualised images as never before. Sex emerged as a matter of public concern, as something that needed to be shown and discussed. *Masculinity and Italian Cinema* will show that, in this context, a wide-ranging interrogation of masculinity also took place, with a number of films beginning to question the definitional boundaries demarcating a socially acceptable male identity and the exclusions inevitably produced by such boundaries.

* * *

A man sits with his back to the camera. He slowly turns his head towards us. His gaze is sustained, tense, inquisitive. He seems frightened. The man stares into the darkness. His gaze seems to convey a desire for knowledge, for self-knowledge. The man seems transfixed. His gaze appears to be both reaching out and blocked, the bars that separate his body from the camera partly hampering his search of the darkness. In staring at the camera, the man involves us in his search. It is a gaze for which there seems to be no distinct object other than the subject looking, the camera operating like a mirror, turning the gaze back on to itself.

This closing shot from *The Conformist* (*Il conformista*: 1970), featured on the cover of this book and which I have just described, exemplifies the predicament of masculinity in the Italian cinema of the 1970s. It is the predicament of a man who is forced to look at himself, to confront his insecurities and face a set of circumstances that demand a move towards introspection on his part. As he looks back towards us, the man faces the desires that he has tried to disavow throughout the film. In confronting these desires, the man is also confronting himself, his limits. It is a kind of confrontation that occurs repeatedly in the Italian cinema of the 1970s. Such a confrontation implies the questioning of a set of blockages. Like the bars obstructing the man's inquisitive look, this questioning may not be able to transcend a set of pre-existing limits, but points towards the possibility of pushing them outwards and renegotiating their constraining power.

This man appears to be both daunted and forced towards self-analysis. Scriptwriter Bernardo Zapponi, who collaborated with Federico Fellini on one of the films that best explored this predicament, *City of Women* (*La città delle donne*: 1980), describes the situation of this man in the following terms: 'it was the period of feminism, women appeared with a new threatening face; as a result, men felt somehow bewildered.'[4] Zapponi's comments point to the image of an unsettled man, one who now faces a set of new challenges. His words reflect the predicament of a number of men involved in consciousness-raising practices during these years. In a collective memoir entitled *L'antimaschio*, one of these men describes the impact of feminism for his generation as one of traumatic confrontation with one's insecurities and previously unquestioned privileges.[5] As I will be arguing in this book, far from being simply fraught with anxieties, this predicament also points to the possibility of re-imagining one's masculinity in new ways. Writing on the pages of a leftist magazine in 1969, one of these men declares: 'we will have to rethink the whole way of being men, [. . .] so that we might feel free from all the obligations coming from our privilege [. . .] and from that particular kind of slavery that stems from being masters.'[6] Predicated on an implicit critique of what masculinity has historically been, this rethinking points to the possibility of change and of envisaging alternative ways of being a man.[7]

The Conformist explores the dilemmas of its male protagonist by making use of the classical Oedipal narrative, thus dramatising the internal conflict experienced by the protagonist in the form of a symbolic struggle between father and son. The father stands in the film for repression and the presence of one inevitable path leading to the acquisition of a stable male heterosexual identity. The son stands for the potential to imagine other possibilities, a potential charged with the desire to break free from a singular, univocal path. In its most conventional articulation, the Oedipal plot describes a deterministic journey, one in which the only possible outcome is the intervention of repression. In the conventional psychoanalytic account, the conflict between father and son ends with the latter bowing to the authority of the former, endorsing his repressive regime and following in his steps. *The Conformist* initially adopts this fairly linear narrative and its deterministic logic. But the film also twists the linear succession of narrative components and creates an elliptical structure with the superimposition of flashbacks that appear to disturb the linear progression of the story. These disturbances reflect the psychosexual conflict experienced by the protagonist, and the impossible resolution of the conflict. Throughout the film, the protagonist strives to repress his homosexual instincts and the memories of an earlier erotic experience with an older man in order to achieve a sense of normality. Exemplified by the unexpected re-emergence of these unwanted memories, the 'repressed', however, returns to haunt the protagonist at the end of the film. As the conflict of the protagonist remains unresolved, an alternative space of libidinal possibilities becomes visible.

It is this conflict between the singular and the plural – between the narrowing down of knowledge and the proliferation of a multitude of knowledges – that interests me about the predicament of masculinity in the Italian cinema of the

1970s. It is a tension between, on the one hand, conventions that constrain the way in which masculinity may be envisaged and, on the other, an underlying thrust to disrupt the operating mechanism of these conventions and to widen the meaning of this gender experience. This is a dynamic, productive tension, I would argue, one that is constraining as much as it is enabling. It points to the power of these conventions to validate a set of norms, whilst simultaneously allowing the possibility of resistance to these norms and of acknowledging the exclusions that such norms produce. In *The Conformist*, these conventions follow the archetypal Oedipal story. Functioning like blockages, such conventions are regulative: they constrain and impose a set of necessary steps in the development of the story. Yet, they are also constitutive: that is, they determine what is possible within the story, what is to be shown and how it is to be shown. This book examines the predicament of masculinity in the Italian cinema of the 1970s by considering both the constraining and the constitutive power of the conventions regulating its representation.

Blocked, apparently unable to take action, the man who appears in the last shot of *The Conformist* is a far cry from the model of masculinity revolving around notions of control, mastery and power that some of the early scholarship on men in films theorised in the 1970s and 1980s. Unlike the insecure look of the man that turns to stare at the camera in *The Conformist*, the male look defined by this earlier scholarship was one that projected its controlling fantasies on carefully styled objects of desire. This was a man that enjoyed a considerable degree of control and mastery also at the level of the narrative through his active role in making things happen and his ability to push the story forwards.[8] In the last twenty years, the paradigm for thinking about masculinity in films has shifted somewhat. A wealth of recent scholarship has focused on images of men who, far from being in control and unshakeable in their position of mastery, appear damaged, fragile and unstable.[9] In a number of instances, the challenge has been for scholars to show that the earlier model of male mastery and control was not so monolithic and resolute after all, but was always already wounded and provisional in its display of self-control and power.[10] In one of the first pieces of scholarship marking this shift, Pam Cook considers the male protagonist of *Raging Bull* (1980) as axiomatic of a kind of masculinity put into crisis in the context of New Hollywood cinema. Cook discusses a sense of 'collapse into impotence' that seems to affect the protagonist's experience of being male, an experience that Cook describes as marked by a sense of suffering and loss.[11]

Images of vulnerable, passive men feature prominently in Italian cinema throughout much of the post-war period. Explorations of inadequate male subjects appear in many Neorealist films and melodramas of the late 1940s and 1950s. Similarly, in the *comedies Italian-style* of the 1950s and 1960s, male prowess and sexual vigour, previously celebrated by the propaganda films of the fascist period and so central to the representation of masculinity in Hollywood cinema, are frequently ridiculed as untenable for Italian men. Unsurprisingly, the idea of a crisis in masculinity has become one of the master narratives of Italian film criticism.[12] Ruth Ben Ghiat, for example, has discussed the impact of military defeat on the unglamorous models of masculinity that appear in two films of the post-war period, *Come persi la guerra* (1947) and *The Bandit* (*Il bandito*: 1946). Ben Ghiat argues that the disempowered men of these films exemplify a move away from the ideal of virility previously validated by films of the fascist period; in the years of post-war reconstruction this ideal had to be rejected in favour of a new experience of masculinity that absorbed both the sense of emasculation experienced by Italian men at the end of World War 2 and the sense of guilt for crimes committed in the name of the now-discredited ideology of fascist militarism.[13] Jamie Fisher has examined the father figures that appear in a number of Neorealist films, including *Bicycle Thieves* (*Ladri di biciclette*: 1948) and *Shoeshine* (*Sciuscià*: 1946), arguing that, as a result of their precarious socioeconomic status, they persistently fail in their role as providers for their families, and embrace lack and inadequacy as structuring conditions of their masculinity.[14] In the most extensive study of masculinity in the Italian cinema of the post-war period, Jacqueline Reich argues that, as the figure of the disempowered Italian man, the *inept* constitutes the most prominent male type in Italian cinema. For her, the *inept* is a striking reminder of the difficulties with which Italian men lived the social and political transformations at the end of World War 2 and, particularly, the changing role of women.[15]

Film scholarship has suggested – over-enthusiastically, I would contend – that, in Italian cinema, masculinity has been in an on-going state of crisis for a very long time and remains even more so after the end of World War 2 and with the rise of feminism. This approach tends to cast on images of men those attributes traditionally imposed on female representations – vulnerability, fragility and so on. Jacqueline Reich argues that 'the [*inept*] articulates the traditional binary opposite of the masculine, as it is constructed in Italian culture and society, and as it relates to sexuality: the cuckold, the impotent and feminized man.'[16] In arguing that the shortcomings of this cinematic man are in opposition to the prescribed hyper-masculine characteristics of the traditional male hero, Reich encompasses within this typology a rather varied spectrum of male figures ranging from the impotent – as in *Il bell'Antonio* (1960) – to the homosexual – as in *A Special Day* (*Una giornata particolare*: 1977). The shortcomings of this approach become especially visible, I would suggest, when Reich discusses the male protagonist of *A Special Day*. Here, she looks in particular at the climactic sex scene between the homosexual character played by Marcello Mastroianni and the female protagonist played by Sophia Loren. Reich describes the way she seduces him and 'assumes the traditionally masculine position of the sexual act'.[17] She concludes by saying that '[t]he homosexual, although heterosexually competent, remains the sexual [*inept*] in traditionally masculine terms, dominated by the woman on top'.[18] Regrettably, Reich's reading clings too closely to the homophobic logic that would define the protagonist as unmasculine precisely because of his homosexuality. Reich is careful in arguing that he is a 'sexual [*inept*] in traditionally masculine terms', yet it is not clear how this character should be understood beyond those terms, or at least this is not openly stated.

My criticism of Reich's approach should not be taken as a dismissal of her informed study but as an opportunity for pointing to the binary logic underlying the way in which the axiom of masculinity in crisis in Italian cinema is predominantly framed.[19] Such an approach to the study of masculinity sets a normative male ideal in relation to which cinematic representations of men are to be measured. The ideal is persistently heterosexual, heroic, virile, predatory and aggressive. The ability of the cinematic representations to incarnate this ideal fully constitutes the yardstick for the 'failure' of the male characters and their inevitable casting as inept, woman-like and emasculated figures. As a result, the disempowered male subject of Italian cinema often seems to be defined as 'unmasculine' precisely under the terms of the hetero-patriarchal framework that contributes to producing the masculine–unmasculine binary in the first place. Such a framework appears hardly challenged and the derogatory connotations traditionally attached to male vulnerability, passivity and fragility remain similarly unquestioned.

As I will show in this book, the Italian cinema of the 1970s offers especially productive ways of complicating this normative framework. Several films made during this period critically, and often polemically, address the meaning of an experience of masculinity defined by patriarchy and by the dictates of hetero-normativity. This is evident, for example, in those films that look at male homosexuality as a central concern – see my discussion of *La patata bollente* (1979), *A Special Day* and *Scusi lei è normale?* (1979) in Chapter 4. In exploring the oppressive constraints of a society that stigmatises men who do not live a normative sexuality (and implicitly the right kind of masculinity), these films attempt to validate dissident male experiences traditionally excluded from the domain of the 'normal'.

This is not to say that the Italian cinema of the 1970s unproblematically envisages more pluralistic and non-oppressive constructions of masculinity. Indeed, one of the objectives of this book is to discuss some of the difficulties in 'regendering' masculinity and disconnecting it from its customary assertion of authority, privilege and exclusion. Another objective is to show that the paradigm of a crisis in masculinity does not fully account for the historical specificity of the predicament of men explored by Italian cinema during the 1970s. In questioning the notion of male crisis, this book will argue that something more complex and, potentially, more radical happens in the 1970s: namely, a wide-ranging interrogation of what it means to be a man and a redefinition of the terms under which masculinity may be understood and experienced.

Such a redefinition does not transcend a set of perceived constraints and limits. The result is a dialectic of conflict, one that underlies and structures the dilemmas of masculinity in the Italian cinemà of the 1970s. The conflict is manifest through, on the one hand, a set of blockages hampering the possibility of change and, on the other, the awareness that such change is necessary, if not inevitable. Two different temporalities are at play here: a past of certainties, comforts and authority and a present/future that appears mysterious, disorienting, even threatening, while also offering opportunities for renewal.

This book examines the predicament of masculinity in the Italian cinema of the 1970s within this particular tension. The Italian cinema of the 1970s finds it hard not to look at masculinity beyond an experience of power, repression and authority. Yet, a number of films of this period also appear to be interested in exploring the direct ramifications of this experience and its points of crisis. These films also shed light on mechanisms of gender exclusion and oppression, and expose to critique those institutions through which such mechanisms seem to be sustained and reinforced. In so doing, they also show a direct critical engagement with some of the cinematic codes traditionally involved in the construction of normative ideas about masculinity.

* * *

Existing film histories refer to the 1970s as a period of crisis for Italian cinema. Film critic Lino Micciché describes 'a stagnant bog where lazy steersmen, sitting on mouldering boats, await with little conviction, the arrival of the tide that will shift the foul, slimy waters'.[20] Making a similar point in a more restrained but no less evocative style, Gian Piero Brunetta asserts that 'the 1970s are marked by a sense of closure and loss: one can see on the horizon "the death of cinema".'[21] The sketching of this pessimistic scenario appears to be partly fuelled by anxieties about the crisis in the Italian film industry. Between 1974 and 1979, the industry suffered dramatic losses at the box office and the number of domestically made films fell by almost half.[22] This decline coincided with the gradual disappearance of the multinational productions that had greatly benefited the Italian film industry since the 1950s. But the decline was also a result of the liberalisation of private television stations in 1976. As audiences were increasingly inclined to stay at home to enjoy the vast range of programmes and films available on TV, cinema ceased to be a mass cultural phenomenon. Many film theatres fell into disuse and closed down.[23]

For much of the post-war period, Italy had the highest levels of cinema attendance in Europe, this trend being facilitated by a dynamic domestic industry and by a very high number of cinema screens across the country. In

1965, for instance, 663 million Italians went to the pictures, compared to 259 million in France and 326 million in the United Kingdom.[24] In the same year, Italy had 10,517 screens (only around 3,000 fewer than the United States), whereas in France there numbered 5,454 and in the United Kingdom 1,971. In 1976, the number of tickets sold at the box office fell by 11% compared to the previous year.[25] Between 1967 and 1977, around 2,000 screens closed down, the great majority being those second- and third-run cinemas that had served the popular audiences of the suburbs and of the provinces throughout much of the post-war period. At the same time, ticket prices increased considerably. Between 1945 and 1970, the average ticket price had risen steadily by 20 lire per year. But in 1972, the price went up by 43 lire compared to the previous year; in 1973, by 59 lire; in 1974, by 103 lire; and in 1976, by 120 lire.[26] As shown by a 1977 poll commissioned by the Doxa agency, one of the effects of this increase in ticket price was a considerable change in cinema-going habits. The poll revealed that Italian cinema audiences had not simply become smaller but were now also considerably more educated, younger and wealthier than ever before.[27]

In the 1970s, Italian cinema, it is often said, stopped speaking to the nation, abdicating its function as the privileged medium for the exploration of Italy's collective dilemmas.[28] Film histories of the 1970s often point to the increasing visibility of sex in the films of these years as an unequivocal symptom of artistic and moral decline. Monica Respetto has argued that the use of sex was a major aspect of the survival strategy of the film industry in this period of crisis.[29] Canonical critical accounts of the 1970s insist that erotic comedies and soft porn took advantage of the widespread desire for erotic titillation among audiences and made any attempt to promote a progressive idea of sexual freedom impossible.[30] Cinema-going lost its function as a mass popular phenomenon, becoming an individual and self-isolating ritual, mainly for the benefit of male audiences.[31] For scholars such as Gian Piero Brunetta and Stephen Gundle, the symbol of this deterioration is the female body, objectified and presented as a sellable expression of modernisation in a vast range of erotic films being made in these years.[32]

These critical assessments invariably link the opening of Italian cinema to sexual subject matter during the 1970s with the endorsement of a regressive, indeed phallocentric, version of sexual freedom. Whilst it is certainly important to acknowledge the fetishistic display of female flesh in several erotic films made during this period, this critical perspective has too often failed to pursue an investigation into the expanding territories of sexual expression and gendered experience concurrently being explored by Italian cinema. In a period that offered a set of new opportunities for defying taboos about sex, the increasing display of nudity and eroticism also established the conditions for exploring more inclusive and diversified gender representations. In focusing on the display of objectified female bodies in many films of the 1970s, canonical critical accounts have tended to leave the opposite term – men – unmarked and thus unquestioned. This book will show that it is instead the presence of particular concerns about masculinity that deserves attention. The book will also argue that masculinity – with its historically specific dilemmas – functions in fact in many films of this period as a charged allegory for many of the socio-political lacerations of the Italian nation in these years.

* * *

The closing shot from *The Conformist*, which I have used to introduce the predicament of masculinity in the Italian cinema of the 1970s, presents a man engaged in the act of looking inwards, at once subject and object of the inquisitive look of the camera. This man is looking for answers, his search consisting of a movement towards introspection. The unifying narrative thread of the film is the man's unconscious, the editing logic of the film being the convulsed emergence of repressed memories and desires that appear to upset the linear continuity of the story. Challenged to explain the motivations behind this inward approach, the director Bernardo Bertolucci explains his attitude in making the film as follows:

> I discovered the individual level in political revolution. And for me that remains true at the same time that I repeat Sartre's phrase which is quoted in *Spider's Strategy* [sic]: 'A man is made of all men. He is equal to all of them and all of them equal him.' I'm sure that some young occidental Maoists will reproach me for *The Conformist* because it's beautiful to look at and because I mix dirty things like sex with pure things like politics. But I think that's Catholic, moralistic reasoning and I find that the great foolishness of young Maoists in Italy is their slogan, 'Serve the People'. My Slogan is 'Serve Myself', because only by serving myself am I able to serve the people – that is, to be part of the people, not serve them.[33]

Bertolucci is commenting on the suggestion advanced by his interviewer that this film marks an awkward shift in the director's career from openly political subject matter towards a cinema of heightened subjectivity. It is a suggestion that strongly resonates with what is often perceived to be one of the limits of the Italian cinema of the 1970s: namely, its lost ability to address the collective concerns of Italian society. Commenting on this perceived limit, Flavio De Bernardinis has noted that the Italian cinema of the 1970s indeed proved unable 'to stare at the present' and turned instead towards a decentred, subjective outlook on reality.[34] One may easily see in this suggestion the influence of an authoritative strand of Italian film criticism that has historically measured the value of Italian films according to their ability to provide a unifying national imagery for their audiences. For instance, in her seminal work on Italian cinema in the light of Neorealism, Millicent Marcus argues that Neorealist films offered to Italian cinema a model of social engagement, one that 'forced viewers to abandon the limitations of a strictly personal perspective' and promote true objectivity in its engagement with social reality.[35]

By invoking his discovery 'of the individual level', Bertolucci does not seem to reject directly this post-war cinematic mandate for social engagement. Rather, he seems to contest the ambition behind the mandate to represent reality in its totality, as exemplified by the Neorealist motif of 'the common man in the crowd'. Typical of a wider tendency in 1970s Italian cinema that this book will examine, this move towards a cinema of heightened subjectivity does not contest Neorealism as such, but turns polemically against that cinematic practice – and the tradition of film criticism that has often endorsed it – which, in the name of Neorealist purism and Marxist orthodoxy, had dismissed and often silenced the realm of subjectivity. But Bertolucci is also making another important point: the possibility of exploring sexuality as a political question. Only two years after *The Conformist*, Bertolucci made *Last Tango in Paris* (1972), a film that explored the political significance of a sexual relationship divested of the moral conventions and norms imposed by society. The film was an indictment of the bourgeois family. The notorious scene in which Paul sodomises Jeanne provides a particularly vivid example of the male-dominated idea of family life that the film questions. As Paul penetrates Jeanne, he forces her to repeat after him a litany in which he refers to the family as an oppressive and castrating social structure, 'where freedom is assassinated' (Fig. 1.1). Through the abusive act of buggery, Paul acts out precisely the subjugation of women that he attributes to the family. From instructor in the dangers of the patriarchal family, Paul ends up incarnating the role of the oppressive 'Father' to illustrate the point. The scene symbolically expresses what marriage means to a woman subject to the conditions of patriarchy.

Last Tango in Paris epitomises a wider preoccupation in the Italian cinema of the 1970s with the exploration of distinctive relations of power and subordination in private domains such as the nuclear family and the heterosexual couple. In so doing, it sheds light on the position of privilege that men have historically enjoyed in these domains. *Last Tango in Paris* does not mark a move away from the 'political' as such, but rather an attempt to complicate and expand the viewer's understanding of what this 'political' could be. This attempt reflects the cultural and political developments of the 1970s. One of the main objectives of the feminist and gay movements during this period was to point to sexuality as a crucial domain of human life that is organised into systems of power and inequality. The influential Italian feminist Carla Lonzi, for example, made the claim for 'difference' – the peculiarity of one's own

Figure 1.1 *Last Tango in Paris*, Paul instructing Jeanne on the evils of the holy family.

experiences, goals, possibilities and one's sense of existence – to be a central principle in political action.[36] Lonzi's claim was not isolated. Emerging out of the post-1968 leftist wave, most of the Italian feminist groups and gay militant organisations began to question the limits of a Marxist political orthodoxy myopically concerned with class struggle and the way this orthodoxy had romantically constructed the concept of *the people* as an equal and homogenous community of oppressed subjects. Both the gay and the feminist movements challenged this way of conceiving revolutionary politics by denouncing it as a male vision operating through the abstraction of man into the domain of the universal.[37]

In the context of the 1970s, the significance of films that pose the question of sexuality in political terms is, however, far from unproblematic. This is especially true for all those films whose concern with sexual subject matter intersects with widely legitimated national narratives. In discussing a number of 1970s Italian films that reconsider the memory of fascism through erotically charged scenarios, David Forgacs points out that such films are open to a strong objection: 'they exploit the collective memories of the past and their apparent political engagement in an irresponsible way by hitching them to sex.'[38] In discussing films such as *Pasqualino Seven Beauties* (*Pasqualino Settebellezze*: 1975), *The Night Porter* (*Il portiere di notte*: 1974) and *Salò, or the 120 Days of Sodom* (*Salò o le 120 giornate di Sodoma*: 1975), Forgacs argues that these films owe their thematic concerns to the sexual politics of the 1970s and their impact on the Italian cinema of this period. Yet, he also points out that these films raise problems of ethical accountability and historical accuracy.[39] Implicit in such an argument, it seems to me, is the assumption that sex is an unworthy subject that needs to be kept separate from the domain of 'serious' politics and the monuments of national history. One of the main aims of this book is to show how a number of Italian films of the 1970s indeed move sex beyond the realm of the frivolous and the unimportant. The point of the book is not to assess the extent to which sexual subject matter is reconcilable with a politically and ethically responsible use of the cinematic medium. Rather, it is to demonstrate that in these films sex reveals its internal politics, its iniquities and asymmetric modes of expression, whilst also constituting a central vehicle for expressing wider social and political anxieties and for interrogating masculinity as a construct.

*   *   *

Chapter 2 examines the rhetoric of male crisis in a group of Italian films that were made in response to the recent advancement of feminism in Italian society, including *The Last Woman* (*L'ultima donna*: 1976), *Bye Bye Monkey* (*Ciao maschio*: 1978) and *City of Women* (*La città delle donne*: 1980). The chapter focuses in particular on the apocalyptic imagery of these films. It examines the way this apocalyptic imagery is constructed, the desires and aspirations that it conceals, and the expression of specific male anxieties in accommodating social change. Chapter 3 looks at two films made by Bertolucci – *Spider's Stratagem* and *The Conformist* – which harness the Oedipal story to reflect on the conflict between the post-war and the post-1968 generations. Both films deal with the national memory of fascism but they do so in the light of the post-1968 critique of parental authority and a symbolic rejection of the nuclear family as a site of social oppression. This chapter looks at the opportunities that these films provide for thinking about the dilemmas of male subject formation and male sexuality in the context of 1970s Italy. Chapter 4 examines a trend of popular genre films directly influenced by the sexual politics of the 1970s, including *The Seduction of Mimì* (*Mimì metallurgico ferito nell'onore*: 1972), *La patata bollente* (1979) and *A Special Day*. In examining how these films were trying to dismantle a set of normative assumptions about masculinity, the chapter shows how these films manage to negotiate their popular forms of address with their aspiration to political commitment and social protest. The chapter demonstrates the extent to which masculinity becomes a crucial concern for resolving this negotiation. Chapter 5 focuses on the eroticisation of the male body in Pier Paolo Pasolini's *Teorema* (1968), *The Decameron* (1971), *The Canterbury Tales* (1972) and *Arabian Nights* (1974). The chapter examines the films' erotic imagery, and in particular the display of the naked male body, in relation to Pasolini's search for an oppositional cinematic language (the so-called 'cinema of poetry'). The chapter theorises the spectatorial experience of the encounter with male nudity and sexual explicitness in Pasolini's films by providing a detailed account of the conditions under which the male crotch is screened. Chapter 6 considers the problematic relation between 1968 and feminism through the question of male subjectivity. This chapter draws on scholarly and personal accounts that reflect on the partial inability of the worker and student movements to incorporate specific feminist concerns in their struggles. This final chapter examines how Nanni Moretti's *Ecce Bombo* (1977) explores these shortcomings from a particularly male perspective and how this film tackles the problematic question of men's change.

2. MALE CRISIS: BETWEEN APOCALYPSE AND NOSTALGIA

City of Women begins with the image of a train about to enter a tunnel, followed by a medium shot of the protagonist, Snaporaz, dozing off inside a train compartment next to a window. The darkness of the compartment suggests that the train is now inside the tunnel. We cut to a close-up of a woman wearing sunglasses, the image of Snaporaz dozing off reflected and doubled in each one of the glasses' lenses. The close-up of her face is so extreme that her glasses take up most of the on-screen space. The camera dollies in to concentrate even more on the image of the man reflected in the lenses. This shot would seem to establish Snaporaz as the object of the woman's gaze. The following shot shows Snaporaz still sleeping, though this time the position of the camera is frontal; in the previous reverse shot, the axis between the woman and Snaporaz was slightly decentred, as if the woman was sitting further from the window. There is sudden light – presumably the train has now exited the tunnel – and Snaporaz wakes up. One may also interpret this waking up as the beginning of the dream that structures the film.[1] We cut to a shot of the woman's boots. The camera tilts upwards to her face and we are teased into wondering whether it is Snaporaz, now awake, who is looking at her. The camera's position is not frontal any more, but further to the left of where Snaporaz is sitting. The tilting movement could initially be interpreted as an attempt to fetishise the woman's body from a male point of view, but because of the shift in the axis of action Snaporaz cannot possibly own the gaze. As he wakes up, Snaporaz puts on his glasses. He starts looking at the woman rather insistently. At this point, one may wonder whether the man is finally taking

Figure 2.1   *City of Women*, the mysterious woman sitting on the train and staring at Snaporaz.

control of the gaze. The woman first looks at the window and then responds to Snaporaz's look (Fig. 2.1). A frontal medium shot repositions Snaporaz as the object of her look, whilst the following one – a close-up of the woman's face – again denies the man a point of view. This latter shot complies with the axis of action – hence it could hypothetically correspond to Snaporaz's gaze – but it is such an extreme close-up that it bears no relation to Snaporaz's optical standpoint. The sequence of shots is remarkable, however, because of the way in which the woman insistently responds to Snaporaz's increasingly excited gaze. It seems as though Snaporaz is the preying man, but clearly the relay of looks and the composition of the shots refuse him this active position.[2]

This initial sequence from *City of Women* exemplifies one of the most striking ways in which the Italian cinema of the 1970s explores the predicament of men in the face of feminism. The problem that it introduces is the difficulty for men in maintaining a position of uncontested authority in relation to the world of women. Such a difficulty is here articulated in terms of men failing to keep control of their fantasy world, in which women have so far mainly functioned as meaning-makers and as objects of desire. Take *The Last Woman* as another example. Here, Giovanni is a young man who has recently separated from his feminist wife, thus becoming the sole minder of their child.[3] As a single father, he is now burdened with parental and domestic responsibilities whilst also working full-time. At the beginning of the film, we see him bringing home his child's nursery teacher, Valeria. Giovanni is seen naked in the bathtub with his child, while Valeria, dressed, is sitting on the toilet and is looking at him. A sequence of subjective shots – ranging from medium long shots, to medium shots, to close-ups – frame Giovanni, completely naked, as the object under scrutiny. This scene constitutes in a sense a reversal of the subject–object dynamics of their first encounter at the nursery. At the nursery, we had seen Giovanni entering his son's classroom, his entrance followed by a long medium shot of Valeria holding Giovanni's child next to her bare breast in a typical maternal pose. The reaction shot had revealed Giovanni looking at her, followed by a close-up of Valeria's breast next to the child's face. The relay of shots had bound this erotic spectacle to the man's gaze. Valeria had appeared defenceless and available to Giovanni, and a few moments later she had thrown herself into his arms.

In this earlier scene we were left to contemplate a conventional visual model of male agency and female objectification. Such a model has been very much studied and deconstructed by an influential corpus of film theory.[4] Of particular interest for this scholarship has been the way in which this subject position controls the film fantasy through an alignment of the gaze of the male protagonist with the gaze of the camera and the gaze of the audience, and through particular techniques that mask their very production of an ideal male subject position.[5] In a sense, part of the challenge for film theorists has been to make this invisibility a bit more visible or, as Peter Middleton puts it, to turn 'the gaze back onto itself, making it visible and, at that moment, disturbing it'.[6] As feminist film theory has shown, this reversal constitutes a crucial deconstructive gesture because of the traditional conflation of men with a self-effacing universal position that disavows its gendered specificity.[7] Interestingly, in a number of Italian films of the 1970s, this subject position is self-consciously marked and exhibited as distinctly male. The particular formation of this gendered specificity and its resulting position of authority are precisely what the films seem to be interested in exploring. In first establishing a conventional visual model and then reversing it, *The Last Woman* places this model under scrutiny. It turns the gaze on to the male subject, making visible the power that this subject has traditionally had in limiting the image of woman to the position of passive object. *The Last Woman* succinctly performs, then, the most frequently recurring scenario by which Italian cinema of the 1970s imagines the crisis of men at this particular historical moment: as a fantasy of power reversal in which the relation of subject and object of the look appears first undermined and eventually overturned.

In referring to the challenge that feminism poses to men, Judith Butler has talked about a male subject confronting 'a female "object" who inexplicably returns the gaze, and contests the place and authority of the male position'.[8] Italian cinema of the 1970s self-consciously stages this reversal from a male subject position that is now 'forced' to look at itself and reconsider the conditions and the terms of its mastery. The fantasy of reversal is really structured on a self-reflexive gaze within what still remains a male discursive economy, in which man occupies at once the positions of subject and object of the gaze. In turning the gaze back on to itself, the reversal makes explicit the very attempt to make masculinity visible as an object of critical self-analysis during the 1970s.

*   *   *

In a memorable scene in *Romanzo popolare* (1974), Giovanni, a Milanese factory worker in his mid-fifties, confesses to his eighteen-year-old wife, Vincenzina, that he is aware of her feelings for a young policeman. He calmly tells her that he fully understands the situation and is ready to accept the end of their marriage. 'After all, we are in the Seventies!', he asserts, suggesting that the modern times require a new approach in dealing with such matters.[9] It is a line repeated by Giovanni every time he talks about the need for men to change and adopt more progressive attitudes. *Romanzo popolare* makes particularly clear that the social and political changes of this period have called masculinity into question. The refrain 'After all, we are in the Seventies!' conveys an awareness that the 1970s have considerably altered the balance of gender relations and have challenged what 'being a man' means. At the end of *Romanzo popolare*, Giovanni has proved unable to change. Even though Vincenzina never actually cheats on him, he remains unbearably jealous and possessive. Vincenzina leaves him; she becomes a factory worker, finds her own apartment and achieves that sense of self-fulfilment and autonomy that a life with her husband could never give her. The film ends on a self-pitying note as Giovanni's voice, off camera, informs us of his new life as a retired divorcee, with its empty routines and loneliness.

At first glance, Giovanni could be interpreted as a typical example of the Italian *inept* described by Jacqueline Reich in her book *Beyond the Latin Lover*. As a passive and inadequate male, the *inept* is, according to Reich, rooted in a distinctly Italian cultural tradition that runs from the mid-sixteenth-century *commedia dell'arte* to twentieth-century Italian cinema.[10] The *inept* paradigm may partly describe Giovanni's gradual disempowerment in the story but does not fully account for the historical uniqueness of his predicament and the way it is articulated in the film. The specificity of his predicament is, in fact, most visible in the realisation that his wife has benefited from particularly favourable social conditions (e.g. the legalisation of divorce; feminism; industrialisation; a wider range of models of female independence and autonomy) facilitating her emancipation. These conditions coincide with the traumatic turning point of the 1970s ('After all, we are in the Seventies', as Giovanni would put it). Here, we are not simply confronting the cinematic spectacle of a male anti-hero who has been divested of his authority and emasculated, but also looking at the cinematic articulation of a historically contingent male experience of uncertainty, doubt and self-questioning. The film seeks to express the experience of being male *from the inside* (e.g. the consistent use of Giovanni's voice, off camera) and, most importantly, what this means at this particular historical moment.

Romanzo popolare also signals the appearance of a genre – the anti-romance – which frequently structures cinematic portrayals of men experiencing crisis during the 1970s. The anti-romance constitutes a deviation from the classical narrative trajectory of the film romance and borrows some of the narrative conventions of melodrama. Whilst in conventional film romances the hetero-sexual couple faces a number of obstacles that initially keep them apart but which are later overcome to allow the two protagonists to be happily reunited, the anti-romance of the 1970s questions this trajectory by denying the hetero-sexual couple the possibility of staying together. It does so by placing in front of them a set of insurmountable obstacles (hence its closeness to melodrama); in a reversal of the inevitable path to marital union that structures the classi-cal romantic comedy, in the anti-romances of the 1970s the inevitability of a future apart represents the only possible ending.[11] *Night Full of Rain* (*La fine del mondo nel nostro solito letto in una notte piena di pioggia*: 1978) explores, for example, the problems of a married couple consisting of an Italian commu-nist journalist and an American feminist. The film builds up its melodramatic affective potential out of the impossibility for the protagonists of continuing to live together as a couple. By showing the man's inability to meet his wife's need for more emotional connectedness and sexual fulfilment, the film pre-sents her final decision to leave him as a necessary gesture by which she is able to re-affirm her dignity and remain true to her feminist beliefs. While both conventional melodramas and romantic comedies are usually concerned with negotiating female desire through the restrictions imposed by marriage and family, the anti-romantic trajectory of *Night Full of Rain* stems precisely from the opposite need not to chastise female sexuality. In a similar vein, *Pigs Have Wings* (*Porci con le ali*: 1977) follows the problematic relationship between feminist Antonia and Rocco. Set in Rome during the student protests of the mid-1970s, the film deals with the couple's difficulty in experiencing a mutu-ally enjoyable relationship on an equitable basis. Whilst Antonia repeatedly contests his sexist attitudes, Rocco appears hopelessly stuck. Under pressure to change, he lacks an alternative code of reference that might guide him through this transformation.

Similarly to *Romanzo popolare*, *Night Full of Rain* and *Pigs Have Wings* situate their anti-romantic narratives in the historically specific context of the 1970s, in relation to the contemporary rise of feminism and its troubling impact on the relations between men and women. These films do not simply deal openly with questions concerning erotic desire, but approach sexual subject matter as a political question. In *Pigs Have Wings*, Antonia finds that sex is where her feminist credentials and her dignity as a woman are to be tested. Thus she refuses to be simply a receptacle for her boyfriend's sexual impulses and prefers to break up with him rather than live a relationship that frustrates her. Similarly, in *Night Full of Rain*, Lizzy feels the need to end her marriage with Paolo because she finds herself unable to express her erotic potential. Not prepared to respond to these demands, the male protagonists of these films reveal their inadequacy. Italian cinema of the 1970s presents countless examples of male characters struggling to make sense of a rapidly changing society, their inadequacy partly being an effect of the radically new demands that are made on them (especially by women) and a symptom of their unpreparedness. This struggle inevitably places the subjectivity of the male characters at the centre of the narratives through a frequent use of the generic conventions of melodrama. Suffering, which would normally be closely associated in melodrama with the female protagonists, is here presented as a distinctly male experience. Suffering coincides with the closing down for these male characters of potential action and marks a distinctive turn inwards towards interiority, a turn that underscores their emotional fragility and vulnerability.

* * *

In an essay on the melodramatised man, Kathleen Rowe examines a number of post-classical American comedies that seem to appropriate female suffering and the 'feminised' genre of melodrama to narrate male stories of emotional failures and impossible romance. Rowe discusses the so-called 'nervous romance' of the 1970s in US cinema. Best exemplified by *Annie Hall* (1977) and *Manhattan* (1979), the nervous romance appears to reveal a certain wariness about the possibilities of the heterosexual couple through the central role of a beleaguered man nostalgically mourning a time of simpler romance. The question that these films seem to raise is whether these cinematic images of men suggest a true collapse of patriarchy and a reconfiguration of masculinity according to more feminist-friendly conditions. For Rowe, the answer is emphatically 'no'. As she points out, 'the melodramatised male raises troubling issues regarding gender.'[12] On closer scrutiny, these films suggest not so much a crisis in masculinity as the finding and repairing of 'cracks'; and, as Rowe notes, cracks do not necessarily imply collapse: 'Woody Allen and the other melodramatised males of the post-classical romantic comedy use their feminisation to bolster their own authority, which they then invoke to "instruct" women about relationships, romance and femininity itself.'[13]

Rowe's work interrogates the initially appealing spectacle of a male figure divesting itself of some of the traditionally sustaining traits of patriarchal masculinity. Her insights point to a set of underlying strategies by which male authority may be re-asserted behind the surface of a cinematic male subject apparently in demise. Rowe addresses critically the nostalgia and the rhetoric of male martyrdom that pervades a number of cinematic representations of men in crisis. What is especially useful in this kind of approach is how it illuminates the very process by which a narrative of male crisis is assembled, pointing to the complex layers of meaning underneath the image of a male subject in demise. It is an approach that brings into question a symptomatic reading of what we may interpret as male crisis, whilst at the same time allowing us to interrogate the discursive as well as the strictly cinematic procedures by which the narrative of crisis is constructed.

Rowe's work arguably suggests the usefulness of treating narratives of male crisis as performances. As Fintan Walsh has argued, '[t]o think of crisis as a performance is to imagine that the disruption it signifies is actively or even carefully produced; or, to extend the theatrical analogy, even affected'.[14] The term 'performance' denotes in this sense both the doing of something and its own representation. It challenges the presumed 'naturalness' of the object of analysis and the way in which the object (the crisis) seems to present itself as a matter-of-fact piece of evidence. Moreover, the term 'performance' points to the very representational process by which the object comes into being and asserts its self-evident 'natural' existence. To approach a cinematic narrative of male crisis in terms of performance might mean, then, to try to understand the way it works, what aesthetic and narrative devices it draws on and what functions it plays. Stuart Hall reminds us that the notion of representation 'implies the active work of selecting and presenting, of structuring and shaping: not merely the transmitting of already-existing meaning, but the more active labour of making things mean'.[15] Representation does not simply reflect reality, Hall suggests; it is instead a complex process that makes things mean in a certain way not because this is how they are in reality, but because certain selection and exclusionary procedures have been operating.

In presenting men as the threatened sex, 1970s narratives of male crisis generally conjure up the demise of men as an effect of the empowerment of women and of the social transformations that have accompanied the rise of feminism. Such transformations are understood to have dramatically compromised the possibility of peaceful reconciliation between men and women. The rhetoric of these films is distinctly apocalyptic and tends to frame men as victims of a wider social undoing. Consistently, one of the most prominent characteristics of the films under focus in this chapter is a certain emphasis on the inevitability of the demise of men and of the social order that has allowed their domination. The chapter will explore the 'construction' of this narrative of inevitability and some of the implications and effects of the use of an apocalyptic imagery to represent this male crisis.

To approach the cinematic exploration of a crisis in masculinity in terms of performance is to identify the role of certain subject positions in the service of which these stories of male crisis would seem to work. It means recognising that cinema is also an apparatus in which the subject is implicated and constructed. As Stuart Hall notes, the production of meaning does not work in a vacuum where subjects are all the same: 'some subjects have more power than others to produce meaning.'[16] Hall's argument raises the question of who may speak in a text or, as Teresa De Lauretis puts it, what particular type of '"subject of enunciation" has left "its" footprints' in a text.[17] The challenge, here, is to see this subject of enunciation not as existing before the text and coinciding with the point of view of a particular person (director, scriptwriter, actor, a real person and so on) but as a subject position that comes into existence and acquires meaning (and authority) within the films. In other words, it is a subject to be understood not as source of meaning, but as produced within discourse.[18] The chapter explores the enunciating *male* subject position from which the crisis of masculinity appears to be articulated in Italian films of the 1970s. More specifically, it looks at the conditions under which this subject position may determine the structuring and articulation of the crisis, what it may inevitably favour and what it may exclude.

Envisaging the End in Bye Bye Monkey and The Last Woman

Set against the backdrop of a rat-infested and half-deserted New York, *Bye Bye Monkey* follows Lafayette (Gérard Depardieu), a young male electrician who works for a museum and feminist theatre. In the initial scenes of the film, Lafayette is subjected to bullying and a number of humiliations by a group of feminists. Powerless in the face of the anger of these women, who contest his 'historical' role as a patriarch, Giovanni is first ridiculed, then hit with a bottle and eventually 'raped' by Angelica, one of the feminists. *Bye Bye Monkey* situates the crisis of the male protagonist in a world on the verge of collapse. The beginning of the film shows Lafayette leaving his basement apartment and walking around his desolate neighbourhood with a baseball bat for self-defence, while soldiers wearing nuclear protection suits patrol the streets (Fig. 2.2). The film shows wasteland, street corners overgrown with plants, run-down buildings and empty streets.

This apocalyptic imagery – and its connection to the crisis of men – is further

Figure 2.2   *Bye Bye Monkey*, soldiers wearing nuclear protection suits patrol the streets of New York.

evoked through the repeated appearance of the carcass of a gigantic gorilla on a deserted beach facing Manhattan. The gorilla is just one of the many totemic symbols that appear in Marco Ferreri's films.[19] It appears here as a symbol of the male crisis that the film intends to represent. Its death reflects the undoing of the capitalist socioeconomic order of which the gorilla/King Kong is a product. To highlight the parallel between the collapse of this order and the crisis of man, the image of the dead gorilla is set against the gloomy backdrop of the skyscrapers of Manhattan, arguably one of the most vivid metropolitan icons of capitalism in the West.

In *The Last Woman*, the predicament of masculinity is played out in the more private dimension of the heterosexual couple. The protagonist, Giovanni, has been abandoned by his wife, who has chosen her feminist militancy over married life. The story follows Giovanni's whirlwind romance with Valeria and the difficulties that they encounter in constructing an emotionally and sexually fulfilling relationship. In his affair with Valeria, Giovanni confronts a new kind of sexually empowered woman. Valeria rejects traditional institutions such as marriage and the family, and refuses to be treated by Giovanni as his own exclusive property.

In *The Last Woman*, a calamitous vision of Western society is introduced through the initial images of an oil refinery, a gloomy landscape punctuated by chimneys, pipes and their emissions recalling the dim colours of Antonioni's industrial Ravenna in *Red Desert* (*Deserto rosso*: 1964). This industrial landscape is accompanied by occasional shots of shopping centres, car parks and skyscrapers. The outdoor sequences of *The Last Woman* were filmed in Créteil, a satellite town just outside Paris, chosen by Ferreri as an ideal example of the self-sufficient neocapitalist town purpose-built to satisfy all the material needs of its inhabitants. Occasionally, the camera scrutinises the suburban landscape surrounding Giovanni's flat, only to show a dull sequence of purpose-built buildings and deserted lawns. This sense of claustrophobia is further emphasised as the film relates the dramatic story of the male protagonist within the constraints of Giovanni's domestic space. In this space, we occasionally hear voices and other domestic noises such as vacuum cleaners and TVs resounding from other apartments, an aural effect that heightens the sense of the protagonist's entrapment within the physical constraints of this artificial world.

Bye Bye Monkey and *The Last Woman* reveal a vision of the present that is laden with deep anxieties about social decay and emasculation. The men at the centre of their stories experience an alienating relationship not only with women but also with their surroundings. In the sequences set outdoors, long-distance shots position the male protagonists in gloomy urban landscapes with the effect of creating onscreen spaces of separation; here, lost and isolated, these male figures appear divested of any agency. This catastrophic imagery taps into a flourishing apocalyptic trend in Western art-house cinema of the

1960s and 1970s, exemplified by the release of films such as *Alphaville* (1965), *Shame* (*Skammen*: 1968), *Weekend* (1968) and *Zabriskie Point* (1970). Famously saluted by John Orr as the cinema of the 'Cool Apocalypse', these films explored the despair and paralysis of the neocapitalist world and the moral and spiritual decay of the bourgeoisie.[20] In envisaging a social order rapidly approaching its end, such films revealed an undeniable visual fascination with spectacles of destruction and human misery. Marked by a sense of pessimism and fear for the future, they constituted a collective response to large-scale technological and industrial developments, the advance of mass culture, fear of nuclear conflict during the Cold War and, perhaps most significantly, the rise of the ecological movement in Europe and North America.

The cinematic imagery of the Cool Apocalypse provides a rather fitting framework to stage stories of male crisis. This imagery functions as an ideal mise-en-scène for the manufacturing of an end that may appear proximate and inevitable. In *Bye Bye Monkey* and *The Last Woman*, this gendered scenario of inevitable demise is also produced through the incorporation of some of the generic conventions of melodrama: an emphasis on domestic interiors within which the male protagonists appear to be claustrophobically stuck; the use of music for expressive effects, especially to mark moments of emotional tension and release for the male protagonists; a narrative trajectory that sets up a number of blockages on the way to wish fulfilment. This linkage between melodrama and men's crisis is not entirely surprising. In his study of Vincente Minnelli's melodramas, Geoffrey Nowell-Smith notes that a frequent theme of these films is the male protagonists' failure to occupy a stable male identity unproblematically. But whilst, in Minnelli's melodramas, the problem for men seems to be the presence of a number of impairments to the protagonist's masculinity under the aegis of patriarchal law and the difficulty in fully disavowing the feminine, in *Bye Bye Monkey* and *The Last Woman* the central dilemma for the two protagonists appears to be how to redefine their masculinity *outside* this law.[21] As in Nowell-Smith's reading of Minnelli's melodramas, however, it is the inevitability of castration that intervenes to resolve this dilemma. On one level, in *Bye Bye Monkey* and *The Last Woman* castration is literalised as a fantasy of male disempowerment in response to women's self-empowerment. In *The Last Woman*, the threat of castration seems to emerge gradually through a number of cautionary signals (cuts and wounds on Giovanni's fingers and genitals). On another level, the inevitability of castration, which takes place at the end of the film with Giovanni's phallic amputation, seems to stand metonymically for the unstoppable social undoing that is evoked by the apocalyptic fantasy. The inevitability of castration connects the dystopian fantasy of social collapse and the psychosexual dilemmas of the male subject within the Oedipal complex.

Within the Freudian narrative, the possibility of castration coincides with the boy's perception that his mother lacks the distinguishing mark of maleness, the penis. The sexual differentiation that comes from this perception (father/male as having the penis; mother/female as not having it) impresses upon the boy the understanding that the lack is both an indication of the father's authority and that this is a privilege that can be taken away through castration. In the face of the threat of castration (the possibility that his privilege as a male subject might be taken away), the boy gives up the mother as object of desire and as model of identification. He then accepts his place as a male subject by identifying with the authority of the father. The image of the castrated woman has been particularly important in feminist film theory for understanding how cinema reflects and plays with socially established ideas of sexual difference.[22] This image has been used to consider the function of women in film in giving meaning and order to a visual economy that reinforces men's sense of control and power within the cinematic fantasy. *The Last Woman* seems to play both with this visual model and with the very threat of castration. There is a moment at the beginning of the film when Valeria stands in the middle of Giovanni's apartment holding his child. Naked, having just come out of the shower, Giovanni joins them and takes the child from Valeria. He starts flirting with her and approaches her, kissing her, touching her and eventually starting to undress her. Disarmingly passive, Valeria lets him do so but begs him to be a gentle lover. Fiery and passionate, Giovanni carries on and then eventually moves away towards the camera to sit on the floor with his child. Valeria, standing in the same position, continues to undress for him. Moving away from her and sitting on the floor, Giovanni leaves the position of object of the camera's gaze – now occupied only by Valeria – and establishes himself as the active viewing subject. It is a moment in the film that seems to stage self-consciously the voyeuristic separation between the darkness of a cinema auditorium and the interplay between light and shadow on the cinema screen. This staging frames Valeria as the image to be looked at and positions Giovanni's point of view in line with the gaze of the camera and the gaze of an ideal spectator. A reverse shot reveals Giovanni, with his child, almost hidden in the darkness of the room, enthralled by the spectacle that enfolds in front of him. A back light source coming from the bathroom functions here as a kind of camera projector situated in the rear of a cinema auditorium. Valeria stands still, completely naked in the middle of the room, fully available to the scopophiliac pleasures that seem to be activated in the scene. It would seem as though, in a literal rendering of the visual paradigm described by Laura Mulvey, man is here the active bearer of the gaze that has the power to objectify women and confine them to the status of passive image and meaning-maker of the film fantasy.[23] The particular interplay of light and shadow on Valeria's body seems to attract the viewers' gaze and, at the same time, push it away from her exposed crotch – which here is at the very centre of the shot. As

Valeria proceeds to hide her crotch with her hands, the viewers' gaze is arguably directed even more forcefully towards what lies behind them. As Mulvey herself noted, in psychoanalytic terms, the female figure 'connotes something that the look continually circles around but disavows: her lack of a penis, implying a threat of castration and hence unpleasure'.[24] In a sense, the image of Valeria standing in front of Giovanni may be considered a re-enactment of this original trauma for the male subject. But rather than disavowing the threat of castration, this moment in the film seems to quote the threat for the male protagonist with uncanny literalness. The camera then takes Valeria's point of view, hence turning the gaze on to itself as she submissively asks him, 'What else do I need to do for you?'[25] The question could be taken as an ironic one, as if the trick played by the cinematic medium on the body of woman has been uncovered. Giovanni is now in the spotlight; he has been caught and, by extension, the visual procedures by which male authority is reproduced in cinema have also been exposed.

* * *

Bye Bye Monkey and *The Last Woman* momentarily divert attention from the inevitability of their apocalyptic ending by contemplating possibilities for male regeneration through a return to a lost pre-social dimension. In *Bye Bye Monkey*, this dimension is evoked through the discovery of a baby chimpanzee inside the hand of a huge dead gorilla. In contrast to a pervasive symbolism suggesting decay and destruction, the image of the baby chimpanzee seems to imply the possibility of salvation. As Angelo Migliarini has pointed out, the chimpanzee is clearly presented as a Jesus-like redemptive figure.[26] When Luigi (an older friend of Lafayette's) first finds it, he asks: 'Who are you? Baby Jesus?'[27] Significantly, when Lafayette, Angelica and Luigi take the chimpanzee to the registry office to obtain a birth certificate, they communicate to the clerk that its date of birth is 25 December. The scene on the beach is also specifically reminiscent of the Nativity: the huge carcass of the gorilla functioning as the Bethlehem grotto; Lafayette and the elderly people arriving like the wise men; and the final composition of the scene – Lafayette, who has the chimpanzee in his arms, sitting next to Luigi, like the virgin Mary and Joseph, while their three elderly friends (the wise men) stand at some distance (Fig. 2.3).

This redemptive imagery is articulated in distinctly maternal terms. After taking the chimpanzee out of the gorilla's womb-like fist, Luigi gives it to Lafayette, who places it inside his sweater as if to return it to the safe warmth of a maternal uterine space. The same image of the pregnant father re-occurs when Lafayette and Luigi go to visit the feminist theatre. This maternal imagery is further invoked by the recurring association between Lafayette and a number of other womb-like spaces, such as the feminist theatre and his basement flat. With its lack of windows, the theatre is a space in which all the

Figure 2.3   *Bye Bye Monkey*, the discovery of the baby chimpanzee next to the gorilla. In the background, Manhattan.

destructiveness of the outside world has been closed off; in one of the initial sequences set at the theatre, a red filter evokes a kind of placenta that may protect Lafayette from the dangers of the external world. The feminists have decided to 'rape' Lafayette, but the rape turns out to be a gentle moment of love-making performed by one of the feminists on him (Fig. 2.4). A similar sense of separation from the outside world – an imagined return to a time before history – is evoked in Lafayette's basement. The difference is that here the external noises are not blocked off but are heard in the distance. In both of these spaces, Lafayette experiences momentary comfort and safety. At ease with his nakedness like a foetus in its womb, here, Lafayette seems to find a (pre-Oedipal?) refuge from the destructive forces of history and acculturation. This experience seems to lead the protagonist to the possible recuperation of a lost point of origin, a comforting as much as a regenerating maternal affective dimension.

In *Psychoanalysis and Feminism*, Juliet Mitchell has discussed the importance of the pre-Oedipal phase for the development of the child's sexuality and the centrality of the attachment to the mother as the first nurturing, caring object of desire. This is a space of polymorphous desires and multiple possibilities before castration, a space that is in a sense before history. As Mitchell

Figure 2.4   *Bye Bye Monkey*, Angelica rapes Lafayette.

reminds us, '[h]istory starts with the Oedipus complex, or rather with its over-coming and the inauguration of structured language that accompanies it.'[28] It is not surprising, then, that in their escape from the destructive effects of the present, the male protagonists of *The Last Woman* and *Bye Bye Monkey* should seek refuge from history within this pre-linguistic dimension. In *The Last Woman*, the crisis experienced by the protagonist when he is left alone to look after his child is counter-balanced by Valeria's increasingly strong attach-ment to Giovanni's child. Throughout the story, Giovanni appears as a dis-tracted and careless father. When she moves into his flat, Valeria instead shows Giovanni the importance of re-introducing physical and emotional warmth within the parent–son bond. It is a scenario that appears to be pervaded by a sense of nostalgia for man's own original relationship with the mother and the multiple libidinal possibilities intrinsic to that kind of attachment. This becomes clear after Valeria explains to Giovanni the importance of establish-ing a strong physical bond with the child. Giovanni quickly protests that he too needs the kind of love that Valeria is willing to give to his son. With such a request, Giovanni seems to convey his desire for physical warmth and the kind of emotional intimacy exhibited by the relationship between his son and Valeria, which he clearly envies. The relationship between Valeria and Pierino functions in this sense as a bond that replicates the solidarity and unselfish friendship between Valeria and Giovanni's ex-wife, Gabriella, in contrast to Giovanni's inability to move away from his possessive and jealous behaviour. In these terms, the child and the particular kind of relationship that Valeria establishes with Pierino become paradigmatic of the way in which the film envisages alternative types of bonds and emotional attitudes that men may aspire to in the face of the challenges posed by feminism.

This maternal imagery is further complemented by the possibility of trying to imagine a different experience of masculinity in tune with the demands of the present. This possibility is envisaged in *The Last Woman* through Giovanni's willingness to create a new kind of relationship with Valeria. After a row with Valeria, Giovanni enters the bedroom, holding Pierino in his arms, and stands in front of her. Valeria provocatively asks him when he will start being con-cerned with her sexual pleasure. As Giovanni puts Pierino down on the bed and then lies down next to Valeria and the child, the couple start discussing the difficulties of a sexual relationship that fulfils both man and woman. Giovanni vows to be a more generous lover and starts kissing and caressing her. In his attempt to meet Valeria's demands for erotic fulfilment, the male protagonist tries to relinquish his self-centred sexual drives. Pierino, on the bed, next to his father and Valeria, does not simply witness the gentle love-making between the two protagonists, but is involved in his father's attempt to provide a more emotionally and physically fulfilling type of intimacy for Valeria. As Giovanni tenderly kisses and touches Valeria, he simultaneously fondles his son. Valeria finally seems pleased. This spectacle of erotic intimacy, in its triangular composition, acquires the characteristics of a ritual. Through the presence of the child, the sequence appears to invoke the subtle intimacy of a 'pre-social' libidinal experience, an alternative erotic space starkly contrasting with the way in which the film has so far depicted Giovanni's sexuality as an aggressively self-gratifying performance.

The scene would seem to mark the immersion into an 'imagined feminine' space of sensual pleasures. This is partly due to the contemplative, gentle music that accompanies the love-making and, especially, to the cinematography. In the room there is only a diegetic light source, consisting of a very high lamp sitting on the bedside table. The rest of the room is in darkness, except for a feeble light coming from the other room. The interplay of shadows and warm light on the bodies and their immersion in the darkness of the room make the contours of the bodies tenuous. Their gentle movement during the love-making and the triangular composition of the scene complicate and dissolve the subject–object erotic relation. The scene could be interpreted as the staging of what an erotic experience in tune with feminist demands might look like from a particular male perspective. The real stakes of this 'mimicry', I would argue, are evident in what follows.

In the subsequent scene, Giovanni wakes up and conveys his frustrations at having suppressed his 'natural inclination' in order to please Valeria. He says, 'What a silly idea not to fuck. Now my dick is rock-hard.'[29] He then goes downstairs to his other lover and proposes that she has sex with him. In these terms, the act by which Giovanni finally meets Valeria's need of sexual gratification also corresponds to the repression of men's natural desire. Dominated by a fantasy of active male desire, which in the previous scene is repressed as much as it is re-asserted by the sense of dissatisfaction that this repression generates, the image of man willing to change to account for women's erotic autonomy is therefore doomed to failure. In depicting female sexuality as essentially maternal and potentially castrating for men, the film also denies men the possibilities of bodily eroticism beyond the phallic stranglehold of lack and loss. In its critique of patriarchy, The Last Woman ends up freezing the very terms of its critique within the idea of an unchangeable order of things. It is man's body, his very nature, that makes it impossible for the male protagonist to transcend the limits of sexual difference, transform his masculinity and construct more equal relationships with women.

So, men will never change. At the end of the film, Giovanni holds his son in his arms and regrettably tells him that men like them have no choice but to be patriarchs. This scene would seem to articulate the feelings of despair experienced by the male protagonist in failing to redefine his masculinity in response to Valeria's requests for a more equal relationship. Desperately confronting this failure, Giovanni takes an electric knife and finally castrates himself. It is an image of male sacrifice to atone for one's sins. Yet, it is also a sacrifice that, in its perversity, unites humiliation and transcendence, passivity and control. The final act of self-mutilation, shown in a sequence that appears to be a nightmarish fantasy originating from the protagonist's mind, ends up being an ultimate act of self-control. The male protagonist here appears to be defeated and yet still remains master of the fantasy that he has created.

In *Bye Bye Monkey*, the protagonist Lafayette is not the only character who experiences a sense of disempowerment with regard to dramatic shifts in the relations between men and women. A similar sense of gender displacement is shared by Luigi. Played by Marcello Mastroianni, Luigi is first introduced at a roadside, begging a kiss from a young woman, who sternly refuses to satisfy his requests. In cutting to a close-up of Luigi, the camera reveals a man overwhelmed by disappointment and humiliation, staring into space. In its painfulness, this shot resumes Luigi's main function in the story of representing an ageing male body that is out of touch with the present reality in which it no longer has a place. Like Lafayette, Luigi also longs for a pre-social affective space as a way of escaping his present crisis. His relation with the chimpanzee – which he adopts as his own son – has precisely this objective. Yet, the film shows the impossibility of men entering this primitive dimension in light of their essential embeddedness in the master narrative of history. Luigi's asthma, recurring every time his tries to hold the chimpanzee in his arms, is in this sense the marker of the essential impossibility for the male subject of transcending his body, and implicitly his maleness. Luigi's disconsolate expression whenever he is forced to renounce the intimacy of physical contact with the chimpanzee conveys the tragic awareness of this impossibility.

Despite suggesting at different points in the story that the legacy of man's history must be destroyed, Luigi is in fact very much invested in the order that he rejects. Even though he appears to refuse the dominant structures of history and male privilege, he struggles to conceive of the existence of man outside the rules of this social order. As Luigi confesses to Lafayette, a man is nothing without an identity and a recognisable position in society. He therefore encourages Lafayette to give an official name to the chimpanzee, give him a birth certificate and ratify his existence before the law.

The registration of the chimpanzee at the public record office marks not only the collapse of the illusion of a primitive and authentic relationship between Lafayette and his adopted son, but also, most importantly, the downward spiral of the story leading to the final death of the male characters. The relationship between Lafayette and his chimpanzee progressively shows instead the insidious effects of socialisation. The domestication of the chimpanzee and his social recognition thus mark the gradual movement from the pre-linguistic to the symbolic. This experience, the film shows, is inevitable as much as it is destructive for man. The first effect is Luigi's death. Luigi hangs himself from the branch of a tree and his death is quickly followed by another event that symbolises the gradual undoing of masculinity under the destructive influence of civilisation. Almost foreseeing that Luigi's death is not an isolated tragedy, Lafayette goes to the plain of sand where he first found the chimpanzee and discovers that the carcass of the gorilla has almost completely disappeared. On realising the symbolic meaning of this disappearance, Lafayette starts screaming. As the drama unfolds, Lafayette fails to show support for Angelica when she tells him that she is pregnant with his child. He abdicates parental responsibility and, in so doing, fails to see the true possibility of regeneration that an authentic experience of parenthood might confer on him.

After having discovered the death of the chimpanzee, Lafayette runs to the museum to see Flaxman. Flaxman is the only character in the film who refuses to give in to the crisis and continues to worship man's history. Heartbroken and trembling, Lafayette struggles to tell Flaxman what has happened. His hesitant confession takes the form of a broken speech 'Monkey dead . . . been eaten . . . by the rats.'[30] Irritated by Lafayette's unashamed admission of his vulnerability, Flaxman shows the young male protagonist a statue of a humanoid and gravely tells him, 'Look at yourself. That's who you were.'[31] It is a reminder of men's origins, the starting point within a linear vision of history along which men have exerted their power. Most importantly, it is a warning about men's vulnerability and their imperfect nature in the moment in which they decide to abandon the discursive veil of acculturation – and implicitly their privilege – to reconcile themselves with a pre-social dimension. Flaxman encourages Lafayette to remain within the protective limits of present history, its values and conventions, suggesting that this is the only dimension in which man's security and power may be preserved. He tells him, 'There's nothing to understand. One needs only to obey.'[32] Flaxman preaches obedience to the authority of history. In so doing, he also incites Lafayette either to obey or to kill him. As Lafayette decides not to obey, Flaxman's death constitutes a final tragic warning of the fate that awaits the protagonist.

In his refusal to bow to the power of history and socialisation, the protagonist finally confronts the possibility of his own tragic death. It is an apocalyptic scenario marked by the desperate search for a different way of being 'man', which leads nowhere. At the end, Lafayette kills himself after ascertaining the impossibility of reversing the corruptive cycle of history. The smoke coming from the fire that kills Lafayette dissolves into images of a deserted beach on which Lafayette's girlfriend and his child play, completely naked. It is a scenario that envisages the possibility of rebirth after social collapse and a return to an uncorrupted state of nature. If change is impossible – due to men's embeddedness in the social structures that have preserved their power throughout history – then destruction appears to be the only plausible alternative.

NOSTALGIC RETRIEVALS AND REGRESSION: *MALIZIA*

The Last Woman and *Bye Bye Monkey* present a vision of the present that is laden with deep anxieties about social decay and emasculation. Through their anti-romantic narratives, they provide an image of contemporary society, which is envisaged as the site of an unlikely resolution of the predicament faced by men. The unfeasibility of their heterosexual romances expresses in this sense the perception of an impossible reconciliation between a bruised male subject position and the threatening female world associated with feminism. In the face of this impossibility, both films point to a nostalgic journey back into the maternal womb. Envisaged as a comforting refuge, the maternal is associated with an idea of libidinal freedom preceding acculturation. When the male protagonists of these films realise that it is not possible to inhabit this maternal space permanently and fully, destruction appears to be the only solution.

It is a fantasy of destruction that points to a vision of the future in which the world of man has collapsed and a primitive world of natural feelings and relations may finally materialise. In *Bye Bye Monkey*, the correlation between the apocalyptic vision and the dream of a primitive utopia is conjured up at the end of the film with the dissolve superimposing the images of the burning museum and the uncontaminated beach. This ending presents the vision of a refound Eden where the only signs of human presence are the naked bodies of Angelica and her child. As the camera tracks forward towards them, the film is implicitly telling us that this is the future awaiting humankind after the destruction. This vision anticipates the gyno-centric fantasy explored by Ferreri in *The Future is Woman* (*Il futuro è donna*: 1984) where, after the disappearance of man, the image of a woman with her child is meant to evoke a future in which a pre-Oedipal mother may nurture a new humanity. It is a vision of the future that conceals an underlying nostalgia for a golden past of authentic libidinal attachments and fixed sexual difference. In this vision, the mother appears as a primitive female ideal, the guarantor of a return to a stable gender order. This nostalgia features not simply as a sentiment pervading these films but as a 'performative' authenticating the allegedly truer values of the past against the threatening images of a decaying present and an even more frightening future.

Both *The Last Woman* and *Bye Bye Monkey* introduce feminist characters as both symptoms and agents of the process of cultural deterioration in which men experience their crisis. In both films there is a strong perception that contemporary society has turned traditional gender roles upside down and disrupted the natural order of things. Significantly, *Bye Bye Monkey* mockingly points to the clumsy attempts of the feminist collective to adopt typically masculine codes of behaviour by trying to rape Lafayette and demonstrating that women can be violent too. In showing Angelica's inability to act as an aggressive rapist, the film seems to suggest the impossibility of overcoming 'natural' differences between the sexes. Whilst the scene of the rape could be interpreted as an instance of deviation from an appropriate way of being woman, the final image of Angelica as mother, in an uncontaminated setting far removed from any sign of civilisation, defines motherhood as the ultimate locus of female authenticity and as the only viable alternative to the sense of gender disorder illustrated by the film through its apocalyptic fantasy.

The apocalyptic imagery of the 1970s establishes a space for a male subject position to confront anxieties of de-legitimation and subordination. This imagery should not be considered as a specular space reflecting an actual male experience of disempowerment, but as a performative one in which the anxieties may be staged, given a particular configuration and then dealt with within the possibilities provided by the cinematic medium. In *Bye Bye Monkey* and *The Last Woman*, the apocalyptic fantasy re-establishes an order that is felt to have been violated. This shift takes place by recuperating a set of normative beliefs in fixed sexual difference. Whilst the present appears as a site of impossibilities, future and past are conflated into a kind of nostalgic mourning for what has been lost. Far from pointing exclusively to the past, the mourning re-activates the loss by turning it into a hope, a project for the future.

Consistently, a fantasy of regression seems to uphold much of this apocalyptic imagery. The regression may take the shape of a journey back into a maternal space, a space where a male subject may be able to embrace again an experience of unproblematic reconciliation with the feminine. It is a feminine that is conceivable, however, only under the shadow of the Oedipal journey. Here, the feminine is inevitably evoked as the very first nurturing, caring object of desire in relation to which the male 'I' will understand himself and his place in the Symbolic. The regression allows an escape from the challenges of the present and the painful confrontation with a time in which men are expected to redefine their masculinity. The escape is really a journey backwards into oneself, into what is already known and familiar.

Interesting examples of this tendency are provided by a number of erotic comedies released in the same period. These are comedies that focus on stories of sexual initiation. At the centre of these stories are teenage boys, typically enthralled by much older women. Tamao Nakahara has called them 'incest comedies'.[33] Meant as substitute mother figures, the female character at the heart of these films is generally an aunt, a maid or a stepmother, and famous titles include *Grazie zia* (1968), *Le tue mani sul mio corpo* (1970), *Grazie ... nonna* (1975) and *Dolci zie* (1975). The role of the female characters is to awaken the boy's sexual instincts whilst offering a reassuring image of maternal sensuality. The most famous example of this trend is arguably *Malizia*. Made in 1973, *Malizia* was a huge hit at the Italian box office, where it grossed 6 billion lire and became one of the most popular Italian films of the 1970s.[34] The film is set in 1950s Sicily and tells the story of a beautiful maid called Angela, who is employed to look after a recently widowed man and his three sons. The film exploited a widespread desire for sexual titillation in the increasingly permissive Italy of the 1970s and provided a male heterosexual fantasy in which a beautiful woman seemed to be devoted to the male members of a family, whom she served and looked after selflessly. More than any other films of the same period focusing on male adolescents falling in love with older female relatives or maids, *Malizia* eroticised maternal love by evoking a world in which man could become child again and escape the responsibilities and pressures of the present.

The film makes use of sexually explicit scenarios and levels of nudity that would have been unthinkable in previous decades. At the same time, with its 1950s setting, it reverberates with a sense of nostalgia for a long-gone past in which women could be tamed and made docile, a far cry from the anxieties experienced by men in a period in which women were becoming increasingly autonomous and were challenging age-old gender conventions. In the final fulfilment of this erotic fantasy, Angela initiates the young Nino into sex in a strikingly oneiric sequence. Followed by Nino in the dark of the house during a stormy night, Angela is initially forced to undress, only to take the role of the sexual predator at the end. In the midst of this dream-like sequence – accompanied by flashing lightning and roaring thunder – while calling him 'my child' and sitting on top of him, Angela looks at Nino with a reassuring expression that betrays her mother-like affection. She then makes love to him. At the end of the film, Angela, married to his father, is now to be called 'mamma' by Nino.

This type of maternal imagery provides a male fantasy of erotic appeasement with an otherwise changing female world. By using the motif of an older woman and a teenage boy, films such as *Malizia* displace male concerns about female empowerment by conveying it in terms of age difference. Age difference then becomes a viable arena in which to rehearse the male perception of loss of power. By presenting active female desire as conspicuously maternal, films such as *Malizia* were offering a representation of passive male sexuality and inadequacy that could be acceptable, even desirable.

In a period in which feminism left the older generations behind and created uncertainty about gender roles, one way in which 1970s Italian cinema dealt with anxieties of male disempowerment was by incorporating strong elements of male nostalgia. Federico Fellini was arguably the director who most consistently explored this nostalgia through his films. In *Amarcord* (1973), for example, he evoked his childhood in Rimini by representing a long-gone world populated by mother-like goddesses such as Gradisca, the prostitute Volpina and the voluptuously sensuous tobacconist. The nostalgic romanticisation of this past was for Fellini a way of warding off a present that was, in his opinion, disfigured by commercialisation and moral vacuity, and from which he felt increasingly alienated.[35]

In *Fellini's Casanova* (*Il Casanova di Federico Fellini*: 1976), this nostalgia for a golden past intersects with the exploration of Fellini's own preoccupations with the contemporary state of the male subject. The film is an unconventional portrayal of the Italian Latin lover *par excellence*, the eighteenth-century Venetian womaniser who had a reputation for being the world's greatest lover.[36] *Fellini's Casanova* revisits the myth of the quintessential Italian Latin lover to suggest not simply the crisis of an individual male but the demise of a whole social order. The film conveys a sense of disempowerment and futility that, in light of its distinctly gendered narrative, seems to anticipate the exploration of specific male fears and concerns about feminism in *City of Women*. During his exile, Casanova repeatedly looks back at his past, recalling his romantic adventures in Venice and the fame brought to him by his reputation as a great lover. In contrast to the increasing sense of disillusion experienced by Casanova through his numerous encounters with women who abandon him after having satisfied their lust, the film points nostalgically to the memories of a reassuring model of docile femininity embodied by the sickly Anna Maria and the mechanical doll Rosalba. At the end of the film, the protagonist dreams of his native Venice. The water of the lagoon is frozen and a number of women from his past appear to run away and vanish. The final scene of Casanova dancing a last waltz upon the frozen lagoon with the mechanical doll is an image that ironically suggests that this was perhaps the only woman who really understood Casanova: a passive and unthreatening reflection of man's desire that can only be recuperated now as fantasy.

Fearing Loss, Performing Power Reversal: *City of Women*

City of Women revolves around an oneiric fantasy in which man attempts to enter the 'dangerous' recesses of a new female world – the dream structure of the film being established at the very beginning when the protagonist Snaporaz falls asleep in a train compartment and reiterated just before the end when he wakes up. The dream is divided into three stages corresponding to the three main internal spaces of the film – the hotel Miramare, Katzone's house and the boxing ring hangar – each stage also involving, as Gaetana Marrone has noted, a series of circle-like journeys through memory.[37] *City of Women* explores a path that appears both familiar and strangely foreign. It follows the protagonist, Snaporaz, in his quest for the ideal woman. The journey is marked by a number of encounters with sexually palatable female objects of desire, which coincide with different moments of the protagonist's life. The encounters, initially comforting, keep on turning into nightmarish fantasies in which a number of aggressive, menacing-looking women appear. This circularity is also evoked by the familiar Fellinian motif of the circus and through a number of recurring circular configurations (for example, the skating rink and the slide). It could be said that the main motif of the film is the circular chase of the hunter, who is repeatedly transformed into the hunted and reduced to the state of victim of his own erotic obsessions. The motif, repeated several times during the story, represents Snaporaz as stuck between dream fantasy and memory.

Michelangelo Buffa and Roberto Escobar have argued that *City of Women* is really a film about 'symbolically penetrating and venturing on a perilous journey into the contemporary female world'.[38] This is exemplified at the beginning of the film by the image of a train about to enter a tunnel. It is a symbolic image that, according to Fellini, explains the sense of the whole film: 'the tunnel, the uterus, the train, the rigid thing, which wishes to enter but is instead sucked up by it'.[39] In the sequence of the train – eventually repeated at the end of the film with the train's actual entrance into the tunnel – the use of the subjective shot lays emphasis on the position of the train (the phallic symbol standing for man?), which appears here to be swallowed by the tunnel. The effect produced by this camera position is that the train's entrance is figured as losing its active position and giving in to the suction of the receptacle. This ending seems to allude to the final scene of Alfred Hitchcock's *North by Northwest* (1959), in which a train similarly enters a tunnel, leading us to believe that the protagonist's dream of having sex with his female accomplice has finally been realised. *City of Women* seems to play with the inevitability of the Hitchcockian ending, by teasing the familiarity of its erotic symbolism only to reveal a narrative of male possibilities that now appear to be denied.

Man's possibility of losing agency is again hinted at through the subjective shot that marks another 'penetration': Snaporaz's entrance through the doors of the hotel where a feminist convention is being held. As Snaporaz moves toward the door, the camera, dollying in, replicates his movement forwards. At the convention, Snaporaz confronts a number of women who claim total control over their bodies and lives. The protagonist is literally drawn to the hotel by the woman from the train, who asserts that her role in relation to Snaporaz is far from that of passive prey. 'I do not escape, I reach over,' she says.[40] Anxieties about impotence are again conjured up by means of camera movement. The initial shots of the convention are taken from Snaporaz's optical standpoint through a series of panning shots, which reveal the various groups of feminists, who are unevenly distributed and engaged in vivacious discussions. A similar kind of panning movement is then replicated by Snaporaz's face as the protagonist looks around the hotel lobby with an amused expression. Up to this point, the movement of the camera signals the protagonist's partial agency in relation to his experience of space. We clearly know where he is positioned and the subjective panning movement of the camera indicates his control over what he sees. Shots showing the crowd of women are linked to shots showing Snaporaz in the act of looking. Gradually, however, this stable position gives way to a more disorienting experience of space. The subjective shot is first reversed by the image of a woman looking menacingly at the camera, followed by another shot showing Snaporaz, who is seemingly unaware of what is happening around him. A similar reversal takes place in relation to the subjective panning shot. The camera dollies to the left and then pans to the right, again showing Snaporaz as the object of its gaze. The subjective shot is then progressively replaced by a much more complex editing pattern and a less smooth camera movement through the different rooms of the hotel in which the feminists attend workshops. The position of the camera changes continually to the point that we are not always sure where Snaporaz is standing and what he is looking at. Every now and then, a woman stares aggressively at the camera. These are the moments when we are reminded that the dominant point of view is still that of Snaporaz. Yet, precisely because of the hostility of these female gazes, Snaporaz's point of view hardly confers on this subject position any sense of security in relation to the surroundings.

At the feminist convention, hordes of infuriated women animatedly debate the evils of penetration and fellatio, whilst promoting lesbianism and invoking the creation of a new world populated only by women. The presence of smoke creates a gloomy mist-like effect in the lobby; the menacing quality of the mise-en-scène is further compounded by the infernal noise of various female voices forming a maddening cacophony of shouts and chants. At a loss with these enraged women, Snaporaz wanders around the lobby of the hotel only to feel more and more intimidated by their threatening looks and their slogans against men and patriarchy. Snaporaz asks some of these women, 'I understand the problems of feminism, but why do you need to be so angry?'[41] The question highlights even more the exaggerated hostility of the women. It turns Snaporaz into a seemingly innocent victim, whilst simultaneously confining the women within the realm of the grotesque. Pointing to such a problematic vision of feminism in the film, Marie Jean Lederman has accused Fellini of representing feminists as humourless and frivolous figures. For her, *City of Women* confirms Fellini's inability to move beyond his own psychic limits and his chauvinist visions of women: 'The terrain in Fellini's *City of Women* feels familiar. [. . .] The terrain of this city is Woman, and once again we see through Fellini's eyes; once again we are inside his fantasies and his fears.'[42]

Interestingly, in an interview, Fellini partly anticipates this critique. For him, *City of Women* is:

> a film about one man, a man who invents woman. She is his metaphor, his obscurity, the part of himself he doesn't know, and about which he feels a fatal necessity to create ever new hypotheses. [. . .] My feminist critics are even now saying that in the whole film there isn't one real woman. Of course there isn't.[43]

Similarly, the film poster released in Great Britain reported: '*City of Women* is a film about a man who invents woman.' Far from being an objective representation of feminism, it is, according to Fellini, only an artefact expressing his personal take on the shifting relation between men and women at the time. The film is for Fellini only a dream and what we see is just a projection of the dreamer. The film stresses this subjective perspective right from the initial credits, where a giggling female voiceover ironically asks, 'Marcello again? Please, Maestro!'[44] Here, the Maestro could be the conductor, who then starts directing his orchestra as the music plays through the initial credits, but it could equally be Fellini himself, who was often called 'maestro' (master) in recognition of his art. The question seems to be an allusion to Marcello Mastroianni's presence in the film as lead actor and to how *City of Women* will self-consciously play with Mastroianni's well-established role as Fellinian alter ego in *La dolce vita* (1960), *Juliet of the Spirits* (*Giulietta degli spiriti*: 1965) and *8½* (*Otto e mezzo*: 1963). Significantly, the name of the protagonist is Snaporaz, which is the nickname that Fellini generally used to refer to his actor friend. *City of Women* thus integrates the close relationship between Fellini and Mastroianni within the film and plays with the director's unresolved issues with women from the perspective of an ageing man. Snaporaz appears here as a surrogate for Fellini, who is also using Mastroianni as an alter ego for his own dilemmas.

As such, the film is a powerful statement of auteurial omnipotence, one that is very much consistent with the self-consciousness of much of Fellini's cinema and with the director's claim to represent only women as seen by his own eyes, the eyes of an ageing man who is struggling to make sense of a rapidly transforming reality. But *City of Women* is also a sombre reflection on man's fear of losing control over his own fantasy world. The tension between these two opposite drives is made explicit in the sequence showing the feminist convention.

Near the end of this sequence, the mysterious woman we met on the train re-appears. 'Once again we have been betrayed,' she announces to the other feminists as she looks around the chanting crowd.[45] This announcement marks a sudden shift in subject positions. Up to this point, Snaporaz is shown looking around the crowd of women and smiling at their eccentric declarations of self-empowerment. A series of pan shots interspersed with medium and close-up shots of the women are sutured together within Snaporaz's gaze. The shift is marked by an extended close-up on the contemplative face of the woman, whilst her voice becomes a commentary (initially extra-diegetic) on what we have seen and are about to see. In order to achieve this effect, the volume of the women's chanting suddenly decreases. The woman calmly tells the others that they have been very naïve in exposing their concerns and rituals to the ridiculing eye of a man who is not really interested in understanding their frustrations and motivations. The camera keeps on panning, revealing the joy and enthusiasm of the women. The music and the noise then stop. All the feminists interrupt their chants and start listening to her. She declares:

> The eyes of that man are the eyes of the male we've always known. They reflect his inner derision, his mockery. He has the same rotten core. We are only a pretext for another of his crude, animalistic fables. Another neurotic song-and-dance act.[46]

The woman is clearly referring to Snaporaz, who stands immobile in front of her. She stands up and announces that the time of women's subjection to man's demeaning gaze is over. At this point, the camera intrusively dollies in on Snaporaz. He tries to hide behind a column but, as the camera gets closer and closer to him, the woman finally addresses him directly and unmasks his identity to the others. She encourages the other feminists to look at him and shows a photograph depicting him (the one that she had taken on the train). Here, a diegetic feminist subject literally reverses the dominant gaze back on the male one. It is now the man that becomes an object of derision for the women. This moment signals the momentary loss of an overpowering subject position for the protagonist. Most importantly, it marks his inability to exert control over what we have believed to be a strictly subjective male perspective on the feminists. The mysterious woman is also implicitly talking through Snaporaz to Fellini. Hers is a monologue that throws back on the director the traditional accusations made by a number of feminist critics of his cinema. As Peter Bondanella points out, feminist viewers of Fellini's films have tended to criticise him for his portrayal of women as distorted projections of his personal imagery.[47] But the woman's monologue is also a feminist-informed comment on the grotesque way in which the women of the convention have been portrayed thus far. It is not unusual for Fellini to introduce such self-conscious commentaries about the alleged limitations of his own cinematic vision. In *8½*, for example, the common criticisms of Fellini's style (his complacency, his incoherence, his inability to provide a clear conclusion) are already present in the film, voiced through the critic Daumier. The same applies to the accusations of complacency with Catholic morality, which come to be thrown back at Guido – and implicitly Fellini – near the end of the film. In *City of Women*, the self-consciousness of this scene has ambiguous, if not contradictory, implications. On the one hand, it spells out the threat of losing control over his world that the protagonist confronts in his relations to modern women. On the other, in representing women and feminism according to the conventional biased outlook for which Fellini is generally blamed and in playing out intra-diegetically an 'imaginary' feminist critique of such a distorted outlook, the sequence in the hotel lobby further emphasises the pre-eminence of the subjective perspective on the feminist movement that Fellini adopts here. It is a sequence that, through its final self-reflective commentary, demonstrates incontrovertibly that the film is conscious of its own subjective view and that it is not going to make any apologies for it.

As well as constituting a striking assertion of authorial omnipotence, the sequence in the hotel is remarkable for the way in which the relation between men and women comes to be imagined at this particular historical juncture. The relation is significantly conceived in terms of a subject–object trajectory whose 'natural' terms appear inverted. Man is now envisaged as the object of a woman's gaze. The gaze appears threatening. The threat revolves around the possible loss of a subject position from which man understands himself and his relation to his female Other. *City of Women* in a sense mimics what it would be like for man to be finally looked at by a woman's gaze and the consequent loss of power that this experience might generate.

* * *

City of Women makes particularly explicit the nostalgic thrust underlying apocalyptic narratives of male crisis. Nostalgia is the longing for what we feel we have lost. It relies on the evocation of a golden age often linked to a return to childhood divested of present preoccupations. In *The Past is a Foreign Country*, David Lowenthal explains the crucial function of nostalgia in relation to apocalyptic structures of feelings. Nostalgia is laden with anxieties about a future that may never arrive, Lowenthal suggests. 'By contrast, the past is tangible and secure; people think of it as fixed, unalterable, indelibly recorded. [. . .] We are at home in it because it is our home.'[48] If what fuels nostalgia is mistrust for the future and the loss of faith in the possibility of changing the present, nostalgia is precisely the remedy to this mistrust in light of its relation to the familiar, the stable and the 'already known'. Nostalgia reaffirms identities bruised by recent turmoil by re-establishing age-old convictions about gender, morals and society in general. It is also based on mourning something that is inconsolably lost. But as Melanie Klein's study on mourning demonstrates, its working has the objective of reinstating the lost object through an act of recovery. The successful work of mourning is the rebuilding of a representation of that which no longer exists. In these terms, nostalgia may be said to be the mise-en-scène that enables the work of mourning to be successful.[49] *City of Women* seems to perform precisely this act of bringing back to life the mourned object – an authoritative masculinity and a set of comforting images of women – by plunging into a past pervaded by childhood masturbatory fantasies and maternal erotic goddesses. Such nostalgic imagery has the effect of re-affirming a stable male subject position, but most importantly inscribes the relation with the female sex within the terms of a script that positions women as unthreatening objects of desire.

In *City of Women*, Snaporaz finds shelter from the threats of a present dominated by a new generation of castrating women when he arrives at Katzone's house. Katzone lives in a mansion full of phallic furniture, erotic memorabilia and a collection of photographs and recordings of his sexual conquests (Fig. 2.5). Against a present that is laden with deep anxieties about emasculation and disempowerment, it is here, in a microcosm evoking a past in which man is still king, that Snaporaz finds comfort and consolation; the film offers a particular configuration of the past marked by a sense of nostalgia for a period in history where things were easier and gender relations much less complicated. Most importantly this is a past that enables the recuperation of a comforting erotic imagery and the re-establishment of man's traditional position of control over women. This erotic imagery is first conjured up in the corridor where Katzone collects photographs of his numerous sexual conquests and recordings of their orgasms. Snaporaz seems safe from the threatening behaviour of the modern women that he has so far encountered. The rows of women's photographs appear here as 'harmless' objects of desire under the control of an all-powerful male subject. The protagonist switches their voices on and off according to his own liking and, as he does so, does not hide his excitement. He utters childish sounds and hops up and down along the corridor. While at this point the film is obviously parodic, it is also creating a space for the protagonist to regain a sense of self-confidence. Here, the man again appears able to exert his mastery over his own experience of space. The camera underscores this sense of mastery by moving sinuously along the corridor and steadily accompanying Snaporaz's movements with occasional cuts to close-ups of Katzone's sexual conquests.

Figure 2.5 *City of Women*, Snaporaz visits Katzone's collection of photographs.

Katzone's house functions as a comforting haven where the protagonist appears able to retrieve that sense of security that is relentlessly denied to him in the present. At the end of the party that celebrates Katzone's latest conquest, such a sense of comfort is signalled by Snaporaz's encounter with an elderly maid, who announces that Katzone has prepared a surprise for him. The sequence begins with the appearance of Raina and Vassilas, two showgirls whom Snaporaz fell in love with as a young boy, who start dancing down the stairs of the house.[50] Elated by their presence, Snaporaz dances with them in imitation of Fred Astaire. Meanwhile, all the other female housekeepers cluster around. Snaporaz is then given a nightgown, mothered by these women and put into bed like a child, much to his excitement.

Snaporaz's regression into childhood reconnects him to the reassuring certitude of a past and a familiar erotic imagery populated by maternal female figures. This is never clearer than when Snaporaz crawls under his bed and descends along a slide in an imaginary circus-like fantasy. In descending the first part of this dream-like rollercoaster, Snaporaz recovers a series of erotic memories from his past, which are introduced by three old men dressed in tuxedos. The first memory shows the curvaceous maid Rosina, who first reprimands the child Snaporaz for his mischievous behaviour and then kisses and hugs him maternally. Other shapely figures such as the fishwife and the nurse from the thermal baths reveal a similar motherly erotic appeal (Fig. 2.6). As the three men introduce Snaporaz to these memories, it is soon clear how this erotic imagery is also meant to evoke Fellini's past objects of desire from his childhood and their cinematic celebration through figures such as

Figure 2.6 *City of Women*, the fishwife appears as one of Snaporaz's childhood memories.

Saraghina from *8½* and Gradisca from *Amarcord*. Such imagery, so concerned with past objects of desire, is also connected with childhood memories of cinema-watching, following the appearance of a huge bed where a crowd of young boys start masturbating as they look at images of Hollywood stars such as Mae West and Marlene Dietrich. This is not just a reference to what Bondanella understands as the crucial relation between male sexual desire and cinema in the film, but also a moment that emphasises the interconnectedness of an erotic imagery associated with a safe past and the realm of individual fantasy, both functioning as shelters in which men may find protection from the frightening realities of the present.[51]

In her analysis of *City of Women*, Jacqueline Reich points out how the film is in essence one big joke, with Snaporaz as the subject and women as the object of the joke. She also points out that the pervasive humour that characterises the film functions as the tool that reveals the subconscious fears and anxieties of masculinity in relation to the extra-cinematic context of the 1970s feminist movement.[52] Her argument insists that we should not take the grotesque portrayal of feminism too seriously because it is part of the general workings of *beffa* within the film (*beffa* being a comic trope by which female characters have traditionally been able to circumvent the authority of men through wit, deception and unruliness). Reich takes a rather similar standpoint to Peter Bondanella who contends that feminist attacks on Fellini's images of women in *City of Women* are perfectly understandable in the ideologically charged atmosphere of contemporary film criticism, but they often ignore the film's satirical outlook on man's inability to understand women.[53] This emphasis on the humorous aspect of the film, I would contend, has determined a general lack of interest in how the film may in fact contain a space for a more sombre reflection on feminism and its questions. A starting point may be to recall the woman's final monologue at the feminist convention.

Apart from accusing Snaporaz/Fellini, one of the major thrusts of her monologue is to point out, in women's historical oppression and subjugation to the male sex, 'how much freedom, how much authenticity and love, and life has been denied us'.[54] Her tone during the speech is passionate and deprived of any hints of humour. The tone allows us to speculate that here Fellini probably meant to suspend his grotesque portrayal of the feminists temporarily and to enable a more serious reflection on the claims and struggles of feminism. This more contemplative space in relation to the feminist movement re-emerges even more dramatically when Snaporaz discusses with his wife the state of their marriage at Katzone's party. Elena appears here as Luisa – Guido's wife in *8½* – twenty years later. The difference is that Elena has now learnt the lessons of feminism. While the marital problems between Luisa and Guido used to centre on the latter's on-going lies and infidelity, Elena now talks about her frustrations as a woman stuck in her house with a man who treats her like his own mother. 'Do you realize how empty my life is?', she angrily asks Guido at the party at Katzone's house, as she compares her secluded life to her husband's adventures and freedoms.[55] Elena has also acquired the sense of rebelliousness and decisiveness that Luisa was partly lacking in 8½. When Snaporaz, in an attempt to soothe her anger, reassures her that, despite their marital problems, he will never be able to leave her, she defiantly asserts that it will not be up to him to end their marriage but to her: 'Grow old with you? To be your nursemaid? [. . .] Forget it!'[56]

Times have changed and Snaporaz has to realise that his power over his dream-like world and his female goddesses is crumbling. Such a realisation first comes at the end of the rollercoaster ride, when his nostalgic journey into his childhood leaves him at the mercy of a crowd of feminists, who arrive to entrap him in a cage and put him on trial. A further realisation of powerlessness in relation to the present occurs when Snaporaz climbs into a boxing ring in search of the ideal woman he has been dreaming about. The ideal woman turns out to be an enormous hot-air balloon in the shape of Donatella. The balloon stands here as the incarnation of an archetypal feminine, condensing all of Snaporaz's erotic obsessions. It is a Gargantuan rendering of the role played by Claudia Cardinale in 8½. The real Donatella, now dressed as a terrorist, shoots the balloon from the ground, thus destroying Snaporaz's illusion and the possibility of escaping the anxieties of the present. This is a moment that replicates the idea of the unattainable feminine that was already central to *Fellini's Casanova* in the images of the whale and the giantess, both figurations of the archetypal feminine that dominates Fellini's erotic imagery.

At the end of *City of Women*, the protagonist wakes up and realises that what he has experienced was simply a dream. In the train carriage, Elena looks at him half-smiling while the mysterious woman, Donatella and the second showgirl enter the same carriage. The women look at each other as though they were sharing a secret and Snaporaz observes them in dismay. The protagonist experiences the same feelings of disempowerment he has faced in his dream. These women's knowledge appears inaccessible and mysterious and, again, he feels excluded from their world.

This ending is instructive of the nostalgic operation that the film performs and the power such an operation has to afford shelter protecting the protagonist from the threats of the present. In closing his eyes and going back to sleep, the protagonist prefers to retreat into the rather more secure realm of dreams and fantasy. It is a conclusion that enlightens the audience about the distinctly male power to affect the terms of cinematic representability and to counteract the threatening effects of modernity, of which feminism is supposed to be a symptomatic emblem. As Fellini later declared about this ending, 'The important thing for man today is to hang on, not to let his head droop but to keep looking up along the tunnel, perhaps even inventing a way through fantasy.'[57]

Similarly to *The Last Woman* and *Bye Bye Monkey*, *City of Women* provides a vision of the present permeated by concerns about modernisation and the blurring of clear-cut gender roles. Against this threatening image of the present, these films reveal a nostalgic longing for a past dominated by reassuring maternal fantasies linked to the memory of a golden age of unproblematic gender relations. In *Screening the Past*, Pam Cook points out that cinematic nostalgia is typically predicated on a dialectic between longing for something that has been lost and an acknowledgement that this something cannot be retrieved in reality. The pleasure provided by the cinema of nostalgia consists of the playful desire to overcome the certainty of such a loss through cinematic fantasy.[58] One could also add that cinema as a medium appears especially capable of bringing back the very thing that is irretrievably lost. In the case of *City of Women*, however, what is lost is not an actual historical reality but the perception of an uncontested position of male stability and control over reality. The loss is imagined as irrecoverable but such a loss is itself a product of fantasy, thus rendering explicit the self-conscious visualisation of male crisis as a discursive construction. *City of Women*, in particular, lays bare the imaginative drive at the heart of its vision. It invites us to interrogate the limits of its engagement with an alleged male crisis in actuality and its status as a reassuring male-centred narrative.

3. CONTESTING NATIONAL MEMORY: MALE DILEMMAS AND OEDIPAL SCENARIOS

The Oedipal conflict between father and son is a motif that has structured much of Bernardo Bertolucci's cinema.[1] A desire to escape paternal influence is, for example, at the basis of Bertolucci's decision in his early twenties to abandon poetry and choose cinema as his privileged medium of expression (his father, Attilio, was a famous poet).[2] Such a desire anticipates the materialisation of specific anxieties about his artistic influences in his earlier films. The theme of the son's rebellion against the father pervades Bertolucci's love/hate relationship with his two main cinematic mentors, Pier Paolo Pasolini and Jean-Luc Godard. Influenced by their aesthetic and political preoccupations, his earlier films reveal the extent to which Bertolucci as a young filmmaker was trying to deal with the intellectual authority of his 'fathers' whilst pursuing his quest for an autonomous cinematic language.[3] The Oedipal theme became increasingly central in the films that Bertolucci made after 1968. Vito Zagarrio has pointed out how Bertolucci was only the most radical and consistent representative of a generation of young Italian filmmakers that, in the aftermath of 1968, was obsessed with the figure of the father and the theme of the parricide.[4] Envisaged as a family crisis (where the family stands for the nation), this conflict crystallises a tension between the younger generation of Italians who came out of the post-1968 social movements and the cultural legacy of the previous generation. As Paul Ginsborg has noted, one of the most popular slogans of 1968 was 'I want to be an orphan'.[5] The slogan provocatively highlighted the symbolic rejection of the nuclear family as a site of oppression and social closedness. It suggested a critique of parental authority in the traditional family as linked to the repressive workings of the dominant social order. Most importantly, by alluding to a symbolic act of filial rebellion, the slogan reverberated with the more general anti-authoritarian spirit of 1968.

This chapter concentrates on two of the films made by Bertolucci after 1968 that, in harnessing the subject matter of the Oedipal conflict, appear most influenced by the spirit of generational rebellion of these years. Structured around parricidal narratives, *The Conformist* (*Il conformist*: 1970) and *The Spider's Stratagem* (*Strategia del ragno*: 1970) make use of the Oedipal story to develop an investigation into the memory of Italy's fascist past. Bertolucci explains his interest in fascism by referring to his conflictual relation with his father's generation and their cultural legacy: 'My own father was anti-fascist, but obviously I feel that the whole bourgeoisie is my father. And Fascism was invented by the petit bourgeois.'[6] In the highly politicised context of 1970s Italy, the anti-authoritarian rebellion of the 1968 generation against their fathers implies for Bertolucci a confrontation with this problematic legacy. By exploring the memory of Italy's fascist past, Bertolucci's aim is to reconsider the true nature of the anti-fascist stance upon which the national myth of post-war reconstruction has been built.

These two films epitomise a revival of interest in Italy's fascist past and a new critical outlook on this controversial chapter of Italian history, exemplified by the release of films such as *Christ Stopped at Eboli* (*Cristo si è fermato a Eboli*: 1979), *The Garden of the Finzi-Continis* (*Il giardino dei Finzi-Contini*: 1970), *Salò, or the 120 Days of Sodom* (*Salò o le 120 giornate di Sodoma*: 1975), *Love and Anarchy* (*Film d'amore e d'anarchia, ovvero stamattina alle 10 in via dei Fiori nella nota casa di tolleranza*: 1973) and *A Special Day* (*Una giornata particolare*: 1977). Such a new critical perspective is directly connected to the collapse of the master national narrative that had portrayed the Italian Republic as the natural product of the Resistance (1943–5). According to this narrative, the post-war Republic was cemented together by the common aims of anti-fascism. As intellectuals such as Benedetto Croce influentially argued in order to consolidate this narrative, fascism had only been a tragic parenthesis in the history of the country.[7] The counter-narrative of the 1970s suggested instead that the Italian Republic still maintained a fascist-derived centralised form of government and kept much of the administrative and judicial personnel of the fascist state. The polemical suggestion of the intellectuals who opposed Croce's view was that fascism had not ended in 1945 but was still present in the same old political class, the armed forces and some of the repressive policies of the ruling Christian Democratic Party.[8] This was an argument that was also advanced by Pier Paolo Pasolini, who famously asserted that the Italy that had emerged out of the economic miracle, with its masked networks of repressive power, could still be defined as 'fascist'.[9] The effects of this perception on the filmmakers who decided to turn to memories of the fascist period during the 1970s are exemplified by Fellini's comments on *Amarcord* (1973). For Fellini, this film was not simply a nostalgic reconstruction of his childhood in Rimini during the fascist regime, but also 'a way of looking at Italy today: Italy has changed but mentally is still much the same'.[10]

By using the Oedipal story to represent the relation between Italy's present and its fascist past, *The Conformist* and *The Spider's Stratagem* make visible their distinctive masculine gendering of the national body politic.[11] Yet, when critics discuss these films, issues concerning masculinity appear to be interpreted as no more than metaphors for the exploration of more complex historical dialectics concerning the nation. Aldo Miceli, for example, understands the private conflicts of *The Conformist* and *The Spider's Stratagem* as representing wider political realities. He asserts: 'In his vision of anti-fascism as an Oedipal struggle against the father, Bertolucci reflects on the Italian society in which he lives.'[12] In a similar vein, David Forgacs argues that, by representing the relation with the fascist past through an Oedipal conflict, Bertolucci's films, and particularly *The Conformist*, are open to the objection that they *reduce* the problem of the historical relation with the past to a gendered struggle over male identity.[13] Such views implicitly maintain that questions about male identity, in the light of their distinctive relation to the realm of the personal, fall short when they attempt to express the complexity of the historical questions these films are dealing with, hence the importance of understanding them only as metaphors for wider sociohistorical forces.

In this chapter, I would like to suggest that thinking of these films in terms of specific investigations into some of the dilemmas of masculinity in a patriarchal society may not necessarily reduce or simplify the problem of the historical relation between present and national past, but may actually add an important dimension to understanding their political meaning, their aesthetics and ultimately the specific temporal relation between national present and past at the centre of their narratives. I am not proposing to privilege questions of masculinity and, more generally, gender over history, but to read these two spheres as somehow equally important in the understanding of these films.

A second objective of this chapter is to challenge a prevailing tendency to read the Oedipal theme in *The Conformist* and *The Spider's Stratagem* as a deterministic temporality. By this, I mean a certain insistence on reading the Oedipal conflict as a cycle initiated by the son's rebellion and inevitably leading to repression and the reassertion of the Law of the Father. I wish to contest the weight that such readings seem to give to the allegedly conservative, patriarchal and self-defeatist vision offered by Bertolucci. In challenging these readings, my intention is to consider the discordances that may emerge when we confront this kind of interpretation with the evidence provided by the films. In my analysis, particular attention will be devoted to the disruptive way in which *The Conformist* and *The Spider's Stratagem* disassemble the cyclical temporality of the Oedipal narrative and the implications that this operation entails in relation to questions of gender and sexuality.

QUESTIONING THE FATHER AS A POINT OF ORIGIN: *THE SPIDER'S STRATAGEM*

The Spider's Stratagem follows the son of an anti-fascist martyr, who arrives in his father's town – Tara – to investigate his death. In the initial shots, the film establishes the procedure of following Athos in the urban landscape of Tara.[14] Memories of Athos Magnani haunt the streets, the squares and the arcades. In shot four, the camera zooms behind Athos as he stands in front of a wall, giving the impression that he is reading a sign (Fig. 3.1). A very close pan shot from right to left reveals a street sign with the name of his father (Via Athos Magnani). The movement of the camera runs opposite to the way one would read it. The right-to-left pan underscores the reverse temporal movement by which the son goes back to revisit the memory of the father and the function that Tara plays in connecting these two temporalities. Most importantly, it has the function of conveying the temporal movement of the film itself in tracing back the past of the nation.

The memory of the paternal past is also a cinematic one and is directly connected to Neorealism. Neorealism is a visible point of reference and a basic cinematic source in these initial scenes. In De Sica's *Bicycle Thieves* (*Ladri di biciclette*: 1948), the follow shot establishes a connection between the character and the social space in which he moves. This is often accompanied by a balancing movement between characters in the foreground and the background.[15] In the initial shots of *The Spider's Strategem*, this interconnectedness between the character and his experience of the social space is similarly present but the balancing movement is replaced by a different configuration of the shot focusing on Athos's isolation in the urban landscape. On his arrival, the only other character seen walking is a sailor who gets off the train with him. But

Figure 3.1   *The Spider's Stratagem*, Athos reading the street sign.

in the two shots in which we see him, he walks in the same direction as Athos – they follow almost two parallel lines – until the sailor approaches a bench and sits down. Another visual illustration of Athos's reverse movement back into the paternal past is conspicuously clear in shot seven, a long take where the camera follows him under a colonnade by panning and tracking on him. The steady longitudinal movement accompanying the son's symbolic plunging into this paternal past reveals a town populated only by old people and the sign of a youth club commemorating his father's memory (but without any young people). This longitudinal movement has the function of establishing the apparently homogenous configuration of this past in which the father is positioned as a stable point of historical origin.

A crucial point of the film is to reveal how the homogenous memory of Athos Magnani's sacrifice for the anti-fascist cause holds together. The town of Tara appears here as the chronotopic depository of an idealised past that needs to be preserved at the cost of obliterating any contradictions and counternarratives. When it becomes clear that Athos has come to Tara to investigate the mystery of his father's death and unravel his legend, he is first locked in a stable; then he is hit by a mysterious man in his hotel room; and finally he is kicked off the estate of a fascist landowner called Beccaccia. Such acts of intimidation are a demonstration of the threat that Athos represents to Tara and its memory of Athos Magnani. The film suggests the constructedness of the world that Athos enters through repeated references to René Magritte's paintings: as, for example, in shot three, a long-distance take of Tara from the countryside, which reprises the interplay between darkness and stark light characteristic of Magritte's paintings. Similar references are present in the night sequences of the film. Magritte, a painter who was interested in the way the world is conceived through the conventions of representation, provides the film with the ideal pictorial model for the interrogation of the constructedness of Tara's past. Robert Philip Koolker has shown that the references to Magritte's paintings contribute to the upending of the initial Neorealist basis of the film by making visible the artifice by which the self-effacing structure of direct observation of the Neorealist film is determined.[16]

These initial sequences are fundamental to establishing how the film is contesting a specific construction of the national past, one that is strongly informed by the anti-fascist historiography of the Resistance and its prevailing handling of Italy's fascist past. Towards this end, *The Spider's Stratagem* incorporates references to Neorealism in order to distance itself from them and to assert the constructedness of its cinematic rendering of reality. A brief look at *Rome Open City* (*Roma città aperta*: 1945) as an example of a distinctive Neorealist tendency to deal with Italy's recent fascist past may be, in this sense, instructive. In the final sequence of the film, the partisan priest, Don Pietro, is put in front of a fascist firing squad by the Nazis. Their chief officer gives the order to shoot but the fascists fail to kill him. Despite the Nazi commandant's angry demand that they shoot him again, the Italian officer cannot take action and looks at him with an expression that betrays his empathy for Don Pietro. The Nazi takes his gun and kills the prisoner. The fascists' failure to murder Don Pietro is, in a way, a proof of their ineffectiveness as 'killing machines' and implicitly a demonstration of their humanity. This ending is consistent with the way in which the film depicts fascism. *Rome Open City* as a whole does not draw attention to the fascists. It treats them with caricatural tenderness and presents the Germans as the real evil presences in the film. *Rome Open City* does not overlook the moral and political responsibilities of the fascists – it portrays, for example, the police commissioner who collaborates with Bergman as an unscrupulous and loathsome figure – but dilutes our contempt for them by coding them as slightly comic characters in contrast to the cruelty and deathly efficiency of their Nazi counterparts. The film even manipulates historical truth in order to remain consistent with its aim to condone Italians' responsibilities. In this sense, even though in reality it was a fascist officer who killed Don Morosini (the anti-fascist priest to whom the film is dedicated and on whom the character of Don Pietro is based), the film presents a German as the killer. *Rome Open City* exemplifies a certain tendency among Neorealist films to externalise Italians' responsibility for fascism. As Ruth Ben-Ghiat has argued, Neorealism had a sort of purificatory function within the cultural and political context of post-war Italy: 'Both critics and directors conceived of Neorealism as a "return to honesty" after years of fascist rhetoric and a rediscovery and celebration of a "real Italy" that had been suppressed by the dictatorship.'[17] The conciliatory way in which fascists were portrayed in these films was very much dependent on the project of creating a more inclusive national cinematic imagery, in which the opposing political forces that had lacerated the nation at the end of the war could finally be appeased and brought together. Culpability was therefore generally displaced onto foreign figures such as perverse Nazis or Italians, whose embrace of practices such as drug usage and homosexuality (Marina in *Rome Open City*, for example) made them foreign to the national body politic.[18]

Through the story of Athos's investigation into the myth surrounding his father's sacrifice, *The Spider's Stratagem* is implicitly making a commentary on the post-war master narrative for remembering and representing Italy's fascist past. The film questions the coherence of this narrative and the way in which the homogeneous configuration of this past is constructed and preserved. The memory of the father appears here as metonymically representing the post-war memory of fascism and its contribution in shaping the collective consciousness of the nation. By questioning the coherence of this narrative, the film is implicitly inviting us to consider what is generally left out of its homogeneous representation of the past.

* * *

In Tara, with the exception of Draifa and the little girl who works for her, Athos meets only men; the maleness under which Tara presents itself appears to constitute a structuring condition for the maintenance of the narrative of paternal idealisation. In the sequence in which Rasori receives Athos in his flat, the former locks a first door. Behind the door (which has a glass window), we see an old woman approaching. She stops behind the glass whilst Rasori moves to the right and makes a 180-degree turn to face the camera. As Rasori looks at Athos, he emphatically says: 'Your father' ('Tuo padre'). The woman looks in the same direction in silence. Something similar happens when Rasori locks out the second woman. The difference is that he pronounces the words, 'Your father', even more floridly. In both cases, Rasori does not speak before the women have reached the door and look straight at the camera behind the glass. It is a sort of *pas de deux* where the articulation of the narrative of paternal idealisation performed by Rasori implies the parallel closing-down on a female voice. After Rasori and Athos have eaten together, Rasori informs his guest that he needs to lock the women in every time someone comes to visit. He then starts his theatrical account of Athos Magnani's heroic life. This transition from female seclusion to paternal idealisation is crucial not only to showing how Tara silences female knowledge but also to revealing that it is exactly this silencing that allows its citizens to maintain their idealised memory of Athos Magnani.[19]

Like an insect captured in a spider's web, Athos is swallowed up in the plot that his father has conceived and that the town of Tara perpetuates. In a remarkable sequence, Athos walks around his father's statue and stares at it. As he turns around, so does the statue, staring back at the camera (occupying the point of view of the son) almost in defiance (Fig. 3.2). As the statue rotates together with Athos, the father projects his image back on the son in a striking configuration of sameness that articulates the double bind connecting these two figures and the two temporalities they represent. At the end of the point-of-view shot around the statue of Athos Magnani, the camera reveals Draifa, dressed in white and holding a parasol, walking in the background, in soft focus. As the rotating image of Athos Magnani stares at the camera, the female image in the background signals the threat to the coherence of the paternal plot. This image crystallises the crucial role that Draifa performs in the undoing of the official memory of Athos Magnani. At the beginning of the film, she is the one who first summons Athos back to Tara and encourages him to investigate some of the unconvincing truths about his father's killing. Further, she is the only figure who opposes the official narrative of Athos Magnani's death and informs his son that the murderer was not someone from another town, as everybody says, but a local. Most importantly, Draifa provides a reliable account of the facts from which Athos can start his search. She tells him that his father had been shot from behind whilst watching a

Figure 3.2   *The Spider's Stratagem*, Athos Magnani's statue and Draifa, walking with her parasol in the background.

performance of *Rigoletto* at the local theatre and gives him the exact date of the killing. Draifa appears as a source of knowledge that is antagonistic to the male official narrative that is being defended by the citizens of Tara. She represents a kind of female logos that undermines the authority of the father's cult and its seemingly homogenous story. Her role is not to elucidate the truth that may lie behind the official story of Athos Magnani but to provide access for Athos into some of the complexities and contradictions that have been left out of the official paternal story.

By summoning Athos, Draifa propels him into a web of misrecognitions and blurring of identities. When Draifa sees him for the first time, she comments on how similar he looks to his father. The camera pans left to show the son next to a photograph of Athos Magnani and their identical appearance; the same actor, Giulio Brogi, plays both the father and the son.[20] This playful overlapping between past/father and present/son is further played out and translated at the level of the psychic by the use of flashbacks springing up from the memories of Athos Magnani's friends as they meet his son. These montage sequences highlight the entrapment of past and present in the same temporal grid. An example of this entrapment occurs when Athos escapes from Rasori, Gaibazzi and Costa. Athos runs through the woods. Shots of his legs running are intercut with others of his upper body. This frantic parallel cutting gradually introduces images of the father running in the same wood so that the two figures appear to be fused into one.

In capturing the protagonist in a web of identifications with the father, the role of Draifa is to allow Athos to retrace the origins and the intricate workings of the paternal plot. The sequence in the theatre makes explicit the need for direct confrontation with this plot (through a process of doubling) in order to unravel the narrative. Athos sits in the same balcony where his father had been killed. An establishing shot of the theatre is followed by the image of Rasori,

Costa and Gaibazzi sitting in one of the balconies at the theatre. What follows is a sequence of shots in which one friend after another disappears. In revisiting the night of his father's killing, Athos realises that Athos Magnani had seen his murderers in the same way as he now sees Rasori, Costa and Gaibazzi opening the door to his balcony. The re-enactment of the scene of his father's death allows him to understand that Athos Magnani did not turn back to face his murderers and he intentionally let them kill him from behind. He also realises that his father knew his murderers and that his death was part of a plot of which he must have been aware.

Identification with the subject position of the father at the theatre leads the son to the acquisition of the 'repressed' knowledge that he had been prevented from accessing. A flashback springing up from the confession of Rasori, Costa and Gaibazzi to Athos dismantles the myth surrounding Athos Magnani and reveals that he had indeed betrayed his friends by giving the police the details of their plan to kill Mussolini on his visit to Tara. To expiate his crime, Athos Magnani had convinced his friends to stage a farce. They would kill him but his death would appear to be a murder committed by the fascists.

Critics have generally argued that the resolution of the paternal plot, far from marking the fall of the father, follows a distinctly Oedipal paradigm according to which the son 'kills' the father, only to bow to his authority finally. This interpretation stems from a particular reading of one of the final sequences of the film, in which Athos is called by the citizens of Tara to give a speech in memory of his father in the square. The son would not appear to reveal the discovery he has made about his father's betrayal. The implication would be that he is complying with the official memory of the 'hero' Athos Magnani. Lesley Caldwell observes, '[t]he son, once apprised of his father's betrayal, participates in the deception so that the status of the father is publicly preserved.'[21] On a similar note, Robert Philip Kolker argues that this ending illustrates how Athos Magnani

> has himself killed, and in turns he kills his son, not literally [. . .] but by preventing him from acting on any other stage but that of the narrative created by the father, woven by him into the web that entangles all the other participants in the spectacle.[22]

According to these interpretations, in its final resolution, the film would suggest an impasse for the son, who has no choice but to stay silent and realise his powerlessness in the face of the father's plot.

These readings suggest that, after having questioned the 'constructedness' of the paternal myth, the film would ultimately re-assert the authority of the father/patriarch. The patriarchal crisis, signalled by the son's interrogation of the father's authority, would appear therefore as a totally recoverable one.

With the son entrapped in the paternal plot, the act of questioning the myth of his father and the masculine idealisation on which it is based would seem to be only a momentary crisis conducive to the passage of patriarchal right from father to son.

These interpretations seem to revolve around the idea that the film follows rather closely the events of the Borges story on which it is based by borrowing its pattern of repeated lines and its circular structure. In *Theme of the Traitor and the Hero* (1944), Ryan, the great-grandson of the Irish martyr Fergus Kilpatrick, discovers that his ancestor was not a hero who sacrificed his life for the independence of his country, but rather a traitor responsible for the failure of a revolt. Like Athos Magnani, Kilpatrick had convinced his comrades to turn his execution into an instrument for the emancipation of Ireland. At the end of the Borges story, Ryan resolves to keep his discovery silent and publishes a book dedicated to the memory of the hero Kilpatrick. Like Ryan, Athos (according to the interpretation of critics such as Kolker, Caldwell and Houston) would appear to be a final victim of the past and its entangling plot; his failure to reveal that his father was a traitor in front of the citizens of Tara would demonstrate as much.

A closer look at the final sequence, however, reveals something slightly different. At the end of the ultimate confrontation with his father's friends, Athos agrees with them that Athos Magnani's stratagem was not perfect; someone had finally managed to dismantle it. Then, he suddenly asserts that maybe 'this' someone felt obliged to keep this discovery secret because it was part of Athos Magnani's plot. This is the point that most clearly authorises the interpretation according to which the son cannot truly break free from his father's plot but has to appreciate his inevitable embeddedness in it.[23] It is a point that is retroactively informed by how the film has thus far highlighted the son's entrapment in his father's past by means of flashbacks and misrecognitions. But then, Athos defiantly says that this was the point about which Athos Magnani was wrong. This is a passage that critics tend to overlook; Athos suggests that there is something that his father had not foreseen. It is a first suggestion that the protagonist will not participate in his father's deception after all. To understand the implications of this passage one needs to look carefully at the following scene.

Athos is giving a speech in front of the old citizens of Tara, who have come together to celebrate his father. His expression betrays distress, the uncomfortable awareness of being drawn once again in the paternal narrative. The voice off intervenes to ask who Athos Magnani really was. Soon after, a flashback shows his father sitting in a shack together with his friends, who excitedly fantasise about the killing of Mussolini; the flashback begins by showing the father's ambiguous expression as he looks at his friends – an anticipation of his betrayal – in contrast to their jovial excitement as they playfully imitate the noise of the bomb set to kill Mussolini. The camera tracks down and dwells on them whilst leaving Athos Magnani in the background and out of focus. This movement suddenly becomes meaningful as a cut back to the present shows Athos celebrating in front of the citizens of Tara the loyalty and courage of his father's friends. Athos does not waste any words enriching the paternal myth that Tara has endorsed. Instead, he breaks its one-dimensional articulation by avowing other narratives of anti-fascist courage and resistance, as exemplified by men such as Gaibazzi, Costa and Rasori. In another flashback, his father is seen running in the wood whilst the voiceover emphatically utters 'A traitor!?!?'[24] This speech is intercut with the sequence of his statue rotating with the camera. His words intermingle with the present as we return to the square where Athos is giving his speech. This intertwining of flashbacks would appear to show once more the power of the father's past over the present.[25] But then, a young boy wearing a red shirt walks across the square, followed by a group of young men. He smiles. At this point, Athos says 'There's a sentence that . . . A man is made of all men. He is worth all of them and each one of them is worth the same as him.'[26] These are the last words of Jean-Paul Sartre's novel *Les Mots* (1964): 'Un homme, fait de tous les hommes et qui les vaut tous [. . .].' In an unpredictable change of mood, Athos then takes his leave, saying that he has left his suitcase at the station.

Through his speech, the younger Athos has made no contribution to the perpetuation of the official memory of his father. At the same time, he has not substituted a narrative of paternal grandeur with one of paternal betrayal. The flashbacks springing up during the speech and the voiceover repeatedly wondering who Athos Magnani really was invite us to think that a coherent hold on the father and his past is perhaps impossible. Athos Magnani may be both a hero and a traitor. The ending of the film frees the incoherencies of that past to redefine a history that has refused to include anything else but the cult of the father. In his speech, Athos mentions the valuable contribution of Rasori, Gaibazzi and Costa to the anti-fascist resistance. Following this recognition, the arrival of the young boy and the other men during his speech seems to mark another symbolic opening of this one-dimensional narrative. Throughout the film, the exclusion of young people from the public space of Tara has signified the static enclosure of the present in the past. The arrival of the young people and particularly the smile of the young boy reveal a certain intention to mobilise this temporality by opening its linear articulation. Before the arrival of the young boy and the other men, all the old people in the square hold on to identical black umbrellas. The arrival of the young men disrupts this monochromatic ensemble. Significantly, the young boy wears a striking red shirt – an allusion to communist resistance – while the others wear multi-coloured clothes. Through the use of colour, their arrival underscores the undermining of this coherent memory of paternal idealisation. The smile of the child, rather than suggesting the entrapment of new generations in the webs of the past, appears to be a smile of hope that points to the possible reconfiguring of that past under more diversified and inclusive narratives. If the past cannot be changed, its relation to the present can, and this possibility is clearly articulated here. By saying that every man is made of all men at the end of this speech, Athos celebrates the shift from a one-man story of heroism towards a multiple narrative of collective endeavour against fascism. In contrast to how Tara has thus far unified itself in the cult of Athos Magnani, the slogan provides an alternative articulation of anti-fascist resistance in which it is precisely the collective endeavour of many heroes that may provide a much more inspiring paradigm for the future.

At the end of the film, Athos reaches the station with the intention of leaving Tara. The loudspeakers announce that the train is late; he sits down on the platform. The camera moves along the rail track to show some grass growing. Athos looks puzzled, as though he is coming to a moment of realisation. The extended strings of the soundtrack add a sense of thrilling anguish; something is dawning on the protagonist. A short shot of Tara intercutting this sequence constitutes a chilling reminder that no train will arrive; no train will allow him to escape the paternal past that Tara honours. It is a realisation, however, in the light of what we have seen, that does not mean scepticism about the possibility of contesting that past, but rather articulates the understanding that any breaking with that authority will have to imply confrontation with its power over the present. With this ending, the film does not avow the cyclical workings of history but highlights the necessity of redefining the relationship with that past and deconstructing its absolute authority over the present.

* * *

The ending of the film also contributes to redefining the heroic masculinity with which Athos Magnani has been presented in the official memory of Tara. The short flashback in which Draifa accuses him of being a coward is, in this sense, a reminder of the role that an idealised male identity has played in this official memory. This flashback is a shorter version of a previous one that emerges out of Draifa's personal memory of Athos Magnani when the son had asked her to recall what it was like to be with him. It illustrates a moment of playful intimacy between the two lovers as she helps him apply a bandage to support his aching back. This is a moment in which Draifa also conveys her frustrations and sadness about the illicit nature of their affair.

In this flashback, Athos Magnani appears unable to respond to her need for more love and commitment on his part. The focus of this scene is very much on Draifa uttering the word 'coward' ('codardo'), a comment on his inability to confess their affair to his wife but also on his egocentrism and inability to empathise with her suffering. It is implicitly a comment about Athos Magnani's masculinity too. Draifa's accusation in this short flashback follows the image of Athos Magnani running in the woods while the voiceover says 'a traitor'. An implicit link is created here between the possibility that the hero Athos Magnani might not be so heroic after all and that the idealised masculinity celebrated by the people of Tara may similarly be untrue. The spectacle that Athos Magnani has staged to perpetuate the illusion of his heroism encompasses in this sense the illusion of a romanticised male identity that, in the gap that separates its public performance from its private enactment, reveals its fragility.

Through the Oedipal motif of the son questioning the authoritative myth of the father, the film explores the conflict between two masculinities. On the one hand, the father stands for an essentially patriarchal figure of authority, defending its hegemonic position through the silencing and marginalisation of the subordinate knowledges that threaten its authority. On the other, the son represents a new masculine position that, in contesting the father as a univocal point of origin and authority, establishes a space for the fragmentation of knowledge. It is still a male-dominated vision that undoubtedly excludes women as active participants in the national body politic. Yet, it is also a vision that suggests women's disruptive role in mobilising the coherent national narrative of anti-fascism inherited from the Resistance. In the context of post-1968 Italy, the film is actively contributing to a shift towards a re-opening of the national past that is ready to welcome a conglomeration of different voices. It is a redefinition of national history that takes into account the new interpersonal and political realities of post-1968 Italy. By challenging the notion of a past that speaks only through a univocal, authoritative voice, this is a vision that is also now ready to render visible different axes of sexual difference. *The Spider's Stratagem* does not directly incorporate these different voices; nor does it decentralise the dominant position of men from the discursive practices through which the nation is envisaged. Yet, it presents a critical viewpoint on the exclusion of marginal social subjects such as women and the repression of the voices that contradict the 'imagined' coherence of the national past.

The film ultimately questions forms of masculinity that are organised around fantasies of identification with an idealised paternal figure, together with the denials, prohibitions and privileges that this kind of identification implies. Whilst *The Spider's Stratagem* is most explicitly concerned with how a consistent national narrative holds together (and how it can be questioned), it is certainly also evocative of the repression required by the Oedipal journey of male subject formation. To think about masculinity as simply a metaphor for the representation of more complex social and political dynamics about the nation is, then, reductive and misleading. Such a view frames masculinity as an empty rhetorical figure within the film, a vector for the exploration of what should indeed be its true higher concerns (i.e. the dilemmas of the nation). It is a view that overlooks the way in which *The Spider's Stratagem* defines the relation between son (Athos) and father (Athos Magnani) as both a social and an individual paradigm for representing the dialectic between repression and liberation. The film envisages the unravelling of this relation as a journey populated by desires (for knowledge, for freedom, for libidinal chaos, for a plurality of voices and experiences to be told and shared) that can hardly be contained despite the paternal imperative to silence. It is a journey that speaks to the libidinal disavowals imposed on the male subject in exchange for the stable inhabiting of a socially acceptable masculinity and for the preservation of men's privileged status and their control over women's freedoms in patriarchy.

THE OEDIPAL JOURNEY AND THE RETURN OF THE REPRESSED IN *THE CONFORMIST*

Made only a few months after *The Spider's Stratagem*, *The Conformist* adopts the distinctly Oedipal mould of the novel written by Alberto Moravia, entitled *Il conformista* (1951), on which it is based. The novel is a modern Greek tragedy where destiny and cyclical inevitability are crucial to the story of the protagonist. Constructed upon a rigorously linear and deterministic chronology, the novel follows Marcello's life from childhood to adulthood by showing the sadistic acts of violence he perpetrated as a child as signals of his impending murderous instincts. Moravia's novel links Marcello's increasing sense of his own deviancy to his father's abnormality, as a kind of legacy that the son has inherited and from which he cannot escape. In the novel, Marcello is predestined to become a fascist murderer through what Moravia describes as a cruel and unfathomable mechanism.[27] Marcello's fascist allegiance therefore not only is a part of the process by which he turns to a life of total conformity, but also responds to the deterministic logic of Fate in Moravia's novel.

The theme of Oedipal inevitability is partly still present in the film. The past returns to torment the protagonist, Marcello Clerici, when an anonymous letter reaches his fiancée Giulia and her mother. This letter claims that Marcello has inherited a disease from his father and that he is unsuitable as a husband for Giulia. Even though this is a false claim made by Giulia's jealous uncle to prevent their union, it is a gesture that marks the weight that the past will have exert on Marcello throughout the film. Marcello has joined the fascist secret service to kill Quadri, his ex-university professor. Believing that this gesture is the consequence of an original paternal sin that now weighs on him, Marcello goes to visit his father in the asylum where he has been hospitalised; he reminds the older man of the stories he used to tell him as a child, when he proudly recounted the murders and tortures he carried out as a member of the fascist secret police. In recalling these memories, Marcello abdicates personal responsibility for the crime he will commit by blaming his father for the chain reaction he has initiated. It is a symbolic event that emphasises the inescapable connectedness between the destiny of father and son within Marcello's logic. Further, it is an event that marks Marcello's initial perception of the inevitability of his actions and their consequences.

The Conformist reverberates with Bertolucci's concurrent discovery of psychoanalysis.[28] One effect of this discovery is seen in how *The Conformist* further develops, at the level of the 'psychosexual', the dramaturgy of Oedipal conflict already present in *The Spider's Stratagem*. In order to see the implications of this operation, it is crucial to consider the scene set in the asylum as part of a duo. The paternal space of the asylum is all straight lines, order and cleanliness and comes after a sequence set at the mother's house that is instead all leaves, decay and disorder (Fig. 3.3). It is a contrast that reflects the psychosexual conflict experienced by the film's protagonist and his struggle between two opposing poles: on the one hand, Marcello's childhood memory of homosexual seduction by a chauffer called Lino, whom he thinks he has killed; and on the other hand, the repression of this memory, his pursuit of a life of conformity and his attempt to find atonement by having Professor Quadri killed in the name of the fascist cause. Marcello feels that his childhood encounter with Lino has marked his 'difference' in the eyes of society. Metonymically representing the process of sexual normalisation of the child during the Oedipal stage, the contrast between paternal and maternal spaces stands for the conflict between the sexual confusion and polymorphous desires associated with this memory (Id) and the repressive power of the paternal order (Superego). Distinctly linked to the memory of the child's seduction by Lino, the mother's

Figure 3.3 *The Conformist*, Marcello's father in the asylum.

decaying mansion conjures up not only her licentious lifestyle – her affair with a young Japanese chauffeur (other reference to Lino) and her drug usage – but also, most importantly, the multiple libidinal possibilities preceding the paternal repression. By contrast, the father's entrapment in the asylum reflects the power of the socialisation that Marcello aspires to in order to repress the sense of his abnormality. The strait-jacket that his father is made to wear at the end of the sequence symbolically projects the kind of restraint to which Marcello submits in order to repress the intolerable memory of his seduction at the hands of Lino. This scene visually conveys the containment of the drives that threaten the stability of his 'Oedipalised' male identity while also alluding to the costs entailed in their repression.

* * *

Marcello's masculinity appears to be the result of a carefully negotiated compromise with society. When Italo, his blind friend, asks him why he is marrying Giulia, he asserts that he is doing so in order to acquire a sense of security and stability, the impression of being exactly like the majority of people. As Marcello tells the priest during confession, by marrying Giulia, a mediocre bourgeois girl with petty aspirations, he is constructing his normality.

Public acts of recognition such as marriage grant Marcello the social mask he needs to cover up his difference and the past that he is so desperately trying to hide. During a stag party organised by Italo and his blind friends in honour of Marcello, the protagonist asks Italo what a normal man should look like, in his opinion.[29] Marcello is facing the camera, whereas we only see Italo from behind. Both are positioned low in the frame; in the upper half of the frame we see a window looking on to a pavement where some people are walking (Fig. 3.4). To answer Marcello's question, Italo executes a 180-degree turn and stands next to him. Italo says that a normal man is one that turns his head to look at the backside of a beautiful woman walking on the streets, a man that, in doing so, realises that other men have also done the same thing at the same time. As Italo formulates his theory of normality, we realise that the people who are walking in the upper frame of the screen are, in fact, prostitutes. As we see a streetwalker being approached by a man with whom she then leaves, we also realise that the camera is providing a visual commentary on what Italo is saying. That man, in the act of picking up a streetwalker, has performed the social gesture that defines his heterosexuality – and implicitly his normality – in the eyes of society. While Italo continues to speak, the camera slowly tilts down. Italo keeps on arguing that the normal man loves those who are similar to him and distrusts those who look different. Mutual social recognition is what defines and gives social existence to this normality. As Marcello sits down, Italo says that they are different from other people and that this is why they are friends. It is a self-deluding argument, one that is inadvertently

Figure 3.4 *The Conformist*, Marcello and Italo talking; the streetwalkers are visible above.

alluding to the homoerotic nature of their bond whilst obliterating the possibility of making their homosexuality openly visible in the light of what Italo has previously said. Italo wonders whether Marcello agrees with him. As the latter remains silent, Italo says that he is never wrong in such matters. The camera immediately tilts down to show that he is wearing two different types of shoes, a visual proof of Italo's self-deluding argument; Italo is sometimes wrong too. This is implicitly also the moment that betrays the fragility of the public acts that guarantee the construction and validation of a socially acceptable male role for Marcello.

As this sequence shows, a crucial problem in the film is the impossible stability of the male identity that Marcello has constructed for himself. This impossible stability mirrors the similarly deceptive logic by which fascism holds on to the illusion of a stable and unitary national body politic. The insertion into the story of the myth of Plato's cave is, in this sense, a particularly persuasive illustration of the limits of the illusion that the protagonist is pursuing. Marcello goes to visit his ex-university professor, Quadri. Soon after he enters his study, he closes the shutters of one of the windows to recount the Platonic tale from *The Republic*. The story describes a cave, in which enchained prisoners have been forced to live in front of a wall since their childhood. On this wall, these prisoners see the shadows of some statues being carried behind them, which they mistake for real people. Marcello stands in front of the only window whose shutters have not been closed; his figure, like Plato's statues, reflects his own shadow against the wall. Quadri excitedly points out the parallel between Plato's myth and what happens in fascist Italy, where people confuse the shadows of things with reality. Marcello contemplates the shadow of his own body on the wall, the visual materialisation of the illusory identity that he has chosen to live. Their conversation continues in the semi-darkness as Marcello blames Quadri for leaving Italy and implicitly holds him responsible for his own conversion to fascism. Quadri justifies his choice as the most sensible decision to take at the time. Standing between the only open window and the wall, Marcello responds by saying, 'Nice words. You left and I became a fascist.'[30] In so doing, he tries to abdicate responsibility for his actions. As Quadri suggests that a true fascist would not speak like him, he suddenly opens the shutters of the other window. The camera cuts to show Marcello's shadow dissipating on the wall. This is not only a visual exemplification of the moment of Platonic enlightenment speaking for the illusion on which fascism has been constructed, but also a demonstration of the self-defeating process by which Marcello is trying to keep together his seemingly coherent heterosexual identity.

In its unmasking of fascism's illusory quest for a stable world view and the parallel uncovering of Marcello's self-deluding trajectory of masculine normalisation, the film reveals the close affiliations between the contradictory processes by which 'nation' (in this case a coherent fascist identity) and 'gender' are conventionally thought of as natural entities. Benedict Anderson's study of the origins of nationalism and Judith Butler's work on gender are particularly useful for clarifying these similarities. A central tenet of Anderson's *Imagined Communities* is the idea that the nation is an ideological construction based on the forging of fixed boundaries and a sense of wholeness. For Anderson, this idea is indeed only illusory. In looking at the 'self-naturalisation' of Europe's dynasties as nations since the mid-nineteenth century, he argues that their process of nation formation was the result of fundamental contradictions between the identification of coherent national communities on the one hand, and the myths, historical origins and linguistic borders that were often conjured up to support their validity on the other. National identity was created and maintained through a circuitous process in which the present was seen to be the logical continuation of an originary past. Despite being celebrated as ancient and 'natural', on closer scrutiny, Anderson shows, nations appear as artificial, contingent and temporary entities. It is precisely the main objective of nationalistic discourse to hide the traces of their artificiality and make them appear natural.[31]

A similar constructivist approach underlies Judith Butler's work on gender. Butler argues that the naturalised knowledge of clear-cut gender identities for men and women is not only a linguistic – and therefore cultural and political – operation but also a changeable and revisable kind of knowledge. For Butler, the 'unity' imposed by the normative categories of 'men' and 'women', and the compulsory heterosexual division on which it is based, are not natural but instead fabricated. This process sees the body as the site of a cultural inscription based on regulatory norms that establish specific limits, prohibitions and denials to that same body. It is precisely through these regulatory norms that the impression of coherence is achieved. Butler provides a framework for conceptualising gender as a process of becoming, as an incessant and repeated action taking place through gestures, acts and enactments that create the illusion of an essential gender core. Butler is certainly not arguing that gender is like a dress that one can wear or change all the time. She demonstrates, however, the powerfulness of some of the discursive practices and knowledges that seek to impose on sexed bodies a binary fixity that is clearly contradicted by the discontinuous and diverse set of gender attributes deployed by subjects.[32]

The crucial link that allows us to see the similarities between Butler's and Anderson's work on gender and nation is their common emphasis on reiterative and citational practices. Such practices, as Butler explicitly asserts in *Gender Trouble*, produce the effects that they purport to name.[33] Both Butler and Anderson show that the coherence which nationalistic discourse and essentialist understandings of gender claim to express is an impossible one but is repeatedly constructed as 'natural' through such practices. This understanding also provides a way of thinking gender and nation as 'processes of becoming' that 'always fail' to effectively incarnate the essence that they claim to express.

The illusory effectiveness of these processes is strikingly visible in *The Conformist* in relation to the demands for homogeneity of fascist nationalist ideology and the similar demands for consistency implicit in the process of sexual normalisation pursued by Marcello. At the beginning of the film, Marcello goes for lunch with Giulia and her mother at their flat. The couple enter the reception room to talk about their impending wedding. Both Marcello and Giulia initially maintain a certain physical distance between each other (Fig. 3.5). They avoid kissing in front of the maid; Marcello sits on a sofa on the right, whereas Giulia takes a seat on an armchair on the left. This is a carefully maintained distance, but also a fragile one, which Giulia breaks as soon as her maid leaves and she throws herself into Marcello's arms. It is a first demonstration of the game of appearances that bourgeois society requires from them: a game through which Marcello is persistently seeking the social validation of his own normality. The shortcomings of this logic are unintentionally uncovered by Giulia a few moments later, when she starts talking about their wedding and tells Marcello that the priest will not marry them if he will not go to confession. Marcello points out to Giulia that he is not a believer and that such an act would have no value. For Giulia this has no importance and she points out that almost all the people who go to church do not really believe in God. It is enough to convince Marcello. Here, Giulia is involuntarily pointing to the empty meaning of a confession made without any firm conviction. She is also highlighting the great social weight it carries. This

Figure 3.5 *The Conformist*, Marcello with Giulia in her apartment. Giulia's mother walks along the corridor.

is an implicit allusion to the illusory validity of acts of social recognition upon which the world that Marcello wants to inhabit is constructed. It is also a reference to their authoritative value. By getting married, Marcello does not obviously become the 'normal man' he aspires to be. Yet, this social act confers the status of normality on Marcello by means of its performative power. Yet, as I will show in the following section, even though these acts of social validation give Marcello the kind of armour that allows him to disavow his homosexual instincts and his sense of abnormality, the film is primarily concerned with the points where this logic breaks down.

* * *

In *The Body in the Mirror*, Angela Dalle Vacche argues that if *The Conformist* is about the Oedipal crisis of a coherent heterosexual masculinity and the uncovering of the illusion on which it is constructed, this crisis appears in the film to be perfectly recoverable so that the Father (the Oedipal repression) may finally re-assert his authority. At the end of the film, she argues, when Marcello is confronted with the choice of whether or not to save Anna, Quadri's wife, as she stands in front of him screaming before fleeing through the woods of Savoy, the protagonist is indeed on the edge of slipping dangerously away from his consolidated male heterosexual identity towards a feminine homosexual one. In remaining immobile in the car and letting Anna die, he ultimately stifles the latter. It is a position of compromise, Dalle Vacche seems to suggest: one that does not deny the ambiguity of Marcello's masculinity but that, at the same time, entraps him in his 'constructed' identity. As history is reduced to a father–son/man-to-man dialectic, the dominant term of reference in the film, despite its critical interrogation, would still remain hegemonic heterosexual masculinity.[34]

In reading *The Conformist* through the lens of the Oedipus story, Angela Dalle Vacche's study appears to fall victim to its premise: to demonstrate the authority of a historicist tradition in Italy and its influence on the continuous preoccupation of Italian cinema with the past. Dalle Vacche's focus on Oedipal plots and recuperations of the national past surely substantiates the nature of her scholarly concern with historical origins, their authority over the present and the circuitous temporality that her study aims to demonstrate. However, the problem, I think, lies in the application of the Oedipal logic as a closed circle that inevitably re-asserts nothing but the power of the past and the impossibility of breaking free from it. As I read it, Dalle Vacche's study seems to be colluding with the historicist intellectual tradition that she is so keen to discuss rather than pointing to the evidence presented by the film and its potential for resisting the circular temporality of the Oedipal plot. In a way, it is precisely her reading that performs the temporal deadlock between present and past that her study should demonstrate. Whilst Dalle Vacche points out that the conceptual logic of the Oedipus complex is what marks Marcello's subjection to the inescapable oppressive paternal law, I would argue that it is precisely in the way Bertolucci deals with the deterministic temporal dimension of the Oedipal narrative that the film breaks free from Moravia's novel and the cyclical logic of the Oedipus story.

In this sense, Bertolucci's decision to substitute the role of Fate in Moravia's novel with that of the Unconscious is of fundamental importance. The most significant consequence is that the film rejects the dramatic determinism of the novel and shows instead the breaking down of Marcello's illusion. Interestingly, Bertolucci declared that transforming Destiny into the Unconscious also affected the way in which the rapport between sexuality and politics was organised.[35] If we consider this contention together with Bertolucci's point that *The Conformist* is really a film about the present, we may well understand the way in which the function of the Unconscious is to bring to the surface those memories and suggestions that threaten the ideal coherence upon which Marcello's identity is constructed. This is mainly done by the unfolding of events through an oneiric structure based on flashbacks, doublings, condensations and associations. The car journey to Savoy that Marcello and Manganiello undertake to save Professor Quadri's wife constitutes the film's present, the point to which the narrative keeps coming back in flashback after flashback. It functions as the central segment of the narrative over which memories of the past are brought to the surface. Christopher Wagstaff has noted that, in the car journey, the post-dubbed sound and the significant use of the voice-off give the impression that this journey may function as a sort of psychoanalytic session, an argument that reinforces the function of this section as a narrative 'couch' for the re-emergence of 'repressed' memories.[36] In the first section showing the car journey through the streets of Paris, Marcello seems, in fact, to be in a sort of reverie. We hear Manganiello's voice but we do not see him, whilst the camera cuts frenetically between a frontal close-up of Marcello in the car and different shots of Parisian buildings outside. I will not dwell on this sequence any further, as it has already been meticulously examined by Christopher Wagstaff.[37] Suffice to say how sinister and almost dream-like the sequence is, despite its function as a platform from which the flashbacks depart.

The eerie function of the car sequences in liberating memories of the past is made more explicit in another flashback showing the first encounter between Marcello and Manganiello, which confirms the role of cars in the film in resuscitating the repressed memory of Marcello's seduction by Lino. The sequence is filmed with the camera tilted sideways so that the frame is canted. The effect is to convey the anguish felt by Marcello as he walks towards his mother's house, but above all the oneiric memory of Lino and the seduction coming back to haunt Marcello. We do not realise this until later, when the narrative takes us back to the journey to Savoy and Marcello asks Manganiello to stop the car. Marcello gets out and hysterically asserts that he does not wish to follow Quadri and his wife. He walks along the side of the road whilst Manganiello follows him at a distance. The countryside is covered with snow and the fog makes it impossible to see anything round about. This mise-en-scène creates an ideal oneiric setting for the re-emergence of the memory of Marcello's encounter with the chauffeur, Lino. The flashback intersects this sequence by means of doubling. We see Marcello being followed by Manganiello and this sequence soon reproduces the memory of the young Marcello being followed by Lino.

The flashback is important because it establishes for what episode from his childhood Marcello is trying to atone. It is also significant because it confronts Marcello with the memory of his 'difference'. The film visually translates Moravia's description of Marcello's ambiguously candid femininity[38] by showing a young boy with delicate features and long fair hair, who is picked up and then seduced by the chauffeur. The flashback continues by intersecting with another episode from the past: the protagonist's confession to a priest. During this confession, the flashback, showing Lino seducing the boy in his bedroom, distinctly exposes the latter's early attraction to the chauffeur's strange mixture of masculine and feminine traits. Revealing a combination of anguish and desire, the young Marcello moves towards Lino to touch his long hair and is then suddenly recoiling and shooting him. Marcello's attraction is made explicit as he confesses to the priest years later that Lino looked exactly like a woman. In the recollection of this memory, Lino's gender ambiguity constitutes a strange object of attraction, also indirectly reflecting Marcello's own gender ambiguity as an effeminate young boy.

Flashbacks and oneiric techniques such as doubling and condensation re-emerge at various points of the film to disrupt Marcello's mental balance and confront him with that part of himself that he is so incessantly trying to disavow. Anna Quadri's first appearance, when Giulia and Marcello go to visit Professor Quadri at his Parisian flat, is certainly one of the most uncanny moments of the film. The scene gives a dream-like quality to Anna's presence primarily by means of lighting. Anna emerges from the dark at the far end of the hall. A very low lamp positioned between her and the camera accentuates the contrast between light and darkness as she walks towards the middle of the hall, by looking down on her. The camera cuts to Marcello, who is now playing in front of the door with Anna's dog. Marcello suddenly looks over to Anna and seems petrified. The following reverse shot justifies his reaction. Anna has raised her face and now stands next to the lamp that eerily illuminates her right side. The camera cuts to reveal a close-up of Marcello, still with the same shocked expression, and then cuts again to show a subjective medium-distance shot of Anna, who is now looking ambiguously straight into Marcello's eyes.

The eerie quality of this scene introduces the role that Anna Quadri will play in the film in bringing to the surface the 'wound' that Marcello is so desperately trying to repress. Anna's function in the film is to visualise the repressed memory of Marcello's difference. Interestingly, in this scene, she appears as the doubled image of the young Marcello during the seduction episode with Lino. She wears a similar sailor uniform, and has his delicate features, his white complexion and fair hair (Fig. 3.6). Whilst Christopher Wagstaff has noted

Figure 3.6 *The Conformist,* Anna in the Parisian apartment that she shares with Professor Quadri.

that Anna Quadri is a projection of Marcello's fantasy, I would argue that she is also a visual materialisation of that part of his unconscious that Marcello needs to disavow in order to preserve the sense of his normality.[39] If the film uses techniques similar to dream-work to precipitate the 'repressed' into Marcello's present and upset his laboriously constructed normality, doubling is certainly the most effective means. The clearest example is the mysterious appearances of the actress who plays Anna, Dominique Sanda, in two other roles: as a prostitute in a brothel in Ventimiglia and as a mysterious lady at the ministry. These earlier appearances in the narrative articulate similar dynamics of shock and recognition in Marcello, distinctly expressed by reverse-shot sequences that link Marcello's stunned expression to the images of these two women who are ambiguously looking back at him.

The film reaches a climactic moment when Professor Quadri and Anna are ambushed by the fascists. Quadri is repeatedly stabbed; Anna runs towards the car, where Manganiello and Marcello Clerici are observing the scene (Fig. 3.7). Her plea for help leaves Marcello immobile and passive. If *The Conformist*, as Dalle Vacche argues, is about the tension between regimentation and loss of control experienced by the protagonist, this scene would be the moment in which Marcello finally manages to suppress the 'homosexual/feminine' and keeps hold of his stable male heterosexual identity.[40] Throughout the film, the feminine has been for Marcello an object of attraction and anxiety, a reminder of his encounter with Lino and the illicit desires that this encounter entails. However, Anna's death does not put an end to Marcello's sexual turmoil. On the contrary, the scene is precisely a re-enactment of the anguish and torment that Marcello feels in relation to his memory of the seduction. The whole

Figure 3.7   *The Conformist*, Anna, about to be murdered by the fascists, pleads for help, whilst Marcello sits immobile inside the car.

sequence is indeed staged as an oneiric ritual: from the mist shrouding the wood, to the sun's rays infiltrating the trees, Quadri's balletic fall when he is killed and the hand-held camera following Anna's flight. Its purpose is clearly to restage the 'repressed' memory of Lino's killing and the previous seduction. To achieve this objective, the film violates cinematic codes of realism. In the woods, Anna is repeatedly shot in the back by the fascists. When she finally surrenders, her clothes reveal no signs of blood; instead it is her face that is exaggeratedly covered with red paint. Bertolucci admits that the exaggerated blood on Anna's face had the purpose of showing her death as a symbolic fantasy.[41] As she finally collapses, the red paint on her face inevitably reminds us of Lino's bleeding face at the end of the earlier seduction scene. Interestingly, her supine position on her death is also very similar to Lino's posture after Marcello shot him. Like a dream, Anna's death doubles another death that Marcello wants to forget whilst also condensing the image of the sin with the one that would bring its atonement. (Significantly, in the novel, Anna's name is Lina.)

The elusiveness of Marcello's attempt to escape his 'abnormality' is clear in the final sequence of the film, when Italo and the protagonist overhear a man flirting with a young boy under one of the arches of the Colosseum. Their enthralment with this scene of seduction replays the mixture of attraction and disavowal through which both characters have lived their homosexuality throughout the story. Marcello recognises his seducer Lino and realises that the killing for which he had sought atonement had never occurred. The logic through which Marcello has been trying to escape his abnormality crumbles. Lino had never been killed and the murder of the Quadris has not brought him the expiation he had sought. In the final shot of the film, Marcello peeks through the bars of one of the niches in which a young boy lies naked. In this voyeuristic scene, the protagonist finally comes face to face with his homosexual desire. His face betrays the anguish of a man who realises the impossibility of obliterating a memory that continues to re-emerge, regardless of the strength and tenacity with which it is rejected. This confrontation removes the shadow on which he has based his existence. Like one of Plato's prisoners finally being freed, Marcello looks back and sees what lies beyond the false illusions he has lived. Far from maintaining 'heterosexual masculinity' as the dominant term of reference of the film, this ending reveals its final collapse. It is an ending that also speaks for his final confrontation with the illusions of fascism and its authoritative hold on reality. The last shot of the film shows that Marcello's attempts to cover up one thing have only resulted in the further uncovering of the thing to be covered. It is an image that conjures up Marcello's covering of his wife's backside in the initial sequence. The act of covering works as a metaphor for the self-deluding logic that Marcello has endorsed throughout the film and which fascism promoted in order to preserve the normative notion of a stable and homogenous body politic.

The Conformist utilises the Oedipal story as both a psychic and a socially shared experience, one in which historical conditions surface in individually held desires, obsessions and anxieties. Influenced by the cultural ferment of the post-1968 social movements and by reading Herbert Marcuse, Wilhelm Reich and Freudian psychoanalysis, Bertolucci develops a sophisticated exploration of the dialectic between libidinal freedoms and repression that is at the basis of the formation of male subjectivity by borrowing the appropriate narrative possibilities intrinsic to the Oedipal story. In *The Conformist*, Bertolucci problematises the role of sexuality in relation to the consolidation of male identity by denaturalising the normative relation between heterosexuality and masculinity and by exposing the illusion by which this naturalisation is achieved. By rejecting a dramatisation of the Oedipal story based on closure and the power of repression, *The Conformist* sheds light instead on the contradictions and inconsistencies that cannot be successfully resolved by the imposition of the Law of the Father. Laura Mulvey notes that the Oedipal story reveals a journey populated by desires, anxieties and contradictions, which is then followed by closure around the symbolic order of the Father. Yet, she argues that this terrain in which desire finds expression should be taken more seriously, as it provides an imagery of revolt against a patriarchal order as well as an imagery of change, transformation and liberation.[42] This is a space that emerges powerfully in *The Conformist* through Bertolucci's intention to voice the transgressive desires and libidinal chaos that cannot be successfully contained within the paternal order. It is a space in which the feminine, irremediably excluded from the deterministic linearity of the Oedipus complex, may re-emerge and suggest the possibility of resistance and disruption.

4. UNDOING GENRE, UNDOING MASCULINITY

Investigation of a Citizen Above Suspicion (*Indagine su un cittadino al di sopra di ogni sospetto*: 1970) follows a police detective who, after killing a woman named Augusta during sexual intercourse, leaves a number of clues that may lead to his being identified. The detective – the character who should be mentally lucid, restore order and be on the side of the law – is a psychopath, who uses his power to pervert the course of justice and re-assert his position of authority in the face of evidence that proves his culpability. As a representative of the authoritarian state, the detective presents himself like the ideal father figure of the patriarchal family. During a speech in front of his colleagues at the police headquarters, he argues for the need to treat the masses like children. For him, common citizens should be protected by means of repression from their dangerous quest for freedom. As a study of how the authoritarian mentality operates, *Investigation* uses a typically Reichian model. According to this model, the state functions as a macro-structure of the patriarchal family, in which the leader acts as an ideal father figure and the masses are encouraged to submit to his authority like his children. Prompted to trust him completely, the people sustain his absolute power and confer on him the duty to protect them. Dispossessed of any agency that might allow them to question the 'father's' actions, the 'children' learn to feel unconditional respect for him and to fear his authority.[1]

In the model described by Wilhelm Reich, the authoritarian type experiences a strong identification with the father, the basis for future identification with any authority. Even though Reich did not openly address the question of gender, the film makes it explicit that this is a quintessentially male experience. By using the Oedipal model of the patriarchal family to describe the structuring of the authoritarian state, *Investigation* follows the detective's plan to conceal any manifestation of weakness and vulnerability behind a bullish semblance of strength and self-assurance. The film illustrates the distinctive patriarchal connotations of the institutional power upon which the detective's authority rests. It shows the police headquarters as an entirely male space, whilst also highlighting the strong homosocial bonds and relentless macho attitudes of the chief detective and his colleagues. It is in this public space, characterised by order and austerity, that the authority of the detective seems most visible and effective.

The film sheds light on the mismatch between this public performance of masculine omnipotence and the utterly infantile private identity that the detective hides. This mismatching is an effect of the psychosexual conflict that the protagonist experiences between his inner desires and the self-induced repression of such impulses. 'You are like a child,' Augusta ridicules him.[2] Augusta is here alluding to the detective's puerile investment in the murderous sexual fantasies that they both share and play with. The detective's infantilism is significantly reiterated at the end of the film, when the police chief reproaches him for the murder he has committed, like a child who is being punished by his parents for mischievous behaviour. What the film seems to suggest is that under the oppressive workings of this patriarchal structure, the subject will inevitably fail to develop an autonomous code of moral conduct. Paradoxically, it is the very exertion of power that keeps the detective forever stuck in this child-like condition. Dependent on a law that always confronts him, the detective is a child unable to question the rightness of the law that he is so keen to serve. This paradigm is also inevitably gendered and calls into question the untenable consistency of an exacerbated expression of male authority under patriarchy so deeply embedded in notions of power, control and aggressiveness.

Informed by the social tensions and political unrest of 1970s Italy, *Investigation* should be aligned with a tradition of leftist *engagement* that, in the highly politicised context of the 1970s, operates as a vehicle of social criticism. In a period in which State-authorised repression of the social movements became increasingly harsher and when a disquieting picture of the close contacts between members of the secret services, the police and extreme right-wing groups began to be revealed, *Investigation* emerged as a timely polemical statement against the dangers of a return to an authoritarian regime.[3] Such political ambitions rely, however, on a distinctive cinematic practice. In interviews, Elio Petri repeatedly expressed his intention to make political films that could be commercially viable and would appeal to mass audiences.[4] In Italy, *Investigation* was the sixth most watched film of 1970, bringing in 690,191,000 lire.[5] In the same year, the film also won the Oscar for best foreign film. In *Investigation*, Petri's ambition to make popular cinema dictates a style that is easily recognisable: fast-paced editing, a bouncy and suspense-enhancing soundtrack composed by Ennio Morricone, and a caricatured acting style epitomised by the highly mannered performance of Gian Maria Volontè as the detective. This style is conducive to the creation of those effects of *spettacolarità* that critics such as Bondanella have recognised as being instrumental to the film's popular appeal.[6]

Whilst clearly drawing on the crime film, *Investigation* ends up disassembling the traditionally conservative connotations of this genre. In her analysis of *Investigation*, Millicent Marcus points out how, despite its relation to the crime genre, the film militates against the conventional ideological function of this genre. Quoting Thomas Schatz's study of Hollywood genres, Marcus reminds us that the crime film generally serves to express and resolve the conflicts that threaten the stability of the social order. By contrast, *Investigation* seems to work against this conservative thrust by inserting a progressive message of social protest against the authoritarian state.[7] Rather than constructing a story that progresses from disorder to order, the film goes in the opposite direction. In disrupting the genre convention regarding who is the hero and who is the villain, *Investigation* also turns the detective's masculinity into an object of interrogation, further complicating one of the distinctive features of the genre. The crime film is traditionally a genre structured around a testing of the hero's prowess; when the hero is the detective, the genre encourages spectators to measure the standards of competence of the detective through his ability to resolve the crime. According to Frank Krutnik, the detective operates as 'an idealised figure of narcissistic identification that will ultimately unite authority, achievement and masculine-male sexuality. Such fantastically glamourised hero-figures [. . .] promote an "ideology" of masculine omnipotence and invulnerability.'[8] *Investigation* self-consciously plays with the semblance of male omnipotence described by Krutnik. The film contrasts the detective's public performance of male authority during the investigation with a series of flashbacks revealing details about his private life. These show the development of his affair with the victim, Augusta, and their erotic games based on the staging of murder scenarios. In these flashbacks, Augusta's fascination with the power that the detective symbolises gradually gives way to her discovery of the protagonist's arrested sexual development and erotic inadequacy. Near the end of the film, it becomes clear that the murder was committed by the detective precisely to punish her for having exposed his sexual shortcomings and having ridiculed his authority.

The film epitomises the possibility of adopting the conventions of specific genres in order to reconfigure the gender inscriptions with which such genres have typically functioned. Popular genre forms, as has been extensively noted, play an essential role in constructing clearly differentiated gender images.[9]

In offering systemised variants on its modes of meaning and pleasure, genre cinema constantly participates in an on-going process of construction of sexual difference. This is a process that is often concerned with the definition of rather clear-cut roles, values and expectations of men and women. Given such premises, it is not surprising that Maggie Günsberg's *Italian Cinema: Genre and Gender* – one of the first book-length studies of gender and genre relating to Italian cinema – should strongly emphasise the shaping of gender representations operated by mainstream genres in conjunction with patriarchal ideology. For Günsberg, one element that is crucial to the marketability of genre films is the kind of spectatorial expectations that are mobilised and how such expectations are strongly gendered.[10] *Investigation* shows the potential vulnerability to disruption of the conventions that are used to construct these gendered images. Being the result of a codified process of plot construction intertwined with the assembly of equally manufactured (and codified) ideas about what masculinity is, these conventions may sometimes be re-assembled in a way that contradicts our expectations. As a result, masculinity makes visible its own status as a construction, one that can be modified, re-assembled and endowed with new meanings. This chapter discusses several films from the 1970s that playfully appropriate and dismantle a set of generic conventions and popular forms of address with the effect of disrupting their typical constitutive relation to a set of normative assumptions about masculinity.[11]

Gendered Laughter in *The Seduction of Mimì*

The Seduction of Mimì follows the story of a Sicilian miner (Mimì), who loses his job after refusing to vote for a Mafia-backed candidate at the local elections and then moves to Turin in search of better work opportunities. Having left his wife behind in Sicily, Mimì quickly finds a new job as a metalworker, a political passion (communism) and a woman he loves (Fiore). After a series of unfortunate events, he is forced to return to Sicily. Here, Mimì starts leading a double life with both Fiore and his wife. He gradually repudiates his communist ideals and turns away from the struggles of his co-workers. *The Seduction of Mimì* does not develop a classic comedic structure – that is, a narrative tending towards a happy ending – but features a number of gags and wisecracks based on the motif of incongruity. The protagonist Mimì is presented as a classic comic figure in the Platonic sense of someone who is ignorant of himself. Mimì often misreads his own talents. He thinks he is more clever than he really is and reckons that his actions will achieve a certain effect but is usually proved wrong: hence, our laughing at him.

Whilst presenting Mimì as a laughable caricature, *The Seduction of Mimì* also establishes a space for the audience to enjoy feelings of empathy and identification with him. In the first section of the film, Mimì's outspoken dislike for the Mafia-backed candidate and his decision to vote for the Communist Party (despite intimidation) place him in opposition to an oppressive and corrupt social order. After he is fired and he decides to migrate to Turin in the hope of a better life, the sense of injustice felt by Mimì is presumably also shared by the audience. As we follow his migration from Sicily to Turin (and thus his development into a politicised factory worker), his journey is presented as an easily identifiable experience for Italian and American audiences affected, in one way or another, by the experience of migration. In developing a sequential narrative structure based on causality, the film follows one of the main rules of classical narration. The cause–effect developments are left dangling at the end of a sequence and are generally picked up in the following one: for example, the decision not to vote for the Mafia-backed candidate (cause) → he is fired (effect of the previous cause, and cause of further developments) → the decision to move to Turin (effect).

Consistently with its popular mode of address, *The Seduction of Mimì* conforms to another rule of the classical narrative film: namely, the fact that at least one of the plot lines should involve a heterosexual romance. In the first Sicilian section of the film, Mimì's marital predicament is introduced: we see him in bed with his sexually inhibited wife, who covers her face and prays whilst her husband attempts to make love to her. Frustrated, Mimì gives up. Intertwined with the moral and political dilemma (the conflict between political ideology and personal interest) that Mimì faces in the story, this plot line of frustrated sexual desire, left dangling in the first section, is then picked up in the section of the film set in Turin, when Mimì finally meets Fiore. If life in Sicily denies to Mimì both the possibilities of resisting corruption and Mafia power, and the material conditions for experiencing romantic love (witness the wife's discouragingly prudish attitude to sex), Mimì's arrival in Turin coincides with the excitement of a new romance with Fiore and the exhilarating opportunities of anti-capitalist struggle. The romantic theme, then, is a crucial component in the narrative progression of the film, one that moves from lack to fulfilment, a fulfilment that is both a political and a romantic one.

On one level, *The Seduction of Mimì* deploys a narrative of romantic wish-fulfilment that gives a prominent role to the emotions and passion in the actions of the protagonists, especially Mimì and Fiore. On the other, it plays with the very idea that this kind of narrative will necessarily reduce the complexity of the 'serious' political issues raised. Kathleen Rowe has suggested that classical Hollywood comedies whose narratives involve the formation of the couple between and a man and a woman belonging to different social classes frequently dilute the problem of class difference under the romantic imperative of the happy ending.[12] Coinciding with the flourishing of the romance between Fiore and Mimì, *The Seduction of Mimì* ends up performing precisely the depoliticising function that the 'ideology of love' is generally blamed for in popular genre cinema. Yet, this turn in the plot, rather than being an inevitable consequence of the romance, is a self-conscious narrative gimmick; its function is to shed light on the problematic relation between political ideology and the individual responsibilities of the subject. It is an issue that becomes suddenly central in the film and reveals the distance between the sincere nature of Fiore's political commitment and Mimì's more opportunistic relation to leftist politics. This becomes clear as soon as Fiore and Mimì set up house together in Turin. Whilst Fiore has politics constantly in mind, Mimì quickly dismisses any notion of solidarity with other workers and discourages her from joining the public protest organised by the building workers. A further withdrawal from politics is evident in the scene in which Fiore lies on the bed, pregnant, and asks Mimì to inform her about the political ferment in the factories and the on-going protests. The noise of the workers' protests that reaches their loft from outside and Mimì's unwillingness to tell her anything about the strikes highlight his sudden retreat from politics into his strictly private world. Mimì ends up absorbing traditional family values by directing all his thoughts and concerns towards his heir-to-be and Fiore. At this point, Mimì not only betrays his communist ideals but also reveals the gap between his initial political convictions and his actual self-interest.

Wertmüller's popular cinema is typically based on this trajectory; it moves from a moment of familiarisation to a subsequent state of discomfort that arises when the terms of a political and/or moral dilemma are revealed. It is a trajectory that becomes clear in a number of scenes in which a collective eye pauses on the protagonist. This is signalled by the camera dwelling on the faces of characters who silently condemn Mimì's deplorable conduct (for example, his brother, Peppino, and Fiore herself in the final sequence). During these moments, the film enacts a kind of suspension; marked by the lack of verbal interaction, these are moments that generally imply a relief from the prevailingly comic development of the story and which draw attention to the eyes as silent intra-diegetic propellants for the audience's evaluation of the issues raised by the film. Ironically, it is a relief that mimics the kind of suspension – 'the absence of feelings', as Henri Bergson puts it – that is required for laughter to work. Bergson reminds us that laughter, in order to be effective, needs a disinterested spectator who looks at a comic situation with 'something like a momentary anaesthesia of the heart'.[13] Bergson does not say that one could not possibly laugh at a person who inspires pity or affection, but the very act of laughing must impose a momentary silence upon these emotions. In the *Seduction of Mimi*, the former type of suspension works towards an emotional relief that is needed for us to experience laughter. The latter retrieves those emotions in order for the spectator to connect with and 'feel' the politics explored by the film. They are two seemingly opposite thrusts that appear entangled, especially in the second section of the film. It is the very nature of this two-fold movement, I would suggest, that makes Wertmüller's films of the 1970s especially vulnerable to the contradictory, and often opposite, critical responses that have accompanied their commercial success.

* * *

In the first half of the film, Mimì's masculinity constitutes a central target of humour. His uptight behaviour as he tries to perform his Latin-lover tricks with Fiore plays out some of the mythologies of Sicilian masculinity popularised by Pietro Germi's *Seduced and Abandoned* (*Sedotta e abbandonata*: 1964) and *Divorce Italian-Style* (*Divorzio all'italiana*: 1961). It is a gender performance that is exposed as ludicrous, one that is repeatedly mocked by Fiore, who laughs at the grandiose way in which Mimì introduces himself, his ogling as he tries to woo her, and his obsessive jealousy. The final section of the film, set in Sicily, maintains such a humorous take but tends to expose much more painstakingly the absurd logic of Mimì's sexual behaviour.

This part of the film satirises Mimì's response as he discovers that his promise to remain faithful to Fiore and not to have sex with his wife has elicited rumours among the townsfolk about his sexuality. Mimì's reaction, when he realises that many people in his hometown suspect him of being sexually inept – and implicitly homosexual – is one of panic, a response that is laden with comic potential as the protagonist hysterically bawls at a group of men to defend his reputation. He subsequently leads these men to meet Fiore and to learn the details of his double life. But it is Mimì's reaction in discovering that his neglected wife has fallen into the arms of another man and has become pregnant that sheds light on the real double standard he maintains between his own sexual freedom and the fidelity he expects from his wife.

The motif of the jealous Sicilian husband wishing to defend his honour at any cost should be seen primarily as a comic trope that enables the film to satirise the behaviour of a man ready to sacrifice his principles to assert his manhood publicly. 'I always proceed with a great faith in the power of laughter,' Wertmüller declares in an interview.[14] Underlining laughter as a privileged method for connecting with vast popular audiences, this is a pronouncement that is supported by the depiction of figures such as the corpulent Nazi commander in *Pasqualino Seven Beauties* and the bombastic fascist Spatoletti in *Love and Anarchy* (*Film d'amore e d'anarchia, ovvero 'stamattina alle 10 in via dei Fiori nella nota casa di tolleranza . . .*': 1973). In both cases, the oppressiveness of the power that these characters represent is not shown in its frightening aspect, but rather in a humorous light that reveals the vulnerability of this power to derision. Wertmüller is a director whose use of laughter – often reliant on vulgar jokes and obscenities – has been often targeted, especially in Italy, by accusations of degradation and debasement. In commenting on her popular films of the 1970s, Lino Miccichè asserts: 'We give credit to Lina

Wertmüller for her consistency: her cinema is degrading more and more, from film to film, with a constant progression which, if it weren't deplorable, would certainly be admirable.'[15] This is a comment that reverberates with the widely shared impression among Italian critics that her films, because of their vulgarity and cheap humour, are so degrading for their audience that they deserve nothing but condemnation.

I want to pause, here, to consider briefly the question of degradation in popular comedy. In his essay on the mechanisms of slapstick, Tom Gunning notes that film forms dedicated to provoking laughter, such as jokes and gags, are often antithetical to logic and reason. Glossing Immanuel Kant's reflections on the topic, he refers to laughter as a response in which both the mind and the body operate like a machine breaking down; for Gunning, gags and jokes may be best described as the 'undermining of an apparent purpose, a detouring, if not derailing, of a rational system of discourse or action'.[16] The breaking down speaks of the departure from reason that laughter is meant to provoke in response to a comic situation or a joke. It is an image that evokes a kind of bodily debasement, a downward movement from the mind – depositary of reason, good sense and logic – towards the lower parts of the body.

The kind of bodily debasement that is suggested by Gunning's essay seems to have little in common with the chuckle normally produced by witty, self-conscious humour. It is more closely associated, instead, with that loud, roaring laughter that is triggered by toilet humour and gross-out comedy. The image of the 'machine breaking down' fittingly evokes the spectre of an uncontrollable, mob-like audience splitting their sides in the darkness of the cinema in the face of ribald jokes and obscene catchphrases. The image resonates with the threat of a degraded mass taste and an audience that loses control over its intellectual and critical faculties.

One may not be entirely surprised, then, if the laughter most closely associated with the conventions and forms of popular cinema is often considered to be politically conservative, if not reactionary. One of the starting points of Kathleen Rowe's work on the genres of laughter is the acknowledgement of how often popular culture represents women as objects rather than subjects of laughter.[17] Similarly, in their analysis of popular comedies in contemporary Italian cinema (the 'cinepanettoni'), Christian Uva and Michele Picchi condemn the cruel gags and jokes in these films. For Uva and Picchi, the films provoke a kind of regressive laughter in the audience by targeting what the authors describe as typically 'weak categories' ('categorie deboli'), such as women and homosexuals.[18]

Unsurprisingly, some of the most recurrent criticisms of Wertmüller's films concern the presumed dishonesty of her sexual politics and her much-advertised feminist beliefs. Elle Willis, for example, asserts that 'Wertmüller is not only a woman hater [. . .] but a woman who pretends to be a feminist'.[19]

These are allegations that often point to the impossible reconciliation between the feminist premises of Wertmüller's films and the limitations of the stereotypes and exploitative comic situations on which her popular cinematic practice is based.

The second part of *The Seduction of Mimì* develops an increasingly important plot line that shows Mimì taking his revenge against a man who has made his wife pregnant. The seduction of Amalia (the man's wife), a middle-aged and overweight mother of five, is played for laughs. The scene in which Amalia finally surrenders to Mimì's courtship and engages in a striptease constitutes the comic peak of the film. It is a moment when even the most enthusiastic defenders of Wertmüller's work appreciate that the gratuitous visual indulgence relating to Amalia's fat body should be criticised. Joan Mellen, for example, condemned it thus:

> [W]hatever his faults, which included caving in to the Mafia, the hero Mimì was never caricatured for his rolls of flab. Mimì's faults revealed spiritual weakness; the woman was gross and Wertmüller seemed to be delighting in this grossness for its own sake.[20]

By looking closely at this moment in the film, my objective is not to endorse or refute these criticisms. Rather it is to show the distinctiveness, as well as the productiveness, of Wertmüller's engagement with popular cinematic forms: namely, a kind of film practice based on the use of the most vulgar and sometimes offensive comic situations taken to such an exaggerated level of parody and grotesque humour as to produce the undoing of their expected effect.

The accusations of misogyny addressed to Wertmüller's work strike similar chords to the allegation according to which her cinema, despite its alleged politically progressive premises, may be fundamentally conservative. These allegations often point to the impossible reconciliation between such premises and the limitations of the stereotypes and exploitative comic situations on which her popular cinematic practice is based. This kind of criticism seems to suggest that, by showing some of the coarsest stereotypes relating to women who are abused and humiliated by the male characters, the film actually validates these misogynistic scenarios by encouraging its female spectators to nurture their traditional instincts of subordination and submission to men. To take issue with this criticism means to test the extent to which the film's satire on masculinity remains entrapped or not in an overarching textual framework that is still profoundly patriarchal. In focusing on Amalia's seduction and the regressive stereotypes about women that come to be mobilised in the film, I do not intend to drift away from what should be the real focus of this book – masculinity. Masculinity is not an autonomous object of study but is, instead, a configuration that functions relationally within a wider gender order.[21] In

The Seduction of Mimì, the satirical take on the protagonist's masculinity must be measured up, then, against the comic register that is used to represent women such as Amalia.

There are two major comic motifs in Mimì's seduction of Amalia. The first has to do with Mimì's absurd position in not desiring Amalia but having to have sex with her in order to accomplish his plan of revenge. The second is Amalia's abundant body, which is here presented as an object of laughter for the audience. These two comic motifs are, however, interconnected, since the latter is a device to achieve the former. Cross-cutting between Amalia undressing and Mimì's increasingly distressed face, this scene exploits for comic purposes certain culturally shared attitudes and feelings about female bodies. What makes Amalia's body laughable is not only its chubbiness but also the way in which her erotic performance in the striptease clashes with dominant ideas of what constitutes proper sexualised femininity. By replaying the moment in which Amalia uncovers her bottom three times and repeatedly cross-cutting it with a sequence of pulsating shots zooming in on Mimì's increasing panic (Fig. 4.1), the film only intensifies the feelings of amusement that such a spectacle is meant to provide for the spectator. We are encouraged to laugh at Mimì's shift from victimiser to victim as he comes to terms with Amalia's chubbiness; but the protagonist is only a vector for a laugh that originates and ends with Amalia's body.

This is a quintessential Wertmüller moment, one in which women make a spectacle of themselves by violating the conventions that regulate their social visibility, thus exposing themselves to laughter. One such moment occurs, for example, in *Pasqualino Seven Beauties*, when Pasqualino's sister, Concettina – played by Elena Fiore, the same actress who plays Amalia in *The Seduction of Mimì* – performs a sexy routine in a vaudeville in front of a men-only audience. Confronted with such a spectacle, the men start abusing her verbally and laugh at her ugliness and fatness. The sequence is remarkable for how Concettina defiantly continues to sing while proudly showing her half-naked body, dancing sexily and hurling insults back at the men in the audience.

Figure 4.1   *The Seduction of Mimì,* Mimì worriedly looking at Amalia's body during the striptease.

This type of defiant performance, empowered by a sense of ironic detachment from the oppressive cultural codes of gender visibility that make Concettina's fat, aged body hardly fit for such a performance, is also present in Amalia's striptease. Amalia's performance is imbued with the sexist stereotypes that make her body laughable to the audience, as promptly signalled by the editing pattern linking Mimì's distressed gaze to the sight of Amalia's body. Yet, such a performance also reveals a distinctive element of posing and teasing. As she undresses, Amalia deploys a coquettish smile and gazes back to the camera with self-assurance (Fig. 4.2). Her playful gaze makes a mockery of the proper performance of the ideal sexualised female body. Wertmüller signals the lack of seriousness in this moment with a sudden shift to warm light that invites us to reconsider our initial realistic engagement with this erotic spectacle.

This scene evokes a distinctly feminine imagery of grotesque excess that seems to appear frequently in Wertmüller's films. *Love and Anarchy*, for example, shows the gargantuan depiction of a banquet in which a group of prostitutes gulp down food and wine whilst laughing loudly and shouting insults at each other. The women wear exaggerated make-up and very revealing dresses, and speak with larger-than-life regional accents. This is a scene that exemplifies the wider intent of the film to celebrate the joyous licentiousness of these women by configuring their bodies as sites of desirous excess against the deathly oppressiveness of bourgeois society and fascism.

Mary Russo's discussion of the female grotesque helps us to understand this kind of imagery. In her reading of the terracotta figurines of the laughing hags in Mikhail Bakhtin's *Rabelais and His World*, Russo considers the disruptive potential of feminine hyperbolic performances. The bodies of the hags

Figure 4.2 *The Seduction of Mimì*, Amalia's gaze at Mimì.

described by Bakhtin are deformed and decaying, yet the women are laughing. The image of the pregnant laughing hags is, of course, laden with all the connotations of loathing and discomfort that are associated with the biological processes of reproduction, fattening and ageing. Described within the context of Bakhtin's discussion on Carnival – the expression of popular culture that contests power through mockery – the bodies of the laughing hags constitute a collective grotesque female body that is 'open, protruding, extended, secreting, [. . .] the body of becoming, process, change'.[22] Russo's analysis is useful because it shows a female subject unravelling her exploitation by male discourse by making visible, through an effect of playful repetition, what was supposed to remain invisible (that is, the boundaries that woman is not supposed to cross).

Amalia's performance in *The Seduction of Mimì* makes explicit the affirmative and celebratory potential of women's bodily exposure and hyperbolic exaggeration raised by Russo's study and subsequently expanded and complicated by Kathleen Rowe in *The Unruly Woman*. By unashamedly flaunting a number of excesses that violate codes of proper femininity, Amalia appears in the film as much more than a passive object of scorn. Amalia's body makes a spectacle of itself not simply for what it is but due to the way in which the camera provides repeated close-ups on her protruding wart and the massive size of her breasts and her bottom during the striptease. Its parodic intent is clear as we are confronted with the image of her enormous bottom climbing over the bed. The use of a wide-angle lens exaggerates the depth of the shot by distorting the visual spectacle so as to turn Amalia's prosthetic bottom into an animate mountain of flesh about to submerge Mimì, who appears comparatively much smaller on the opposite side of the bed. In its distortion, this female body is barely believable. It is a spectacle that engages with a masculinistic logic, lending itself to its stifling comic mechanisms in order to distance itself from it and expose the terms of this logic to mockery and derision.

Together with the use of the wide-angle lens, the modulation of specific camera angles in this scene makes explicit the self-empowering implications of this 'masquerade'.[23] By exaggerating the difference in size between Amalia's body and Mimì's, this scene visually anticipates the overturning of the power relation between these two characters in the story. Wertmüller makes sure that we understand clearly that the roles of subject and object of the joke are about to be reversed. This is signalled through a sequence of shots that takes Mimì's point of view as he lies on the bed and Amalia's visual perspective as she kneels over him. For the former point of view, the camera takes a low-angle position that exacerbates the gigantic size of Amalia's body, which is about to engulf Mimì; for the latter, however, a high-angle position increases his smallness. Such a use of the camera angles and its expressive meaning are very much consistent with how the film makes use of asymmetries in point of view to convey the relations of power and submission between characters. Every time Mimì recognises a member of the Tricarico family (the *mafiosi*) and bows to them, the camera signals the power relation through his recognition of the distinctive three moles on their faces and by showing the asymmetric visual relation between the powerful and the submissive. This is done either through dramatically high or dramatically low camera angles, or by placing the character that exerts power on a higher plane such as a terrace, a balcony or a flyover.

The power reversal is made even more explicit as Mimì's vengeful plan (to restore his honour) backfires on him when Amalia leads him back to the cabin where their first sexual encounter occurred. By treating him with disdain and impatience, Amalia now bosses Mimì around, urging him to impregnate her. It is now Amalia who has seized control of the situation and who decides to take her own revenge on her husband for cheating on her with Mimì's wife. This turn in the story coincides with the film's entrance into the realm of *beffa* – as we have seen, a comic trope by which female characters have traditionally been able to circumvent the authority of men through wit, deception and unruliness. Comedy is, of course, the domain of play *par excellence*, a site of disruption where unruly women have been able to undermine dominant patriarchal attitudes. As Steve Neale and Frank Krutnik argue, film comedy is also a game played with transgression and familiarity, where transgressions are cushioned and eventually disarmed by a resetting of boundaries. Much of the pleasure of such transgressions, particularly in the comedy of the sexes, has to do precisely with refamiliarisation within these boundaries after an 'eccentric' female character has enabled some extent of deviation from the norm.[24]

In *The Seduction of Mimì*, such a male-oriented resetting is strikingly absent. On the contrary, Amalia's complicity with Mimì in making her husband a cuckold allows her to humiliate both her husband and Mimì publicly in front of her fellow citizens. This public humiliation takes place in the square in which Mimì has planned to stage a personal bid to restore his honour by informing Amalia's husband that he has impregnated his wife. In the face of her husband's shocked reaction, Amalia here takes the opportunity to highlight, in her usual over-the-top fashion, not only the success of her own plan of vengeance against her husband but also her revulsion at the two men, whom she rebukes as 'good-for-nothing fathers'. The sequence, showing Mimì's stratagem collapse after he is wrongly accused of having shot Amalia's husband, is once again played for laughs but only on one level. On another, Wertmüller punctuates the comic staging of Mimì's revenge with close-ups of the disapproving gazes of Peppino and Mimì's little brother, who realise how far Mimì is ready to go to defend his honour. Such gazes do not allow the comic detachment that this paradoxical resolution would initially require – particularly after Mimì's plan backfires again and the Mafia emissary kills Amalia's husband in his place – but rather impinge upon our direct and serious involvement in Mimì's moral shortcomings. The close-up on the little brother, in particular, is striking because it painfully evokes the betrayal of Mimì's earlier promise of mentorship to him at the beginning of the film. Moreover, it implies the shattering of the mutual feelings of complicity and affection shared by the brothers before Mimì's departure to Turin.

The Seduction of Mimì seduces its audiences only to confront them subsequently with a betrayal of their expectations and a reversal of the 'conservative' re-ordering that conventionally characterises the comic mode. The film lays out some of the politically 'regressive' pleasures associated with laughter, only to create a distance from these pleasures and to reject them. On these terms, then, the film seems to be involved in a self-conscious analysis of its own structure, one that also concerns the kind of oppressive masculinity epitomised by Mimì, with which we are first invited to sympathise and then made to experience unease.

Wertmüller's films are detested and rejected by some critics as manipulative and exploitative commercial operations for the way they seem to bring together a set of binaries that should be kept separate: serious/comic; political commitment/entertainment; the director's presumed allegiance to feminism/sexist jokes. The apparently impossible synthesis between these dichotomies generates the well-known accusations of hypocrisy addressed to Wertmüller and the assumption that the message of her films is muddled and chaotic, or even inherently contradictory. Wertmüller's cinema, as *The Seduction of Mimì* shows, does not transcend the restrictions (and the hierarchies) that are implicit in the sometimes conservative workings of the 'popular', but productively shows some of the possibilities for disengagement from such restrictions. The film seems to deploy some of the possibilities for contesting power and hierarchies envisaged by Mikhail Bakhtin in *Rabelais and his World*. Like the laughter of the people during Carnival, the production of laughter in *The Seduction of Mimi* uses the logic of the 'inside-out'. It is a kind of laughter that upsets the rigid marking between the object of the mocking and the enunciating subject of laughter. This is a laughter that is a genuinely popular cultural practice in the Bakhtinian sense, in which the subject from below enters a utopian realm of freedom and equality. Here, opportunities for movement, transformation and renewal are clearly visible.

GAY COMEDY AND THE REFLECTING MIRROR OF MASCULINITY: *LA PATATA BOLLENTE*

Structured upon a conflict between eccentricity and conformity, comedy constitutes an ideal arena for representing unconventional models of masculinity. The conflict is generally based on an awareness of the norm and a departure from such a norm on which laughter is usually predicated. Unsurprisingly, images of male transvestism and effeminacy have been far from scarce in film comedies, as documented by Vito Russo in *The Celluloid Closet*.[25] Such images may suggest how, in a given society, we define ourselves, see others and laugh at them – the three often being related. More broadly, they say something about the privileged function of comedy in giving visibility to things that are perceived to be out of place, mixed up or not quite right. Cross-dressers and effeminate homosexuals score highly in the Italian comedy of the post-war period. In films such as *Totòtruffa '62* (1961), *Figaro qua ... Figaro là* (1950), *Totò contro i 4* (1963) and *Totò a colori* (1952), the Neapolitan comedian Totò famously impersonates a number of transvestites and effeminate dandies. He typically invests in demands for the easy laughter of the screwball comedy by exploiting common feelings about men not fitting a normative male role and the humorous reaction that emerges from the encounter with their presence. Comedy indeed requires stereotypes that must be based on clearly visible and recognisable diversions from a norm; male effeminacy – as a form of divergence from how 'normal' men are supposed to be – meets these criteria. Male homosexuality and effeminacy feature also prominently in *commedie all'italiana*, such as *The Easy Life* (*Il sorpasso*: 1962), in which a marginal character called Occhio fino (his name being an inversion of the homophobic slur 'finocchio') plays the role of an effeminate servant. Occhio fino's appearance is linked to certain assumptions about homosexual men, here epitomised by his mincing walk, his effete voice and his ambiguous affection for the pretty young protagonist, Roberto. Such a characterisation inevitably turns him into the butt of the jokes of the other protagonist, Bruno. Occhio fino appears for no more than three scenes and within the purposes of the narrative plays a very marginal role; in symbolic terms, however, his presence is considerable. He shows how 'normal' men are not supposed to be, hence functioning as a yardstick to re-assert normative ideas about masculinity.

At stake in these stereotypical representations of male homosexuality and effeminacy, however, is not only the perpetuation of normative ideas about masculinity. In *Heroes, Villains and Fools*, Orin Klapp notes that there is a fundamental distinction between fictional social types and stereotypes. Social types reflect the lifestyle, mentality and morality of the majority. They are inside the social order and the confines of normality. By contrast, stereotypes are outside this world and tend to be dysfunctional. Such a distinction may be made by marking the subjects outside the boundaries of normality with a set of morally deplorable characteristics that clash against the sense of rightness that the dominant moral order instead reflects.[26] Klapp's distinction between social types and stereotypes shows remarkable similarities with the treatment of the gay characters in *La dolce vita* (1960), for example. What is most striking about them in Fellini's film is not their effeminacy or flamboyance but their sense of belonging to the decadent world that the film portrays. Their sporadic appearance is consistently linked with moral shallowness. Throughout the film, the only function that they seem to perform is gossiping. On one occasion, the film even suggests their sadistic pleasure in such a task. In the episode of the fight on via Veneto, for example, Pierone – the homosexual character who appears most frequently – responds to Marcello's request for information regarding the fight by saying that he does not know (what is going on), but it has been beautiful to watch. Appearing on the screen only to deliver shallow comments, these homosexual characters seem to constitute as dysfunctional a presence as the exploitative flashes of the paparazzi. Klapp's model may be also applied to well-known Neorealist films such as *Rome Open City*, where the homosexuality of the Nazi commander Bergmann is associated with sadism, perversity and evil. This association is also strongly gendered. The actor playing Bergmann, Harry Feist, was chosen specifically because he was homosexual. In the film, the effeminacy of this character is typically charged with moral meaning to signify his inhumanity. His deviance is also constructed out of a binary opposition: namely, in relation to the male standard that looms large in the film, exemplified by the principles of manly martyrdom, Christian solidarity, humanism and, most importantly, heterosexuality.

Whereas for much of the post-war period the disavowal of male homosexuality has been instrumental in the demarcation of a distinct boundary between an 'acceptable' masculinity and an 'abject' one, the 1970s constitute a clear turning point. As Vincenzo Patanè has shown in his short history of Italian gay-themed films, after 1968 Italian cinema, despite its persistent use of caricatured images of effeminate gay men, shows a new engagement with the liberationist rhetoric of the Italian gay movement and a commitment to promote the social integration of homosexuals.[27] This new tendency is linked to the interrogation of the normative boundaries defining the terms of a socially acceptable male identity. *Scusi, lei è normale?* (1979) is an instructive example. It follows the misadventures of a gay couple and a woman who works as a model for soft-porn magazines. The film is noteworthy not only for the centrality of the homosexual characters in the plot but also for the way in which it turns moral bigotry and homophobia into the real objects of scorn and condemnation. Exemplified by an over-zealous magistrate, who embarks on a moral campaign to prevent the spread of explicit erotic material in Italian society, and a couple of clumsy homophobic police detectives, these conservative moral attitudes are cast in the film as out of date and unacceptable in the increasingly liberal Italy of the 1970s. *Scusi, lei è normale?* revisits the comic figure of the moral crusader already popularised by Fellini's *Le tentazioni del Dottor Antonio* (*Boccaccio '70*: 1962) and by *Il moralista* (1959). The title of the film acts out its central political and moral statement. Halfway though the story, the female protagonist makes an unappreciative remark about the gay couple. In response, one of the gay men polemically alludes to her similar 'abnormality' in relation to the conservative moral standards that she has just used to criticise them. As a sexually emancipated woman, like the gay couple, the female protagonist is repeatedly scorned by the repressive public authorities and prosecuted for moral indecency. One of the gay characters thus provocatively asks her: 'Excuse-me, are *you* normal?'[28] It is a rhetorical question that, in also addressing the audience, points to the way they may have thus far enjoyed the new sexual freedoms and the numerous occasions for erotic titillation provided by the Italian film industry in these years without entirely questioning the true extent of their supposed liberalism. The film, perhaps simplistically, seems to tell us that we are all slightly abnormal after all. In striking a non-judgemental attitude towards gay people and validating homosexuality as a viable lifestyle, *Scusi, lei è normale?* appears to have been greatly influenced by the enormous advances of the gay movement in this period. The film also crucially disrupts the heterocentric binary logic traditionally regulating the cultural production and consumption of gendered images in cinema by showing one of the homosexual male protagonists as impeccably masculine and untainted by any implications of moral perversity.

But it was another popular comedy, *La patata bollente*, that, on its release, surprised a number of critics for the sympathetic way in which it approached the story of a homosexual. Morando Morandini, for example, praised it as 'an honest film that faces the theme of homosexuality head-on'.[29] Dismissed by canonical film criticism for its crass humour, *La patata bollente* has recently attained the status of 'cult film' for the Italian gay community, with the main tune from the film's soundtrack – *Un tango diverso* – being chosen as the official song of the 2008 Italian Gay Pride event in Bologna.[30] *La patata bollente* revolves around the accidental meeting between a communist factory worker (Gandhi) and a homosexual bookshop assistant (Claudio). The encounter takes place when Claudio, attacked by a gang of skinheads, is rescued by Gandhi and taken to his place to recover. Their meeting is an occasion for Gandhi to interrogate some of his misconceptions about homosexuals. In meeting Claudio and becoming his friend, Gandhi confronts the contradictions between his communist principles (for example, his claim to be on the side of the oppressed) and his homophobic attitudes. He comes to understand the everyday humiliations suffered by many homosexuals and becomes a champion of their rights in front of his fellow factory workers.

The film was conceived, as scriptwriter Enrico Vanzina points out, as a satire on the historical unease with which the Italian Left had handled questions pertaining to sexual politics.[31] For much of the 1960s and the early 1970s, the Italian Communist Party (PCI) had generally ignored the issue of homosexual oppression. The conventional argument with which the party had opposed the call for 'interclass' collaboration on the part of the gay movement was the idea that sexual liberation and the struggle against homophobia could not be priorities.[32] Such a call was also often dismissed with rigid moralising arguments supported by the commonplace that equated homosexuality with bourgeois degeneracy.[33] Released in 1979, *La patata bollente* was a film grounded in a changing political climate that revealed a considerable shift of attitudes within the Italian Left, with the Communist Party finally showing a willingness to engage in a dialogue with homosexual activist groups. Significantly, in 1979, the first two openly homosexual candidates were included on the electoral lists of the PCI for the Italian parliament. In the same year, the mayors of Rome and Turin (both members of the PCI) officially met a number of gay activists for the first time and spoke up about the need for a more visible role for homosexuals in society. Moreover, from the late 1970s, the official newspaper of the PCI, *L'Unità*, started publishing articles touching upon the question of homosexuality in contemporary Italy whilst also inviting its readers to send in letters about this topic.

The characterisation of the two protagonists in *La patata bollente* is very much consistent with the intent of the film to include references to some of these political developments and make a comment upon them. The film strives to present Gandhi as the ideal factory worker celebrated by orthodox leftist rhetoric: politically committed, hard-working, trustworthy, virile, highly respected by his colleagues and, of course, heterosexual. By contrast, Claudio is seen as the new kind of empowered homosexual subject produced by gay liberation: unashamedly confident about his sexual orientation, willing to embrace his 'difference' as positive, and committed to making his homosexuality a political issue.

Most of the reviews written about the film soon after its release highlight how *La patata bollente* followed in the footsteps of *La Cage aux folles* (1978).[34] *La Cage aux folles*, a French–Italian co-production starring Ugo Tognazzi and Michel Serrault, was one of the greatest commercial hits of the late 1970s. It centred on the story of a middle-aged gay couple and their drag nightclub in St Tropez. Much of the popular appeal of *La Cage aux folles*, which in Italy attracted 1.4 million viewers and became the second most popular film of the 1978–9 season, stemmed from the glamorisation of the camp lifestyle of the gay couple and the comic contrast with an ultra-conservative family that arrives in their household. *La patata bollente* noticeably borrows from *La Cage aux folles* the comic possibilities stemming from the encounter between a normative heterosexual world and a gay one: on the one hand, Gandhi's austere lifestyle in the factory and, on the other hand, the theatrically gay subculture of which Claudio is part. Like *La Cage aux folles*, the prime target of *La patata bollente* was clearly a mainstream audience. A crucial strategy for addressing this audience was the casting of Milanese comedian Renato Pozzetto and the emerging French starlet of the concurrently flourishing genre of the Italian sex comedy, Edwige Fenech. Playing the role of Gandhi's girlfriend, Fenech's presence was fundamental to asserting the mainstream heterosexual address of the film. The title of the film revolves around a pun. It alludes to the troubling issue of homosexuality that the protagonist Gandhi has to deal with through his encounter with Claudio ('patata bollente' means hot potato). But it also plays on the colloquial use of *patata* to mean 'pussy' in the Italian language, which in this case clearly referred to Fenech's presence in the film. The poster of *La patata bollente* significantly shows a sultry Fenech posing next to the title with Pozzetto and Ranieri behind, thus appealing to a straight male audience whilst also invoking, through the presence of Pozzetto, the 'safety' of the comedy genre (Fig. 4.3).

With the objective of meeting a mainstream audience's expectations of entertainment and creating opportunities for laughter, the film underscores the effete mannerisms of a number of marginal homosexual characters. Virtually all of Claudio's homosexual friends in the film perform limp-wristed gestures, mincing walks and suggestive pouting. Constructed in opposition to the outrageous effeminacy of the other gay characters, Claudio's homosexuality initially appears inconspicuous. It is, in fact, Claudio's 'invisibility' as a homosexual in the eyes of Gandhi that constitutes the major element of surprise and humour in the first part of the film, especially after the audience (but not Gandhi) discovers that Claudio has a boyfriend. The gap between what the audience knows and what Gandhi ignores is the basis for a number of gags and jokes about gay men during their first night together. Whilst inevitably reiterating a set of clichés about homosexuals, the jokes end up turning the straight protagonist into the true object of laughter for the audience. Comic misjudgements

Figure 4.3 *La patata bollente,* promotion poster.

proliferate throughout the film. Revolving around a tension between how things appear and how they really are, such misjudgements primarily concern the straight protagonist Gandhi and a number of incidents raising doubts about the possibility that he might be homosexual himself. On one occasion, for example, as he is trying to re-animate Claudio after an alleged suicide attempt, the porter sees him and thinks he is passionately kissing another man. On another occasion, whilst helping Claudio to move into his flat, he slips on a banana and, falling, reveals to the astonished porter the compromising contents of a suitcase that include jewellery, feather boas and gay-themed books.

In *La patata bollente*, the encounter between a heterosexual man and a homosexual one is the occasion for a number of comic situations revolving around the conflict between conformity and eccentricity, between how we expect things to be and how surprisingly odd they turn out to be. This encounter opens up a space where the heterosexual protagonist has to question the terms by which he understands and defines his identity as a man. Confronted with a homosexual identity that he has so far seen as abject and extraneous to his sense of masculinity, Gandhi is forced to embrace this 'otherness' and redefine his identity accordingly. The result of this encounter is the creation of a reflective space within which masculinity, without its traditional definitional boundaries, has to question and reinvent itself.

Much of Gandhi's shock on learning that Claudio is gay after taking him to his flat has to do with the fact that, according to Gandhi's standards, Claudio's masculinity is somehow beyond suspicion. Such a discovery destabilises Gandhi's misconceptions about what constitutes a real man. As a factory worker, a Marxist and an ex-boxer – which the film presents as markers of unquestionable manhood – Gandhi makes clear that he is someone who is unlikely to get mixed up with homosexuals. The film makes explicit the conventional function of homosexuality as a yardstick used to define what is and what is not masculine whilst at the same time questioning precisely this function. By suggesting, through the character of Claudio, that not all gay men are effeminate, the film suddenly becomes a locus of tensions around conflicting notions of what constitutes masculinity and the definitional divide that separates heterosexual men (understood as real men) from homosexual ones (understood as women-like men).[35]

In targeting a vast mainstream audience, the film is inevitably cautious in not turning Claudio's homosexuality into the major concern of the story but concentrates instead on the point of view of the straight protagonist. This privileged point of view is established, for example, with the persistent use of Gandhi's voiceover throughout the film. The centrality of Gandhi to the plot has the effect of casting the stability of his masculinity as the central dilemma that the film will attempt to resolve. Since the very first scenes, Gandhi is presented as a factory charge hand beyond reproach, whose sense of responsibility and courage gain him the respect and the admiration of his colleagues. When the porter expresses her doubts about Gandhi's sexuality (she poses the question in relation to his being a 'real man' or not), her husband's reaction is to dismiss them as silly talk. For him, Gandhi's reputation as a great boxer, his factory worker status and the fact that he has a stunning girlfriend like Maria are already unequivocal demonstrations of his manliness. The establishing of Gandhi's heterosexuality is of fundamental importance in relation to how the film strives to present him as a quintessential example of working-class manhood. His relationship with Maria, the character played by Edwige Fenech, is in this sense instrumental.

Yet, it is the very fragility of this constructed model of masculinity that creates most of the comic opportunities throughout the film. Laughter emerges here in the very gap between this idealised model and a reality that constantly seems to tarnish that model. On one occasion, as Maria performs a striptease in an attempt to seduce him after his return from Moscow, we are confronted with the comic spectacle of Gandhi falling asleep. In an earlier scene, Gandhi takes Maria to a restaurant, lest she find out about Claudio, who is temporarily staying at his apartment. He then promises her that he will book a room in the adjacent hotel in order to make love together all afternoon. After overhearing another customer talking about the suicide of a homosexual man, Gandhi panics, thinking that Claudio may have done the same. He looks at Maria, sitting sexily with her legs totally exposed to the camera, and decides to make up an excuse in order to get rid of her. In both instances, laughter stems from the contrast between the sexy spectacle of Edwige Fenech's body – with the erotic promise it gives to the straight male gaze – and Gandhi's inability to act on the heterosexual desire that is mobilised in such scenes.

The handling of the inconsistencies underlying the protagonist's masculinity may indeed be considered as unsurprising for a film that seems to borrow so much from the gags and wisecracks that are typical of the 'comedian comedy'. As Frank Krutnik notes in his study of the classical Hollywood comedian comedy, it is not unusual for the central character to violate familiar conventions of film heroism, unified sexuality and mature manhood. This kind of eccentricity is, however, temporary. In the end, 'the fictional impetus is to subjugate deviance and disruption to the demands of stability and coherence.'[36] In *La patata bollente*, such an impetus is partly present in the second half of the film. Consistent with the logic of a re-ordering, near the end, the film shows the wedding between Gandhi and Maria. It is an ending that is supposed to establish incontrovertibly the protagonist's heterosexuality by presenting the marital union between man and woman as an ideal happy ending. This resolution requires the disappearance of Claudio from Gandhi's world and his move to Amsterdam. It is a final re-ordering that, in its rather schematic development, clearly reveals its connectedness with the ideological and economic demands of the system in relation to which the film mainly works: the mainstream film industry.

La patata bollente operates this re-ordering by executing a set of unconvincing narrative turns, such as Gandhi's sudden desire to make love to Maria only to prove his straightness. This turn in the story is clearly an occasion for exhibiting Fenech's body and therefore satisfying the predominantly male heterosexual addressee of the film. But this re-ordering ends up undoing the very process through which the normative heterosexual male address of the film has been constructed. After their wedding, Gandhi and Maria arrive in Amsterdam for their honeymoon and turn up at the restaurant where Claudio now works. Once he has congratulated them on their recent marriage, Claudio reveals that he is now married too. Gandhi and Maria appear happy and relieved at this news, believing that he has married a woman. Claudio points to a person with long blond hair sitting at the counter and indicates that this is his spouse. The film teases our expectations by showing Gandhi eager to kiss and congratulate the bride. As he is about to approach 'her', the camera reveals that it is a man. Followed by stills showing the two couples surrounded by waiters in drag, this ending plays with the heterocentric assumptions of both the straight couple and those members of the audience who have fallen victim to the same misunderstanding. This is an ending that revolves around the use of surprise as a quintessential comic device. It is a comic ending that retroactively conjures up Gandhi's initial misunderstandings with Claudio and the lesson he should have learnt about never trusting one's first impressions. Based on the interplay between illusion (expressed in terms of coherence) and reality (expressed in terms of messiness), this ending prompts us to re-assess the strategies of re-ordering used by the film to give consistency and uniformity to Gandhi's masculinity.

Misrecognition, equivocation, mistaken identity and surprise are among the fundamental procedures of comedy. Depending on an action that, in being directed towards a goal, leads to the opposite of the goal that is striven for, comedies use these procedures to destabilise an order. Such a destabilisation is usually temporary and is followed by a subsequent reinstatement of the norms that have been disrupted. In providing a conventional resolution and a re-ordering of the gender and sexual messiness raised by the film, *La patata bollente* is symptomatic of the institutionalisation of heterosexual desire pervading much of mainstream cinema. Yet, the film also points to the artificial and often unconvincing mechanisms by which the normativisation of heterosexual desire is constructed, together with the structuring of a coherent male identity. It sheds light on the ineffectiveness of the signifying practices that inform the naturalisation of gender roles in comedies, hence revealing the strategies and conventions needed to preserve a clear distinction between normative masculinity and those male images that threaten its alleged coherence. *La patata bollente* ultimately demonstrates how it may be possible to disrupt some of the limits and constraints imposed by the economic and ideological system in which films have been produced. The film resists its final thrust towards a re-ordering by interrogating the genre and gender conventions that regulate its popular form of address. Further, it shows how, in the context of the 1970s, even popular comedies participated actively in a distinctive shift in social attitudes towards masculinity whilst simultaneously undermining the stability of age-old restrictive conventions for representing men. The film is punctuated by political statements in support of the right of homosexuals to integration and acceptance. Such statements constitute moments in which the comic action is temporarily suspended. This suspension occurs, for example, when Claudio confronts Gandhi about the homophobic jokes that he has been making up to that point and when he informs him about the reality of the social exclusion experienced by many homosexuals like him. Such moments seek to recuperate feelings of empathy and emotional involvement on the part of the audience. The strategy that is used here is one that disturbs that 'absence of feelings' on which laughter is generally predicated. This strategy encourages the audience to reconsider the emotional indifference that has characterised their enjoyment of the comic situations exploiting common feelings about homosexuals throughout the film. But the political statement made by the film also follows more spectacular modalities, as, for example, in the final tango performed by Gandhi and Claudio in front of the other factory workers. This is a moment of camp excess and joyful resistance to the homophobic attitudes that the film has thus unveiled; Gandhi unashamedly comes out as a friend of Claudio's in defiance of his colleagues' hostility. This is arguably the most memorable sequence of the film, which stands out as its most powerful political proclamation.

FILM ROMANCE AND THE ODD COUPLE: *A SPECIAL DAY*

Set on 3 May 1938, during Hitler's visit to Rome, *A Special Day* follows the accidental encounter between Antonietta, a housewife, and Gabriele, a homosexual radio announcer.[37] The two characters are presented as archetypal victims of the gender mythologies of the fascist regime. Antonietta, raised to think that her role as a good housewife and mother constitutes the measure of her loyalty to the nation, struggles to cope with the tasks she is expected to perform for her family and the frustrations of marriage to a man who treats her merely as a servant. As a homosexual, Gabriele not only is a poor fit for the ideal of manhood celebrated by fascism but also is denounced as a public enemy of the nation. For this reason, he has lost his job as a radio announcer and expects to be deported to Sardinia.

A Special Day was initially conceived as a contemporary story focusing on the experiences of social marginalisation and stigmatisation of homosexuals in 1970s Italy. The subsequent decision to modify the historical setting of the film had been a rather pragmatic one. A historical climate such as fascist Italy, which had intensified homophobic and sexist attitudes amongst Italians, appeared to provide more dramatic potential and a sharper political message.[38] *A Special Day*, Scola recalls, was also loosely inspired by Pier Paolo Pasolini's experience of persecution for his homosexuality since his expulsion from the Italian Communist Party.[39] Pasolini himself had been invited to contribute a three-minute documentary focusing on the increasing number of homophobic killings in Italy in the 1960s and the 1970s that should have accompanied the film. Ironically, it was Pasolini's murder in 1975 that prevented this collaboration from reaching the screen.[40]

A Special Day was purposefully promoted as a romantic film starring two actors, Marcello Mastroianni and Sophia Loren, who had already become successful partners in a number of highly acclaimed Italian comedies, including *Marriage Italian-Style* (*Matrimonio all'italiana*: 1964), *How Lucky to Be a Woman* (*La fortuna di essere donna*: 1956) and *Yesterday, Today and Tomorrow* (*Ieri, oggi e domani*: 1963).[41] During the promotion of the film, extra-cinematic expectations about Mastroianni and Loren were used to let the audience assume that the two characters would be, once again, involved in a heterosexual romance. Ettore Scola recalls that the sex scene between Loren and Mastroianni had been a contentious issue while shooting the film, with the producer, Carlo Ponti, insisting that a romantic epilogue was needed in order to ensure the film's financial success. Ponti was convinced that the character of Gabriele, after his encounter with Antonietta, had to grow out of his homosexuality to fulfil the romantic potential of the story and, ultimately, satisfy the expectations of the audience.[42] Ponti clearly thought that a conventional romantic resolution would have provided an audience-friendly representation of homosexuality, one linked to the idea that all deviances and conflicts can be resolved by the genuine love between a man and a woman.

The theme of the romantic encounter between Mastroianni and Loren has significantly allowed a number of commentators to argue that the main motif of *A Special Day* is the love between two outcasts. Jacqueline Reich, for example, asserts that the bond between Gabriele and Antonietta seems to follow a classic romantic paradigm in which 'the heterosexual coupling/union constitutes the natural form of closure to the text as it resolves the gender conflicts raised in the film's narrative'.[43] Another critic notes that the film is really a love story between a man and a woman who are both different.[44] Arguably, these comments make explicit the role of heterosexual romantic resolutions in establishing a seemingly natural causal progression in classical narratives. As David Bordwell has noted, the importance of the plot line involving heterosexual romance is structurally decisive in establishing a kind of closure effect.[45] But *A Special Day* resists and complicates the conventional romantic resolution discussed by Bordwell. The final section of this chapter will show how the film handles its 'popularising' impetus to address a large mainstream audience whilst attempting to deal with Gabriele's homosexuality as a paradigm of the diversified range of male experiences generally excluded under an oppressive gender and sexual ideology.

*　　*　　*

A *Special Day* reveals a meticulous work of research into the language, myths and iconography of the fascist regime. The film shows, for example, a copy of the famous comic book for children, *Nel regno dei pigmei*, whilst making use of recordings of the fascist song *Giovinezza* and of the original voice of the radio presenter Guido Notari, commenting on Adolf Hitler's 1938 visit to Rome. In typical Neorealist fashion, the insertion of documentary footage showing Hitler's visit as a prologue at the beginning of the film is consistent with the objective of presenting a realistic depiction of this historical moment. The ideal 'haunting' protagonist of the film is then the fascist virile body itself: the condensation of discourses, attitudes and ideals concerned with the celebration of the cult of virility during the fascist period.[46] The fascist virile body is first conjured up in the initial documentary footage of Hitler's visit through the appearance of Mussolini welcoming his ally. The epitome of the idealised fascist virile body, Mussolini walks with martial contempt and repeatedly stiffens his body to deploy the fascist salute in front of the crowd. The virile body of fascism is then reconstituted and inserted in the fictional plot through the presence of Antonietta's husband, Emanuele. Played by Canadian actor John Vernon, Emanuele appears to be a rough-mannered patriarch exerting absolute authority over his family. He is the quintessential embodiment of the cult of virility promoted by the regime, engaging in physical exercise every morning and expressing his disdain for foreign words and unmanly behaviours (Fig. 4.4). The film makes sure that we understand Emanuele's masculinity in the context of the gender ideology actively promoted by fascism. When Antonietta first meets Gabriele a reference to the taxation of celibacy, as introduced by the regime, offers a first way of understanding the patriarchal polarisation of gender roles in fascist Italy that the film illustrates: the normativisation of woman's role as mother and wife, on the one hand, and the assertion of man's virility through his ability to find a wife, reproduce and be the head of a family, on the other.

The film emphasises the importance of the virile ideal embodied by Emanuele as a distinctive public performance. The on-going radio commentary makes repeated allusions to the martial virility of the army during the parade, thus implicitly 'virilising' the public body of the nation. Having established Emanuele's masculinity within the dominant gender norms of fascist ideology, the film introduces Gabriele by underscoring his exclusion from this public

Figure 4.4   *A Special Day*, Antonietta's husband, Emanuele, gets ready for the parade.

sphere (Fig. 4.5). Together with Antonietta and the porter, he is the only tenant in the block who has not gone to the parade. When he first appears, sitting at his desk, his despair and frustration are starkly in contrast with the excitement, fervour and agitation of the other people leaving their homes to join the parade. His marginalisation from the public body of the nation is further illustrated as we discover that Gabriele has been fired from the State radio station because of his homosexuality. Gabriele explains this dismissal not in relation to his sexuality, but by referring to his alleged inability to conform to the virile ideal of fascism. Significantly, he tells Antonietta that he has lost his job because his voice 'was not in accordance with the EIAR regulations: solemn, martial and conveying Roman pride'.[47]

Before he comes out to Antonietta, Gabriele's homosexuality appears to

Figure 4.5   *A Special Day*, Gabriele pays a visit to Antonietta.

be somewhat ambivalent. Gabriele is certainly noticeable for his polished manners, soft-spoken voice, refined clothing and sharp humour. But such traits are not heavily marked enough to suggest his homosexuality clearly. If they do seem meaningful, it is only for the way they signal Gabriele's distance from the virile performance of masculinity on the part of Antonietta's husband. Gabriele's characterisation in the film is then important to render visible the oppressive logic of the gender mythology that makes Emanuele's masculinity not only desirable but also a norm in fascist Italy. If the male norm corresponds to the ideal of hyper-virility and martial rigour embodied by Emanuele, Gabriele's function in the film is to highlight the costs of such a norm for the lives of those subjects who are not willing or capable of conforming to it.

A Special Day makes use of the 'dual-focus' narrative that is typical of romantic comedies.[48] When Gabriele and Antonietta do not appear in the same scene – in most of the scenes they do – alternation of point of view and patterns of similarity, parallelism and contrast establish the mutually dependent narrative positions of the two protagonists. *A Special Day* draws in particular on the formula of the odd-couple plot that is typical of some romantic comedies. This formula generally brings together a man and a woman who apparently have very little in common, only to push them gradually closer to each other up to the final fulfilment of their romance.[49] At the beginning of the film, Gabriele and Antonietta are separated by a number of obstacles. Antonietta is an uneducated woman who has been brought up to think that her role as a housewife and mother reflects her loyalty to the nation (Fig. 4.6). By contrast, Gabriele is a cultured anti-fascist with a subtle sense of humour and fierce dislike for Mussolini. Their first accidental meeting introduces the distance that separates them. As Antonietta, yearning to speak to someone in order to break the tedious routine of her days, prolongs her petty talk about her six children,

Figure 4.6 *A Special Day*, Antonietta opens the door to Gabriele.

Gabriele does not even listen, still contemplating the chance to kill himself. This initial distance is eventually drawn into a system of solidarity as the story develops. The narrative trajectory is far from smooth; when Antonietta learns from the porter that her guest is an anti-fascist, she cruelly confronts him and asks him to leave. In bringing the protagonists closer, the film punctuates the story with incidents that hamper the increasing proximity between the two protagonists. Gabriele's coming out to Antonietta constitutes, in this sense, a crucial moment of crisis in the development of the story. Set on the roof of the building where the protagonists live, this scene establishes a blockage between Gabriele and Antonietta, between what he knows about himself (his homosexuality) and what she ignores. The windswept rows of sheets waving between the two protagonists constitute a striking visual reminder of the veiled knowledge that Antonietta is harbouring before Gabriele comes out. The female protagonist's enraged response to this coming out is only the first step towards rethinking her own identity. By acknowledging Gabriele's homosexuality and his painful experience of social stigmatisation, Antonietta has to face up to the terms of her own oppression as a frustrated mother and wife.

*　　*　　*

If a man is 'a man' only on condition that he is father, husband and soldier – as Antonietta's album reads – Gabriele is clearly not a man at all. By showing Gabriele as an attractive man capable of stirring a woman's sexual interest and upsetting her stable view of the world, the film invites us to question the limits of this logic and the varied range of male experiences that such a logic tends to leave out. Understanding how the film underscores the legitimacy of Gabriele's masculinity, despite his 'dissidence' from fascist gender roles, is especially important in relation to how the film frames the final erotic encounter between the two protagonists. This scene is potentially problematic because it runs the risk of undermining the significance of Gabriele's coming out to Antonietta as a homosexual man. To the extent that his self-disclosure establishes the specificity of his identity in contrast to a dominant model that prescribes compulsory heterosexuality to men, the erotic scene may make us wonder whether Gabriele will give up his 'deviant' sexual identity for the love of a woman. The problem that the erotic scene introduces is whether Antonietta's desire for him – and, by extension, heterosexual desire as whole – can rescue the man who has gone astray.

This scene is presented as a post-climactic moment of reunion following Gabriele's furious revelation of his homosexuality on the roof. It also follows Antonietta's coming to terms with her subjugation to her husband and to the gender myths of the fascist ideology that she has been instructed to revere. The love-making is a rather gentle, almost ritualistic moment of physical reconciliation. It starts with a medium shot of Gabriele, who holds Antonietta close to him in an attempt to console her. Antonietta has just admitted that her husband is not faithful and that her life is a misery. Their embrace slowly shifts into a more erotically charged contact. Gabriele gently strokes her breast and Antonietta swiftly responds with a kiss. It is at this point that Antonietta says that she does not care about Gabriele's homosexuality. This is a key moment: Antonietta is potentially disavowing Gabriele's coming-out and, by the same token, his homosexuality as a concrete obstacle to their love. At stake is the significance of Gabriele's homosexuality – his difference as a man – within the film and Antonietta's role in this respect. By the same token, Antonietta is potentially about to re-inscribe Gabriele's specificity as a homosexual man in terms of a negotiable lack that can be redeemed with the right kind of woman. What seems to be suggested, here, is that Antonietta, like Carlo Ponti, truly thinks that he 'can go straight'.

Antonietta's words freeze Gabriele. He stops holding her and withdraws towards the bed with an expression of deep gravity. There is a very unstable balance at play here. On the one hand, it is clear that Gabriele and Antonietta share something more than mutual compassion. Their 'special day' has intensified the level of emotional tension in their relationship. On the other, there is the risk of transforming the two protagonists into ill-fated lovers. Gabriele makes clear that their emotional and physical closeness will not change him. Antonietta acknowledges that this moment of intimacy is more about herself and her need to feel close to another man who respects her. Slowly, Antonietta clings on to Gabriele, touching his face and kissing him. Her desperate expression seems revelatory of her need for him, as much as Gabriele's mixed expression of pain and pleasure is indicative of his confusion here. Gabriele gradually gives up any resistance and submits to her desire. As a wife and a mother of six, Antonietta has been instructed to deny her sexual desires and be content with her role as child-carer and housewife. Through her encounter with Gabriele, Antonietta reasserts her right to a pleasurable use of her body. Her position on top in the love-making and her role as initiator of the sexual act indicate the recovery of a part of that sexual agency that she had to give up to fulfil her role of fascist mother and wife. The erotic encounter between the two protagonists provides an occasion for two equally oppressed subjects to find consolation and emotional strength in each other. The encounter ends up overturning the heterocentric expectations of the traditional film romance formula, as it does not transform the two protagonists into romantic lovers. Similarly, it does not turn Gabriele into a 'real heterosexual man'. His passive posture below Antonietta's body complies with his commitment to enable Antonietta's pleasure. Antonietta does not 'save' Gabriele by putting him back on track, but it is the homosexual man who accompanies the woman in the rediscovery of her body and of the terms of her oppression. As he makes clear to Antonietta after their love-making, this adventure has not changed who he is. Despite Carlo

Ponti's insistence on accommodating male homosexuality within a traditional heterosexual romantic resolution, the final sex scene actually works against this accommodation by means of a paradigm of sexual liberation that is typical of the 1970s: the alliance between two oppressed sexual subjects.[50] *A Special Day* dismantles one of the topoi of the classic romantic comedy – the meeting between an unhappy woman and an attractive man who will save her. In so doing, the film reworks in a productive manner a traditional cinematic mode of representation that has made homosexuality traditionally invisible.[51] The male–female relationship is emptied of its conventionally romantic implications and redefined within a liberating sexual imagery.

A Special Day proves how male homosexuality may be dealt with openly and productively, even within those plot twists and financial pressures that are meant to obfuscate it partially. As the final sex scene shows, the emotional tension binding the two protagonists is not just unproblematically translated into heterosexual erotic attraction. Desire becomes an instrument of liberation within a narrative framework that had already carefully defined the common oppression of the two characters. Like *La patata bollente*, *A Special Day* exemplifies a distinctive tendency in 1970s Italian cinema towards the representation of a wider range of experiences and identities traditionally excluded from normative constructions of masculinity. The value of these films stems not only from their progressive concern with the liberationist rhetoric of the gay movement but also from the way in which they resist pressures towards a heterocentric re-ordering of their own narratives.

5. PIER PAOLO PASOLINI'S EROTIC IMAGERY AND THE SIGNIFICANCE OF THE MALE BODY

Dozens of teenage 'boys' are gathered together in the giant hall of an apparently disused building. They are arranged in rows, military style. A group of older men – middle aged, bourgeois, dressed for winter in heavy coats – arrive and begin to inspect the boys. Some boys are favoured over others. Those favoured are asked to undress, so as to reveal the nature and dimensions of their naked bodies. The boys comply, with somewhat surprising willingness. Their bodies are appraised in silence, the men pass on, the boys raise their trousers and lower their shirts to cover themselves again.[1]

This is how John David Rhodes begins his essay 'Watchable bodies: *Salò*'s young non-actors'. The scene he describes is from Pier Paolo Pasolini's infamous film *Salò, or the 120 Days of Sodom* (*Salò o le 120 giornate di Sodoma*: 1975). In this essay, Rhodes takes issue with the film's supposed anti-eroticism. Whilst the critical consensus has been that there is nothing erotically appealing in this film, Rhodes points out that the standard reception ends up disavowing something rather striking: namely, the fact that in this film there are a number of beautiful boys. 'Many of us', Rhodes says, 'might find the sheer fact of so much nakedness at the film's beginning – its curatorial selection and display of beautiful and nubile flesh – to be (dare I risk saying this?) somewhat arousing or at least titillating.'[2] Conceived as an allegorical critique of the fascism of consumer capitalism in post-economic-boom Italy, this is a film that features horrific scenes of physical violence and humiliation. For Rhodes, it is precisely the presence of these scenes that is supposed to 'neutralise' the erotic appeal of the beautiful young boys. And yet Rhodes argues that Pasolini 'has chosen his actors precisely because they are attractive – precisely because their bodies will, at least, raise the risk or summon the spectre of our own arousal'.[3] Rhodes seems to suggest here that the anxiety resulting from the possibility that we might desire these bodies – the same bodies that will be sexually exploited and tortured for the pleasure of their executioners – is something that haunts our viewing experience of the film. In retrieving the materiality of these bodies (their physicality), and therefore their potential for inducing arousal, from the critical consensus that has made them 'unwatchable', Rhodes argues that this materiality is, in Pasolini's films, always a crucial prerequisite for political critique. 'It is always necessary to talk and act in concrete terms,' Pasolini writes in his letters to Gennariello, an imaginary Neapolitan teenage boy.[4] The letters offer a scathing critique of a contemporary Italy devastated by the emergence of neocapitalism and mass culture. Even though Gennariello is only a rhetorical figure, Pasolini gives a very 'concrete' description of this boy.[5] One cannot ignore, Rhodes notes, how closely this description evokes the physicality of the boys Pasolini spent so much of his life cruising. He concludes by suggesting that, for Pasolini, political criticism depends on the actual substance and physical specificity of these bodies.[6] In challenging the critical consensus about *Salò*'s putative anti-eroticism, Rhodes performs a kind of 'perverse' reading. This reading shows that the possibility for these adolescent bodies of being erotically appealing is not simply present in the film; rather, this possibility constitutes a crucial site of anxiety for viewers, who have to confront the desirability of bodies that, in the course of the film, will be forced to live through hell.[7]

In *Salò,* the young boys are not the only ones who undress. So do a number of very attractive young girls. Yet, Rhodes spends no time at all talking about their bodies and what their nudity might mean to the viewer. Rhodes's essay is, in fact, concerned with the figure of the non-professional actor in *Salò* and with the anxieties raised by the film about the age of these actors, their agency and their ambivalent status as sexual objects for the camera. These are issues that are also arguably relevant for the young girls who were cast to play the roles of incarcerated victims in the film. Nothing in his essay explains the reasons for this exclusion. We are only left with the impression that the bodies that really matter are those of the boys. Rhodes is not alone in suggesting – even though only implicitly – the privileged role of the male body in Pasolini's erotic imagery. Joseph Boone, for example, argues that in *Arabian Nights* (*Il fiore delle mille e una note*: 1974), despite Pasolini's tendency to show both female and male nudes, the scenic composition, lighting and camera angles would seem to invite the spectator's gaze to focus mainly on the male body.[8] But the reading of the potential erotic appeal of the boys' bodies in *Salò* (and their privileged status over those of the girls) is a rhetorical move that Rhodes cannot make without invoking Pasolini's own erotic desire for the boys ('The concrete terms [Pasolini] uses evoke exactly the physicality of the boys he spent so much of his life cruising').[9] Rhodes even notes how closely the physical description of Gennariello is to Pino Pelosi, the teenage hustler who was convicted for Pasolini's murder. Again, Rhodes is not alone in reading the erotic appeal of the male youths in Pasolini's films through the director's own desires for these boys. Bryant George, for example, argues that the cinematic representation of the youths 'is bound up with Pasolini's own sexual and political desire'.[10] For a director whose work seems constantly to posit an individual authorial presence as its primary point of origin, this emphasis on Pasolini's subjective voice and the director's biography is perhaps not that surprising.[11] Robert Gordon has noted that Pasolini 'manipulates, disturbs and renews the pro-filmic in the hope that it will serve him as an idiom for self-expression'.[12] The particular homoerotic scenario allowed by this awareness of Pasolini's controlling gaze behind the camera has been repeatedly noted. This has often made his films susceptible to a biographical analysis.[13] Less has been said, however, about the male homosocial viewing structures that inevitably underlie this putative homoerotic scenario, and even less so about the reflective space that this scenario would implicitly open, a space in which a male subject has to confront the terms of his fascination with an object that is fetishistically exhibited for his own pleasure.[14]

I would like to contrast the scene from *Salò* described by Rhodes with another one from *Arabian Nights*. A young boy and a girl lie asleep on their beds on the opposite sides of a big tent. The camera is placed midway between the two adolescents. First, we have a high-angle medium shot of the boy and then a pan to the right that reveals the girl. They appear for the same amount of time and their positions in relation to the camera and to each other are specular. Then we see a man and a woman; they smile, laugh and stare at the two adolescents. The scene makes intense use of point-of-view shots, which tend to coincide with the optical standpoint of the man and the woman. Yet, their point of view is always a shared one; the man and the woman tend to appear together within the frame, staring at the adolescents and anticipating with the movement of their heads the cut or the pan from the girl to the boy and vice versa (Fig. 5.1). As a result, the scene appears built upon a triangular visual relation between two apices (the objects of desire: the boy and the girl) and a vertex (the ungendered point of view shared by the woman and man). *Arabian Nights* makes considerable use of nudity and this scene is no exception. In *Salò*, the exhibition of the naked bodies of the boys relies on another particular editing technique. As the boys undress, lowering their trousers and lifting their shirts, the tilting camera movement on their bodies (first downwards and then upwards) is sutured to the controlling gaze of their male executioners; such a

Figure 5.1 *Arabian Nights*, the King and Queen watch the love-making between the two adolescents.

gaze functions as a vehicle for the executioners' power to turn these bodies into passive objects for their own pleasure. The construction of subjective points of view appears very rarely in Pasolini's films, but when it does occur, it seems to have a particular function. As Robert Gordon notes in discussing *Accattone* (1961), '[w]here the camera does express a point of view, as of the policeman following Accattone in the final scenes of the film, it is to objectify the figure of Accattone.'[15] The objectifying power of the gaze in the scene from *Arabian Nights* seems to be persistently challenged, and not only through the construction of an ungendered shared point of view for the man and the woman. When an (individual) subjective point of view occurs – for example, when the boy and the girl wake up and stare at each other – this is eventually disturbed in two ways: (1) the desiring subject of desire becomes the object of desire of the other adolescent; (2) the gaze is doubled and externalised by cutting to the woman and man as they look at the action unfolding from their shared optical standpoint.

In considering this scene, Geoffrey Nowell-Smith has pointed out the undifferentiated visual treatment of the boy and the girl as objects of desire and the potential polymorphousness of the erotic scenario.[16] In not attributing a privileged role to a male heterosexual vision, the film seems to open up the spectrum of pleasures enjoyed through the act of looking across multiple axes of gender and sexual identity; it allows, for example, the explicit articulation of homosexual and heterosexual pleasures by means of looking whilst validating such pleasures through both male and female subject positions. Yet, on closer examination, the scene does seem to reflect a degree of differentiation by bestowing greater visibility to the naked body of the boy. The scene is split into two segments, whose shots and camera angles are very similar. In the first, the boy wakes up, goes to the girl's bed and makes love to her (Fig. 5.2). In the

Figure 5.2   *Arabian Nights*, the boy makes love to the girl.

second, the girl does the same with the boy. But, despite the apparent specularity of these two segments, whilst the first segment shows shots of nudity for 49 seconds (in which the boy's nudity is most visible), the second stops short of 35. One could argue that this unevenness is due to the particular structure of narrative repetition, whereby the recounting of repeated diegetic segments takes considerably less time than their first occurrence. Still, as a result, the boy alone remains naked – before uncovering the girl – for 10 seconds as opposed to only 1 second for the girl in the second segment. This degree of differentiation is also confirmed by the much more prolonged and gratuitous exposure in close-up of the boy's genitals. Whilst the girl's pubic area is very hastily shown as the boy covers her with a sheet in medium shot, the camera seems to hold its gaze on the boy's crotch for much longer.

I have contrasted this scene from *Arabian Nights* with the earlier one from *Salò* to suggest the presence of an oppositional thrust in Pasolini's cinematic grammar of desire, which posits the male body as the crux for the elaboration of a set of polemical positions about the politics of gender and sexual representation in film. Whilst, in the first instance, the display of the boys' naked bodies is the occasion for rehearsing dominant objectifying structures of erotic looking, in the second the gaze appears not simply 'de-subjectivised', but also shared, multiplied and eventually folded back on itself so as to neutralise its objectifying power. Built around the provocative exhibition of the male body as a privileged object of erotic interest, both scenes reflect two intersecting aspects of Pasolini's cinematic practice at this stage of his career: on the one hand, a profound awareness of the dominant hetero-patriarchal conventions of pleasurable looking in cinema – which are spectacularly exhibited and challenged in his films – and, on the other, a desire to assemble and foreground an oppositional system of looking and a dissident erotic imagery. What we have, therefore, is not pure oppositionality, but a challenge that is inseparable from the dominant structures it contests. The conventions of pleasurable looking that Pasolini's films tend to disrupt are, of course, those described by Laura Mulvey. They are conventions supporting the preservation of a 'hermetically sealed world which unwinds magically, indifferent to the presence of the audience, producing for them a sense of separation'.[17] Technically speaking, they rely on procedures such as continuity editing and the subjective shot. Their objective is to integrate the gaze of the camera and that of an ideal (male) spectator with that of the male character whose desiring gaze is directed to an erotic object (in Mulvey's model this is normally a woman). This is a cinema of narrative integration, a sealed world of illusions playing on the voyeuristic fantasies of spectators, which reflects, in Mulvey's words, 'the straight, socially established interpretation of sexual difference which controls images, erotic ways of looking and spectacle'.[18] Pasolini's films tend to disrupt pleasurable looking by bringing its functioning mechanisms to the fore and by constantly blocking it, problematising it, charging it with anxieties. In causing such a disruption, they create for the spectator a reflective space where the terms and codes disciplining – and inevitably normalising – the cinematically visible are constantly interrogated. As Patrick Rumble has noted, in Pasolini's films we often find 'images that foreground their own artifice, narrative elements that exceed any definite plot function, and experimentation in POV that cause the spectator to ponder the historical and ideological determinants of representation and of vision itself'.[19]

Exhibiting the Gaze, Exhibiting the Body in *Teorema*

In 1968, Pasolini made *Teorema*. Originally based on a play written by Pasolini three years earlier, this was a film that caused significant controversy. As Pasolini's biographer, Enzo Siciliano, points out, 'it was the first time that a male nude, that of the protagonist Terence Stamp, appeared on the big screen.'[20] Confiscated by the Public Prosecutor's Office for obscenity soon after its premiere screening at the 1968 Venice Film Festival, *Teorema* inaugurates a period in Pasolini's career that is marked by a strong interest in issues related to sex and nudity. To justify his interest in these issues, Pasolini argued: 'there is no limit to the freedom of expression and representation. There can be no limit. At the very bottom of my work [. . .] lies a demand for the "total" representation of the real, which is to be understood as a civil achievement.'[21] Central to Pasolini's concerns at this stage of his career was not simply a desire to make more sexually explicit films, but also a distinct preoccupation with film audiences' access to reality. Cinema, which he understood as 'the written language of reality', was for Pasolini the ideal medium to let reality present itself in its most genuine, original way.[22] As Naomi Greene has suggested,

Pasolini refused to separate cinema and life to overcome the impossible gap between real and 'represented': 'It was a desire to transcend these tragic limits that inspired his passionate opposition to those who analysed film as a system of signs, removed from "reality", that obeys its own codes.'[23]

The visibility of the male body and the conditions disciplining its representations were, for Pasolini, symptomatic problems of the broader taboos and epistemological constraints that narrowed the visibility of reality itself. In an interview for the magazine *TV Sorrisi e Canzoni*, he polemicised the way in which mainstream TV and films were promoting a set of erotic images claustrophobically limited to the 'controlled' exposure of naked female bodies.[24] In the interview, Pasolini seems to suggest that such an exclusionary process of representation tends to normalise a set of images whilst casting others as unimaginable, offensive, unrepresentable. In *Teorema*, Pasolini's polemical response was to break one of the ultimate taboos and have the camera linger on the crotch of the protagonist, played by Terence Stamp. To justify this decision, Pasolini invoked again the need to represent reality in its most truthful, absolute manifestation: 'even the penis, in its extreme and defenceless nudity – which is part of real life – has the right to be expressed and represented.'[25] It is not a mere desire for more explicit representations that correlates Pasolini's 'obsessive' concern for reality with his interest in nudity and with his depiction of erotic scenarios. It would seem that Pasolini did not believe that his films were simply contributing to a teleological progression towards a final, clear view of reality. His theoretical writings on film language reveal the importance that the director placed not so much on the object to be represented but on the stylistic conditions accompanying its expression. Cinema was, for Pasolini, charged with the task of modifying our way of thinking about reality, by making explicit the cultural dimension of our physical relation to this reality. The way to do so was for him to articulate an oppositional cinematic language to the so-called 'language of prose' of commercial escapist cinema.[26] The objective of this chapter is not to give a full account of this oppositional cinematic praxis, but to examine the significance and the functions of the male body within the elaboration of this praxis.

Teorema tells the story of a bourgeois family and its collapse after the arrival of a mysterious young man in their house. It recounts the parable of each member of the family falling victim to an overwhelming form of sexual longing for the man and the crisis that ensues after he leaves. In an interview, Pasolini declared that it was his intention to make the visitor 'a generically ultra-terrestrial and metaphysical apparition: he could be the Devil. Or a mixture of God and the Devil.'[27] Consistent with this declaration of intent, the visitor has often been discussed as an otherworldly figure, a kind of god whose major task is to expose and destroy the artificial life of the bourgeois family. Millicent Marcus, for example, acknowledges something metaphysical in the systematic way in which the visitor elicits desire in each member of the family, whereas Robert Gordon recognises in *Teorema* a persistent allegorical tendency that should caution us against any literal reading of the film; this is a film about class and about the crisis of the bourgeoisie, where sexual desire for a man is simply a pretext to explore much deeper ideological dilemmas.[28] But what if, in thinking about *Teorema*, we were to stop at the level of pretext? What would a literal reading of the dynamics of erotic looking and seduction in the film allow? What can an acknowledgement of the gendered materiality of the visitor's body – his maleness, his sexual appeal – tell us about this film?

One way of approaching *Teorema* 'literally' is to consider the role of the visitor's body as central object of desire in the film. In a variation on the classical Mulvey model, the main function of the male body in *Teorema* is to enthral the looking subject in a condition of scopophilic tension. Often portrayed in a static posture, the visitor represents the obsessive focal point for the gazes of the other characters. This position of visual availability has an essential diegetic function: it is the condition on which the erotic awakening of the family – and the resulting crisis for each member – is based. This position relies, however, on an inherent contradiction between the visitor's narrative – and frequently visual – passivity and the work of seduction that he carries out on each member of the family. In other words, while the narrative function of the visitor is to seduce each one of the family members, this seduction seems to operate through the visitor simply being in the house and available to their gazes; this state of non-action produces narrative action, but this action is not the result of any explicit agency on the visitor's part.

The exposure of the male body in *Teorema* could be considered gratuitous in a sense. Linda Williams has discussed the category of the 'gratuitous' as a form of excessive display (of violence, sex and so on) that is normally dismissed as having no logic or reason for existing beyond its alleged power to excite.[29] In *Teorema*, through repeated lingering shots of the visitor, the camera forces us to stare at this body for much longer than one would reasonably expect. In foregrounding its primary status as an image to be looked at, the visitor's body seems both to freeze action and to suspend meaning in moments of enigmatic contemplation. One could argue, of course, that in most films the purpose of displaying a beautiful body is indeed that of a spectacle breaking the flow of the diegesis. Yet, as a long tradition of depicting the male body in a homoerotic fashion (action movies, epic films, westerns and so on.) has shown, the erotic display of the male body tends to be motivated at the level of the diegesis by the action in which such a body is normally involved. The action 'rationalises' the act of looking at the body by repressing its erotic component. In his famous essay, 'Masculinity and Spectacle', Steve Neale discusses the particular strategies of rationalisation and erotic disavowal in Sergio Leone's westerns:

We are offered the spectacle of male bodies, but bodies unmarked as objects of erotic display. There is no trace of an acknowledgment or recognition of those bodies as displayed solely for the gaze of the spectator. [. . .] We see male bodies stylized, fragmented by close-ups, but our look is not direct, it is heavily mediated by the looks of the characters involved. And these looks are marked not by desire, but by fear, or hatred, or aggression. The shoot-outs are moments of spectacle, points at which the narrative hesitates, comes to a momentary halt, but they are also points at which the drama is finally resolved, a suspense in the culmination of the narrative drive. They thus involve an imbrication of both forms of looking, their intertwining designed to minimize and displace the eroticism they each tend to involve, to disavow any explicitly erotic look at the male body.[30]

In *Teorema*, any rationalisation of the erotic gaze that might lead to its disavowal is implausible. In this film, it is the very development of the narrative that retroactively justifies the erotic display of the visitor's body. This display establishes, in fact, the conditions for the family members to fall in love. Consistent with the logic of a theorem that structures the film, the premise (the erotic display of the male body) already contains its conclusion (the seduction).[31] One cannot be disavowed without affecting the other, and thus compromising the outcome of the story. The gratuitousness of the display is therefore structurally embedded in the logic of the film. It is its rationale, its functioning narrative mechanism.

Scopophilia in relation to the male body is both exhibited and problematised in *Teorema*. In the first scene of seduction, the visitor sits on a chair in the garden, while the maid Emilia stares at him. His legs, wide open, establish an object position that seems to attract Emilia's gaze magnetically. Scopophilia, Laura Mulvey reminds us, is a form of pleasure that consists of treating other people as objects, subjecting them to a controlling, curious gaze. Its precondition is a clear-cut separation between the viewer and what is seen.[32] In *Teorema*, scopophilia is repeatedly disturbed, the separation between the gaze and the object constantly mobilised and filled. Built around a frantic back-and-forth movement between Emilia staring at the camera and the view of the visitor reading, this scene seems to turn our attention to the object of the gaze as much as to Emilia's gaze itself.

Among the films made by Pasolini throughout his career, *Teorema* is the one that makes the most intense use of subjective shots and shot–reverse-shot editing. Yet, rather than being sutured together to give a seamless impression of logical continuity, the shots often appear dislocated from each other and stretched beyond their reasonable length. Far from solidifying the controlling power of the gaze, the shot–reverse-shot sequence seems to undermine this power by making the desiring gaze of the characters hyperbolically visible, and thus reveals its vulnerability.[33] Significantly, for each member of the family, the act of looking is conducive to a form of overwhelming desire for the visitor. It is a kind of scopophilia divested of its active, controlling drive and turned into a powerless compulsion to look.

The shot–reverse shot is the basis for the scene that introduces the first appearance of the visitor during a party at the family house. The camera has thus far followed Pietro (the son), who has been asked by his mother (Lucia) to put on some music. The camera remains external to the room so that the shot is internally reframed by the open door that gives access to the room. By means of deep-focus composition, the shot allows the distinct viewing both of the compositional elements within the internal framing (those further from the camera: a few guests chatting; the son putting on music; a number of pieces of furniture) and of those external to the framing (those closer to the camera: a table with some glasses on the left and what seems to be a couch on the right). It is at this stage that the visitor enters from a door on the right-hand side of the room, his entrance made inconspicuous by the multiple compositional planes within the shot and by the fact that the camera had been following Pietro. The visitor walks towards the centre of the room and stands there. It is at this stage that a medium shot reveals Odetta (the daughter) looking, and, next to her, another girl. The girl asks her, 'Who's that boy?' In close-up, Odetta turns towards the girl to give a short evasive answer ('A boy'), and then turns back to look at the camera. The following cut takes us back to the earlier shot of the visitor (Fig. 5.3).

Up till this point, the visitor has been an unremarkable element of the mise-en-scène. He has simply been 'potential': (1) the potential for action; (2) the

Figure 5.3 *Teorema*, the visitor makes his first appearance at the family's house.

potential to trigger interest/desire in others; and (3) the potential to become a central presence in the scene. Immersed in the compositional density of the shot, he initially lacks both visual and narrative prominence. It is only when the subject looking at him (Odetta) is revealed that this object position is unmasked. It is only then that he acquires visual and narrative centrality. In the most basic articulation of the shot–reverse-shot sequence, we are invited to acknowledge (and identify with) the character's act of looking, recognise his/her point of view and objectify what he/she is looking at. Consistent with the logic of continuity editing, this is a technique that, in creating a smooth flow from shot to shot, confirms a point of view, whilst effacing the audience's own identification with the character's gaze. In *Teorema*, instead, the shot–reverse-shot sequence seems to expose the very ability of the act of looking 'to make' the object of the gaze. This function is foregrounded by the fact that the object was already present in the on-screen space as a 'non-object' of the gaze, autonomously existing and separate from the character's gaze. In these terms, the male body initially inhabits a space prior to the formation of subject and object of the look. What is in front of our eyes, then, is a genealogy of erotic looking and the resulting formation of subjects and objects of the gaze.

The scene that makes the most insistent use of the shot–counter shot is Emilia's seduction. Far from being balanced and symmetrically articulated, the shots showing the visitor absorbed in his reading and those of Emilia staring at him are inconsistent and irregular (Fig. 5.4). With similarity to the earlier scene of the visitor's first appearance, the character's gaze enters a pre-existing scenario in which the visitor has already appeared – first with a very long-distance shot in which he is hardly visible, and then with a medium shot and a slightly

Figure 5.4   *Teorema*, Emilia staring at the visitor in the garden.

different angle. The view of the visitor is then tied in with a frontal close-up of Emilia staring. But the continuity of the shot–reverse-shot sequence appears from now on to be repeatedly violated. The scale of the shots of the visitor bears no relation whatsoever to the point from where Emilia is supposed to be looking. The eye-line repeatedly changes. Rather than closing the sequence and confirming the character's perspective, the proliferation of irregular reaction shots destabilises this perspective and leaves the sequence open, ambivalent. Angelo Restivo has noted that, in *Teorema*, 'when put together, the images become highly ambiguous, as if somehow the meaning is being carried in the very interstices of the images . . . [T]he images fail to "compute", fail to come together in traditional narrative terms.'[34] In *Teorema*, this interstice also consists of what cannot possibly be 'sutured' within the shot–reverse-shot structure: a series of redundant images that highlight the dislocation between the image of the character looking and that of the object of the gaze. It is in this interstice that the affective response produced in the characters by the act of looking is spectacularly exhibited through enigmatic, protracted close-ups on their faces. And it is in this interstice that the desiring gaze both acquires a kind of contemplative frontality and reveals its objectifying status in relation to the camera.

The display of the desiring gaze also occurs through frontal close-ups of the visitor looking straight at the camera. The camera takes the point of view of the mother and Emilia looking at the visitor and finally acknowledging their desire for him. In these instances of direct address, the gaze of the characters and, inevitably, that of the camera are similarly acknowledged.[35] The contemplative frontality of the direct address creates reflective moments of narrative stillness. The viewer is caught up in the act of looking, a predicament that replicates the condition of the intra-diegetic desiring subject. Paul Willemen calls this form of direct address 'the fourth look', which he describes as the look that constitutes the viewer as an independent and visible subject. Willemen's point is helpful for considering the empathic implications of this look. '[A]s the viewer has to confront his or her sadistic voyeurism, the presence of the imagined look in the field of the other makes itself increasingly felt, producing a sense of shame at being caught in the act of voyeurism.'[36] *Teorema* seems to harness these feelings of shame not simply to describe the struggle of the family members to confront their own desires and overcome their inhibitions, but, most importantly, to reflect on the symbolic and cultural structures that maintain the male body as a place of shame and concealment. Further, *Teorema* seems to dramatise the feelings of anxiety that emerge when the male body is turned into the object of erotic looking. Significantly, whilst establishing the male body as the central erotic magnet of the story, the film directs our attention to the consuming state of astonishment of the family members. If, in inscribing the male body as object of desire, *Teorema* opens up the possibility of accommodating two subject positions that usually have been either denied

Figure 5.5   *Teorema*, Terence Stamp undressing.

(the heterosexual female gaze) or repressed (the male homosexual gaze) in narrative cinema, the highlighting of the emphatic elements of the gaze also reminds us of the illicit nature of the female and homosexual gazes within the patriarchal film canon.

One is constantly reminded of this illicitness by the emphasis placed on the feelings of panic shared by those who stare at the visitor's body. At one point, Pietro and the guest share a bedroom and they both take off their clothes before going to bed (Fig. 5.5). The scene is not conceived as erotic in conventional terms. The camera does not indulge in close-ups of the visitor's body but keeps itself at distance; no exchange of looks takes place between the two men. The scene very briefly reveals the naked body of the visitor, while Pietro ashamedly gets under the blankets to take off his underpants and puts on his pyjamas. The scene assumes sensual significance in light of Pietro's bewildered response to the naked male body. Pietro cannot fall asleep; he gets up and feels the urge to stare at the guest. His expression suggests powerlessness and enthralment up to the moment he bursts into tears for not being able to resist his desire for the man. In another scene, again, the film conveys an instance of homosexual panic as it shows Pietro and the visitor glancing through the pages of a book on the English painter Francis Bacon. Whilst the first close-ups reveal some of Bacon's homoerotic paintings and his usual bestial distortions of the human figure, Pietro attentively observes with increasing anxiety the pictures of *Three Studies for Figures at the Base of a Crucifixion* (Fig. 5.6). Based on the Greek legend of the avenging Furies, these paintings remind us how Bacon was dealing with the violent anxieties, insecurities and wider social pressures associated with his homosexuality during his lifetime. The Christian subject of the crucifixion in

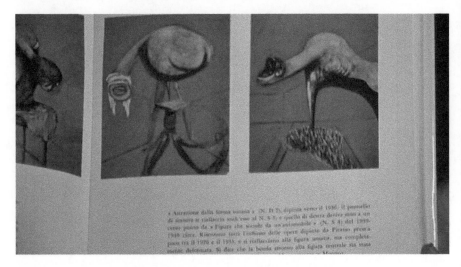

Figure 5.6   *Teorema*, the son and the visitor looking at reproductions of Francis Bacon's *Three Studies for Figures at the Base of a Crucifixion*.

these paintings significantly ties in with the visitor's god-like presence in the film and the kind of 'mystic liberation' that he brings into the life of the bourgeois family, but also suggests the kind of destruction – the sacrifice – that he causes. By showing close-ups of these paintings, the film is clearly also alluding to how Pietro's encounter with homosexual desire has exposed the fragility of his male identity, which is now infused with unease and doubt.

For a film that caused so much scandal on its release and which was prosecuted for obscenity, *Teorema* appears rather chaste in its depiction of sex and nudity. In the scene in Pietro's bedroom, as I have already noted, Terence Stamp becomes the first male nude in the history of Italian cinema, but the camera keeps itself at distance; in undressing, the actor does not face the camera and subsequently reveals his nudity frontally, very briefly and partly in the shadow, for a few instants only in the act of getting into bed. The scenes of (heterosexual) love-making are similarly coy; the visitor always stays dressed and lies on top of the women (Emilia and Lucia), gently kissing them. As for homosexual sex, this always remains at the level of allusion. At one point, Paolo (the father) and the visitor go for a walk in the countryside along a riverbed. After some fooling around and running, we see the visitor lying on the ground surrounded by bushes. The next shot shows Paolo walking alone along the riverbed, apparently seeing something among the bushes and going towards it. The audience is clearly teased into contemplating the idea of homosexual sex in a way that suggests its occurrence, whilst its actual manifestation remains concealed. No kissing or touching between men occurs. In the scene in Pietro's bedroom, the possibility of sex between the visitor and Pietro is clearly suggested, first by the act of uncovering the visitor to admire his naked body and subsequently by the visitor's getting into Pietro's bed. A few scenes later, their love-making is revealed as a fait accompli, as the father catches them sleeping next to each other in the same bed.

In both instances, the screening of homosexual sex materialises in these ellipses, in its concealed actualisation, which is removed from our eyes, whilst at the same time haunting viewers as an unavoidable certainty. Robert Gordon has suggested that the poetics of the camera in Pasolini's films tend towards anxiety, rather than pleasure, by constructing a viewing subject that appears suspended, in crisis, in the face of the unresolved situations that he/she witnesses.[37] It is this sense of suspension that informs the spectatorial experience of homosexual desire in the film. Occluding any explicit depiction of homosexual sex, *Teorema* hardly renders it unimaginable. In an ironic gesture of self-censoring, it is as if the film playfully internalises the sense of embarrassment and shame that the screening of homosexual sex (and desire) has traditionally provoked in the history of cinema by keeping it at the level of prolonged, unavoidable tension. In persistently confronting the ideal heterosexual male spectator with the spectacle of its presence, it is the male body – that of the visitor – that primarily functions as the haunting ghost of homosexual desire in the film. It is a ghost that re-appears once the visitor has left, in the cruising scenes involving Lucia and Paolo. In all these instances, homosexual sex remains a possibility that is hinted at, of which the persistent and ubiquitous reminder is the male body, unashamedly offered to the camera and to the gaze of the characters.

THE CROTCH AND THE QUEER PHALLUS IN *THE TRILOGY OF LIFE*

The Decameron (*Il Decameron*: 1971), *The Canterbury Tales* (*I racconti di Canterbury*: 1972) and *Arabian Nights* – commonly known as *The Trilogy of Life* – mark a period in Pasolini's career that was marked by scandal and a desire to provoke. Full of frontal nudity, these films depicted sex with an explicitness that struck many commentators of the time as pornographic. In a column for the newspaper *Il corriere della sera* in 1973, Pasolini made explicit his intention to render visible through these films a set of bodily experiences and sexual pleasures that, due to society's hypocrisy and moralism, had so far remained invisible.[38] It was not just a desire to provide more explicit representations of sex and nudity that motivated Pasolini to make these films; his objective was also to portray a dissident erotic imagery that would be antagonistic to the sexual representations that were becoming increasingly prominent in 1970s Italy. Following the consolidation of a mass culture and the propagation of bourgeois lifestyles among Italians, sex – Pasolini argued – had become 'a social duty'.[39] Having been co-opted into the repressive economy of modern capitalism, sex was now being experienced through a set of anxieties and neuroses. On various occasions, Pasolini expressed his anger towards what he defined as the 'anthropological revolution' taking place in Italy after the economic boom of the 1950s and 1960s. He argued that this revolution was the result of a shift from a predominantly rural culture to a mass culture, a shift that had caused the almost complete disappearance of regional differences, dialects and many pre-capitalistic social forms of interaction. Pasolini's anger at the development of mass culture was emphatically expressed in *Il caos*, where he defined the bourgeoisie as a vampire, a disease that was quickly spreading.[40] Behind these cultural and socioeconomic transformations he saw the emergence of a new repressive and conformist mentality among Italians, which had turned people's bodies and desires into consumer goods.

Three fundamental premises inform the making of *The Trilogy of Life*: Pasolini's belief that sex is political and constitutes a fundamental area for the right to self-expression; the desire to represent a 'more human' version of sex than the one validated by modern capitalism; and, finally, Pasolini's wish to celebrate an archaic world of corporality and sensual pleasures.[41] In making the three adaptations of these classic medieval texts, Pasolini intended to portray a world as remote as possible from post-economic boom Italy. As he declared in commenting on the films the make up *The Trilogy of Life*, 'the protagonist of my films is popular body culture,' a culture that Pasolini considered lost in 1970s Italy.[42] Through his role as a newspaper columnist, Pasolini denounced the pervasiveness of dominant models of erotic viewing on TV and in film, and their fetishistic exploitation of the female body. He argued that these models, through their normalising reiteration, restricted the possibilities of what could be thought of and represented as erotic.[43] Pasolini was writing in a period in which low-budget erotic comedies were becoming increasingly popular among Italian audiences. Bringing fame to a new generation of actresses including Barbara Bouchet, Edwige Fenech and Lilly Carati, these comedies were providing audiences with voyeuristic scenarios primarily revolving around female nudity.[44] They featured formulaic striptease scenes – normally set in a bedroom or in the fitting room of a shop – for the pleasure of male characters, who would peek through a keyhole or a slot in the wall. In aligning the gaze of these characters with the gaze of the camera and that of an ideal male heterosexual spectator, they abounded with close-ups and zoom shots of naked breasts, but carefully regulated the visibility of the bodies of the male actors, which persisted in remaining covered. Compared to these films, the films of the *Trilogy* depicted sex and nudity with an explicitness and a provocative style that were new to Italy. As well as numerous scenes of unabashed male and female nudity, for the first time these films offered mainstream audiences close-ups of genitals and open references to both homosexual and heterosexual sex.[45] Following the release of the films of the *Trilogy*, Pasolini was repeatedly criticised, however, for having moved away from the politically committed spirit of his earlier works and for indulging in what appeared to many to be a kind of exploitative cinema of erotic escapism. As Naomi Greene notes, a number of critics from the Left attacked these films for their lack of ideology.[46] During a lecture at the University of Bologna, Pasolini replied to them that 'the ideology was there, rather, it was really there in that huge cock that appeared on the screen, above their heads which they did not want to understand.'[47]

Such a contemptuous answer seems to be consistent with Pasolini's provocative attitude at this stage of his career and with his repeated polemical attacks against the hypocritical moralism of Italy's intellectual elites. But this answer also points to the actual presence in these films of repeated frontal shots of male genitals – often in close-up – and the significance that this presence has assumed in critical responses exploring the implications and meanings of Pasolini's erotic imagery. For James Roy MacBeane, the almost obsessive close-ups on the crotch in these films is indicative of the director's phallocentric vision of sex, a vision that re-asserts the hegemony of men at the expense of women's bodies and desires.[48] On a similar note, Joseph Boone has argued that the privileged role of the male crotch in Pasolini's films attests 'to the misogyny that frequently accompanies Pasolini's homoeroticizing aesthetic'.[49]

MacBeane and Boone read Pasolini's display of male genitals as an over-literal indication of phallocentricism. Phallocentricism may be understood here either as an imagery centred on the figure of the phallus or as a male-dominated and male-engendered system of signification. In MacBeane's and Boone's readings, these two meanings are somehow conflated. The penis seems to equate essentially with the phallus, which, in turn, equates with the privileging of a strictly male vision of desire. Through another questionable conceptual slip, this vision is, according to Boone, therefore inevitably misogynistic.

The claim that I make in this final part of the chapter is that these readings overlook a crucial aspect of Pasolini's cinematic and conceptual praxis: namely, the articulation of an oppositional practice that, in embracing and inevitably exhibiting that thing that it contests, also tarnishes it, distorts it, makes it ineffective. As Thomas Yingling has argued, a sign originating in a repressive practice may nevertheless be dislocated from its initial site and installed in one subversive to the system in which it took its original meaning.[50] The meaning of a sign, Yingling seems to suggest, cannot be reduced to a single valence. This point may be productively used to reflect on the significance of the display of the male crotch in the work of a number of queer directors, including Rainer Werner Fassbinder, Derek Jarman and Pedro Almodóvar in the 1970s and the 1980s. Far from simply reproducing literally a phallocentric logic of male authority, these directors use such a display in their films to provoke the audience by directly alluding to the taboos that have traditionally imposed invisibility on the male genitals in mainstream cinematic imagery. Inevitably, the display also opens up a voyeuristic space incorporating a range of pleasures normally denied in cinema. Pedro Almodóvar's *Labyrinth of Passion* (*Laberinto de pasiones*: 1982), for example, begins by cross-cutting between the looks of a man, the female protagonist Sexi and their incessant gazing at the various crotches of the men they meet on the streets. As Paul Julian Smith has argued, here 'the editing suggests that there is no distinction between the two, that the crotches are offered indifferently to heterosexual and homosexual voyeurs, in the market of cinema.'[51] Having been turned into a site of shame and embarrassment – in the same way that the male body often has, the male genitals in the work of queer directors such as Almodóvar constitute a particular site of resistance and defiance for the representation of pleasures traditionally absent in cinema.[52] Further, they provide an opportunity to look and reflect on what it means to represent a male body. Pasolini's depiction of the penis should be both located within this particular queer tradition and examined through the distinctive aesthetic and political challenges that it poses.

In *The Trilogy of Life*, a number of on-screen markers direct the attention of the spectators to the male crotch. Most of the young male actors, for example, wear trousers that are very tight around this area. In *The Decameron*, a number of these men wear a second layer of over-trousers. This has the effect of creating a triangular focal point in the area around the crotch. Clothing often goes hand in hand with a particular way of framing the male body that exacerbates the centrality of the crotch within the shot. In the tale of the young man who pretends to be a deaf-mute to enter a convent of nuns in *The Decameron*, two nuns catch sight of the young man whilst he is working on a ladder. The nuns walk on a lower terrace. As a result, the reverse shot, after they spot him, reveals the young man from a very low-angle point of view. Both his head and his legs are out of the frame and the lower buttons of his shirt are open. The two bottom sides of the shirt create a triangular focal point on his naked lower belly (Fig. 5.7). The triangular focal point is reproduced, but upside down, around the crotch area. The crotch ends up dominating the shot and forcing the viewer to confront its irrefutable presence. In other instances, the male genitals appear focalised through the occlusion of other parts of the body (for example, by foliage or a beam), with the effect of producing a kind of internal refocalisation on the crotch. It is in these instances that the films of *The Trilogy of Life* playfully highlight a crucial aspect of the act of screening sex and nudity: namely, that sexual explicitness in film is always about revealing as much as it is about concealing. As Linda Williams has argued, the history of screening sex and nudity is 'never a matter of a teleological progression toward a final, clear view of "it", as if it pre-existed and only needed to be laid bare'.[53] The dialectic between revelation and concealment that is behind Pasolini's

Figure 5.7   *The Decameron*, the two nuns' view of the gardener, who pretends to be a deaf-mute.

playful foregrounding of the male crotch inevitably points to the exclusions, mediations and kinds of manipulations that are always intrinsic to the act of revealing the naked body in films. The dialectic points to the invisibility of the male genitals in a mainstream erotic imagery that has had far fewer inhibitions in handling female nudity, and to the gendered power asymmetry that is implicit in this invisibility.[54] What we are facing, then, in looking at these crotches is the playful exposure of a sign that carries the symbolic scars of its own cultural invisibility, a way of revealing that evokes a set of historical strategies of concealment.

Another strategy used by these films to direct our gaze towards the male crotch is the abundance of prodigious bulges, especially in *The Canterbury Tales* and *The Decameron*. The narrative function of these bulges is to signal a kind of desire that is antagonistic to the marital union and to structures of male authority over women; significantly, the bulges appear in situations of adultery in which women are betraying their old husbands for young men whom they desire. In the tale of 'Maggio e Gennaio' from *The Canterbury Tales*, a young man secretly yearns for Maggio. Maggio is a woman who has been forced to marry sleazy old Gennaio. The boy's desire is made explicit as he rubs his bulge under Maggio's window (Fig. 5.8). The camera provides a close-up of his erection, which is barely concealed by his tight medieval costume. The shot occurs again later to mark the force of his frustrated erotic longings. A similar situation takes place in the same film in the episode with Nicola and Allison, where Nicola painfully tries to contain his hard-on whilst devising a plan to fool Allison's old husband and make love to her. The bulge stands in

Figure 5.8 *The Canterbury Tales*, the frustrated desire of Maggio's lover.

these scenarios for desire seeking fulfilment. Such a desire, however, is, strictly speaking, only male in its articulation.

Frequently, the bulges really do look like erect penises but, given their size and tumescence, they may well have been created by artificial devices; they occupy much of the men's upper thighs and the actors often hold them with two hands. The kind of veiling that the costumes produce in the crotch area establishes, then, a particular relation between the sign (the outline of an erect penis/the bulge) and the referent (the erect penis). The bulges function here as both iconic and indexical signs. As iconic signs, they represent, by very close resemblance, the erect penises that are supposed to be under the tights. Indexically, they stand for male arousal and for the *possible* presence of erect penises underneath. Modelled on the penis but not quite penises themselves, the bulges bring into productive tension the relation between phallus and penis as defined within Lacanian psychoanalysis. The relation between phallus and penis discussed by Jacques Lacan is one of symbolisation: the phallus is not the penis, but it symbolises it.[55] In *Bodies that Matter*, Judith Butler queries Lacan's desire to separate the phallus from the penis conceptually. Butler's objective is not to prove that they are the same thing but to explore what the minimisation of their relation operated by Lacan actually implies. Butler notes that whilst 'symbolization depletes that which it symbolizes [(the penis)] of its ontological connection with the symbol itself' (the phallus), it also retains a particular relation of dependency between the two.[56] Butler makes use of the Hegelian principle of determinate negation: 'If the phallus only signifies to the extent that it is not the penis, and the penis is qualified as that body part that it must not be, then the phallus is fundamentally dependent upon the penis in order to symbolize at all.'[57] In other words, despite the denial of any relation between the two, the phallus requires the penis for its own constitution. Despite Lacan's 'forced' separation, for Butler the relation between the two is synecdochal; the phallus stands for the penis as an imaginary transfiguration of that body part. But, in order to do so, it has to operate through the negation of its constitutive relation to the anatomical part. The negation, as I understand it, is a kind of veiling mechanism through which the physical partiality and contingency of the organ that provides the material basis for the imaginary elaboration are masked.

In *The Trilogy of Life*, the relation between the phallic sign (the bulge) and the anatomical part (the erect penis) is not imaginary, but one that is based on a degree of morphological resemblance between the two. The veiling (the garment covering the hypothetical hard-on) produces a kind of *unveiling* of the constitutive relation between phallus and penis, as discussed by Butler. Because of their consistently exaggerated size, the bulges appear in terms of an embodied idealisation; the idealisation through which phallic symbolism operates is embodied, conferred with a kind of materiality that undoes the synecdochal relation between symbol and anatomical part, and turns it into a relation of paradoxical morphological synonymy. In the process, the phallic symbolism that the bulges evoke is resignified and eventually re-appropriated within a dissident representational realm. In rendering explicit the terms of a relation that is meant to remain implicit, the bulges paradoxically 'materialise' the process of idealisation of the male body through which the phallus as a symbol works.

The films of *The Trilogy of Life* take this symbolic re-appropriation one step further with the actual exposure of male genitals. In *Arabian Nights*, this exposure further materialises and, implicitly, undoes the phallic imagery of the film. This is particularly evident in the gap between the often-hyperbolic size of the bulges and the unveiling of small, inconspicuous penises in a state of flaccidity, once the garments are removed. In *Arabian Nights*, the female slave Zumurrud undresses her lover Nur al-Din on their first night of love-making. The boy wears a loincloth, which is arranged in such a way as to create a horizontal band around the waist and a looser, vertical one that coincides with the crotch, which magnifies the size of his bulge. The following unveiling of the penis comes across as somehow anti-climactic, as Nur al-Din's small genitals, now revealed to the camera, do not live up to the expectations raised by the loincloth. The inherently dissatisfying nature of phallic imagery seems to be the central point here.[58] The preposterous grandeur of this imagery appears to have been, then, initially embraced, teased and subsequently unmasked for what it is: an inherently disappointing game of masking and repudiation aimed at disavowing the contingent materiality of the male anatomy. Something similar takes place in *The Decameron* in the episode of the deaf-mute and the nuns. Here, we have one very rare instance of an erect penis in close-up (in *The*

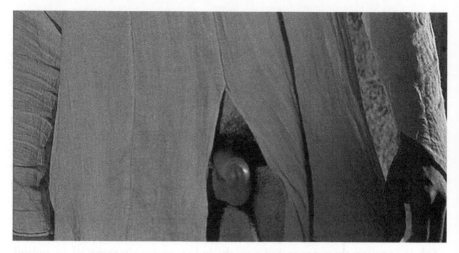

Figure 5.9 *The Decameron*, close-up of the gardener's erect penis.

Trilogy of Life, the penis is normally shown in a condition of flaccidity). The two nuns hastily lure the boy into a hut in order to have sex with him. Inside the hut, a close-up reveals the boy's penis for a second, as the boy is about to lie on top of one of the nuns. The camera is set straight on the head of the penis in a way that foreshortens the depth of the shot, thus diminishing its apparent turgidity (Fig. 5.9). As a result, rather than being stylised in order to emphasise its turgidity, the erection becomes functional to the sexual act the gardener is about to perform. Far from being in itself a celebration of phallic turgidity, this erectness ends up being, then, simply the condition of sexual enjoyment for the nuns. Modest-sized genitals metonymically reflect an overarching aspect of these films, especially in *Arabian Nights*: the greater cunningness and skilfulness of the female characters and the inadequacy of the male characters. This asymmetry becomes particularly clear as Nur al-Din reveals his incompetence, whilst searching for his lost lover after her abduction. In the process, a number of women, who prove to be much more intelligent and resourceful than him, try to help him, only to demand the enjoyment of his body as a reward.

The stylised depiction of the crotch is contiguous with a set of broader strategies used to represent the male body in *The Trilogy of Life*. One of these strategies may remind us of the contemplative frontality of the visitor's body in *Teorema* and the way in which it was offered to the camera's gaze in a condition of immobility and availability. In *The Decameron*, two young lovers, Caterina and Riccardo, are sleeping naked. The shouts of the girl's father wake them and they immediately get up, holding a blanket to cover their nudity. In an attempt to restore his family's honour, the father threatens to kill Riccardo if he does not agree to marry his daughter; the boy excitedly says yes, dropping

Figure 5.10   *The Decameron*, Riccardo's jubilation as he agrees to marry Caterina.

the blanket and remaining naked (Fig. 5.10). From a diegetic point of view, the boy's nudity is justified by the excitement that has made him drop the blanket. Yet, from a formal point of view, the scenario appears self-consciously contrived and unconvincing. The movement of his hands is too mechanical and the stiff frontality of his body foregrounds the artificiality of the scenario, as does his clumsy acting style. As a result, the narrative justification for the boy's nudity – his excitement making him drop the blanket – ends up being simply the pretext for the real objective of the scene: revealing the actor's naked body to the camera in its unmediated visual availability. What we are faced with is a particular strategy of derationalisation, a particular way of confronting the viewer with the spectacle of the male body that challenges conventional cinematic paradigms for eroticising it. As scholars such as Kenneth MacKinnon and Richard Dyer have shown in their analyses of mainstream media representations, erotic depictions of the male body tend to resist passive objectification; even though the spectator may enjoy the erotic spectacle of the male body, such a pleasure is constantly rationalised through situations that generally justify its exposure within the logic of the story.[59] 'One obvious means of disavowal is [. . .] to suggest that there are cogent narrative reasons for a hero to take off his shirt'[60] (for example, to check on a bullet wound). The result of this mechanism is a disjunction between visual structures for sexualising the male body and the narrative logic that denies the male body the simple position of erotic object. Rationalising the erotic availability of the male body to the camera is not just a way of disavowing the possibility for this body to be an object of erotic looking: it also contributes to guaranteeing a set of clear-cut functions and alleged predispositions associated with the male body (for example, agency, aggressiveness and the potential for action). In Pasolini's films, cogent narrative reasons that may allow the disavowal of the male body as an object of desire are at times absent and at times playfully reworked in such a self-conscious way that undermines their plausibility. Pasolini was famous for hating 'naturalness' and his films persistently disrupt cinematic naturalism.[61] The films of *The Trilogy of Life* frequently offer a view of the actors laughing in front of the camera with minimal narrative justification. In casting the actors for his films, Pasolini often asked them to introduce themselves by laughing. Pasolini's films seem to harness this often-unmotivated laughter as a marker of the superfluous, inappropriate materiality of the body against the highly regulated and rationalised performance of the professional actor. Pasolini would often instruct his actors about what to do while shooting was in progress, 'producing an unnatural spontaneity out of tune with situational realism'.[62]

The derationalisation of the visual and narrative strategies for representing the male body in *The Trilogy of Life* is also the result of a particular aesthetic of fragmentation and irregular framing. In the episode of the three brothers and the poet in *Arabian Nights*, for example, the boys are shown kneeling next to each other as the poet recites a poem celebrating their beauty. A middle shot reveals their bodies in line but a horizontal wooden beam 'cuts out' the upper parts of their bodies with the result that our gaze is playfully directed towards their flaccid genitals. In light of the static camera, the abrupt cuts, the absence of continuity editing and the lack of point-of-view shots, the gaze directed at the male bodies cannot be considered fetishistic in conventional cinematic terms; the fragment is cut off from the whole and an intra-diegetic gaze is denied. In the tale of Riccardo and Caterina from *The Decameron*, the naked bodies of the two adolescents lie next to each other. A sequence of extreme close-ups and medium shots on Riccardo's sleeping body is alternated with shots of Caterina moving to touch him. Once again, the focus is on the male body. The framing is, however, irregular. Riccardo's face appears partly covered, either by his elbow or by Caterina's body. At other times, the close-up is so extreme that part of his face is left out of the frame. The panning shot, revealing his upper body from Caterina's point of view, ends at the same height as his pubic area, but his genitals partly remain out of the frame (Fig. 5.11). The camera movement teasingly leads the spectators towards the boy's genitals, but their being partially cut out of the frame ends up both highlighting and dedramatising their presence.

In partly resisting the disciplinary procedures of mainstream narrative cinema, these strategies of derationalisation inevitably force the male body into an ambivalent realm of signification. These strategies partly reflect Pasolini's own theoretical writings on film, and particularly his understanding of film language as essentially based on a system of pre-grammatical and irrational signs (im-signs). Pasolini's argument was that the codification of cinematic

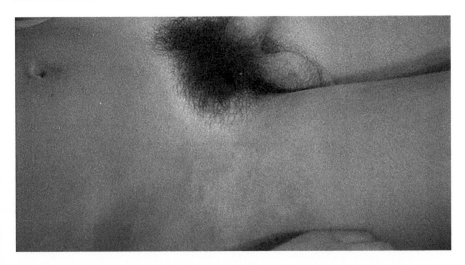

Figure 5.11 *The Decameron*, the partial screening out of Riccardo's genitals.

language produced by mainstream narrative cinema (the cinema of prose) had robbed cinema of its essentially oneiric, irrational elements. Against this codification and rationalisation of cinematic language, Pasolini's aim was to turn to a cinematic style that would be considered inappropriate in mainstream cinema – irrational, so to speak (for example, the sequential juxtaposition of shots logically unrelated to each other or the alternation of different lenses on the same face), but which, in his opinion, was the basis for retrieving the pre-grammatical and authentic aspect of the cinematic image as an unmediated reflection of reality.[63] In Lacanian terms, Pasolini's irregular framing and fragmentation of the male body bring it back to its condition as 'corps morcelé', a pre-symbolic body that is plunged into a state of disunity and incoherence.[64] In resisting codes of cinematic verisimilitude and naturalism, this is a body that confronts the gazes of the camera and spectator with the image of its finitude, incompleteness and contingent physical presence. It is a body that hardly satisfies the primordial cinematic wish for pleasurable looking; this pleasure appears instead to be constantly disturbed so that the act of looking functions primarily at the level of anxiety. Not only are the spectators constantly reminded of the subject position from which the act of looking is produced, but the cinematic image foregrounds the impossibility of serving the purposes of recognition and identification.

6. MALE SUBJECTIVITY AND THE LEGACY OF 1968: NANNI MORETTI'S *ECCE BOMBO*

In *Forms of Being*, Leo Bersani and Ulysse Dutoit argue that, more than any other art form, cinema encourages us to think about the importance of individuality. The film star, they argue, is nearly always presented as a sharply individualised presence; furthermore, 'it remains commonplace of film criticism to praise works that give us unforgettable individual characters, and to condemn those that fail to do so.'[1] One could also add that cinema satisfies a particular wish for recognition and identification that relies on the visible presence of an individual person on the screen. The cinematic experience uncannily reflects that crucial moment in the process of subject formation in which the child recognises its own image in the mirror, an image that constitutes the matrix of the first articulation of the 'I' of subjectivity. The question of subjectivity has also been crucial to the consolidation of cinema as an art form. In his 1948 essay, 'The Birth of a New Avant-Garde: la *caméra-stylo*', Alexandre Astruc famously salutes the emergence of a new cinema exemplified by the films of Orson Welles, Jean Renoir's *The Rules of the Game* (*La Règle du jeu*: 1939) and Robert Bresson's *Les Dames du Bois de Boulogne* (1945). Astruc sees in the work of these directors the potential for cinema to become 'an expressive form'. By this, Astruc means the possibility for cinema to function like a distinct language articulating an internal vision, that of its central creative force. For Astruc and the critics of *Les Cahiers du cinéma*, who were inspired by his essay to promote *la politique des auteurs*, this central creative force was the director. In establishing the conditions for the emergence of the auteur film canon, the essay embraces the image of the '*caméra-stylo*' (the camera-pen) as its guiding metaphor. Like the pen in the hands of the writer, Astruc sees the camera as the means by which a director could 'write' her/his thoughts on the screen.[2] Astruc's ambition was to raise the cultural status of cinema. Taking the novel and painting as models, Astruc saw the possibility for cinema to become a self-reflective medium through which true artists could articulate their personal vision. This view did not exactly ignore the collaborative nature of cinema and its status as an industrial practice based on investment, rationalised labour and profit-making. Rather, it recognised the ability of certain talented directors to overcome such restrictions and articulate, nevertheless, an original individual vision.

What is most interesting about Astruc's essay, however, is its development of a theory of subjectivity in film. Astruc describes films 'as a series of images, which from one end to the other, have an inexorable logic (or better even, a dialectic) of their own'.[3] In the essay, Astruc focuses in particular on the ability of the camera to relate objects to objects, and character to objects. In film, 'all thought', Astruc points out, 'like all feeling, is a relationship, between one human being and another human being or certain objects which form part of his or her universe.'[4] In giving an account of how film may express thought, Astruc seems to suggest that the articulation of cinematic subjectivity always relies on a set of connections with other objects. The subject appears here to be always linked to something outside itself, as it were, essentially placed in relation to others.

Building on Astruc's essay, one could suggest that the experience of being a subject is always a social experience, one that is repeatedly exhibited and reinforced as such by cinema itself. Being inseparable from the forces of socialisation, the experience of being a subject is inevitably also a gendered experience. In *The Second Sex*, Simone De Beauvoir famously asserts that 'a man would never set out to write a book on the peculiar situation of the human male.'[5] This pronouncement may exemplify the widely held feminist belief, according to which, in culture, men have often spoken in the first person but have largely done so from a position that has tended to universalise the gendered specificity of their perspective. De Beauvoir does not question the lack of a degree of self-consciousness in the way men have produced culture. Rather, she refers to men's historical inability to relativise the peculiarity of the subject position from which they have often spoken.

An inward-looking male perspective constitutes one of the most remarkable features of the Italian cinema of the 1970s. With the endorsement of a subject-centred point of view, open to explore issues concerning the realm of the personal and sexuality, this historically specific mode establishes the conditions for looking at masculinity as an object of epistemological investigation and as a political problematic. Such a mode could be criticised for being self-absorbed, ego-driven and myopic. But the Italian cinema of the 1970s often acknowledges the partiality of this subject position and marks the gendered specificity of its point of enunciation as its central site of self-conscious inter-rogation. This shift captures the new spirit of change brought by 1968, whilst simultaneously enacting a commentary on some of its shortcomings. Initiated by student revolts and disputes in the factories, 1968 destabilised the founda-tions of Italian society, leading to a decade of conflict and protest. Struggles to change universities and teaching practices were followed by mass mobilisation among workers, and on-going challenges to the organisation of labour and to the system of authority within the factories. By attacking various forms of authoritarianism, the student and worker movements also changed interper-sonal relations between bosses and workers, students and teachers, children and parents, and women and men.[6] Interpersonal relations started reflecting the increasing democratisation of Italian society and the spreading of a new egalitarian spirit.[7] Luisa Passerini has argued that 1968 offered many women the possibility of both collective and individual empowerment. In her account of this experience of social and political mobilisation, she refers to the atmos-phere of sexual experimentation and self-discovery that deeply transformed the lives of many young people.[8]

These important achievements were, however, marked by contradictions. As Paul Ginsborg has pointed out, the values of the post-1968 social movements remained predominantly masculine, and the male militants were generally rather ambivalent about the specific feminist demands brought up by their female counterparts.[9] The leaders of the extra-parliamentary group, *Lotta Continua*, for example, argued that women's oppression lacked any specificity of purpose and was simply a consequence of the class inequality that char-acterised the social order.[10] The position of *Lotta Continua* with regard to questions of female emancipation and sexual freedom was far from isolated. In belittling feminist claims, the student and worker movements generally re-asserted old patriarchal gender hierarchies by confining women to subordi-nate roles. In recognising this unfortunate inability to accommodate feminist claims, Guido Viale argues that 'the partial failure of 1968 was that of ending after having turned men and women into actors within a play whose script was already written: that in which everything was class struggle.'[11]

The difficulty for the worker and student movements in incorporating specific feminist concerns and in questioning their own masculinistic values, as noted by Viale, stemmed from a tendency to conceive their revolutionary political project around a totalising synthesis between 'private' and 'public'. Such a project was based on the assumption that a change in the structure of class relations would inevitably involve a change at the level of personal rela-tions. Writing in the midst of the social and political agitations following 1968, feminist theorist Carla Lonzi polemically questions the idea that the cause of women should be subordinated to the class problem. Lonzi argues that the central question to tackle was the male-centred perspective that dominated the Marxist project of the social movements, one that was accustomed to find causes and solutions only in the outside world in the form of hostile social structures against which people must struggle.[12] In the aftermath of 1968, Lonzi's essay represented an important contribution to a broader questioning of the claim of objectivity in the social analysis of power relations advanced by orthodox Marxists.

IRONY, THE MALE 'I' AND AUTOBIOGRAPHY

By addressing the crisis of the worker and student movements and the loss of faith in the possibility of creating a more egalitarian and democratic social system, Nanni Moretti's films of the 1970s are ideally suited to considering the sense of disillusion of the post-1968 generation. This sense of disillusion was partly fuelled by the militarisation of the social and political conflict following the advancement of terrorism and the end of the hopes for a communist government after the historical compromise (1973) between the Left and the Christian Democrats. Moretti's first short film, *La sconfitta* (1973), revolves around the sense of political frustration of a young leftist militant, Luciano. This debut anticipates a similar preoccupation with the predicament of the post-1968 generation and the dissolution of their revolutionary hopes in Moretti's first two long feature films, *I Am Self Sufficient* (*Io sono un autarchico*: 1976) and *Ecce Bombo* (1977). This chapter focuses in particular on *Ecce Bombo* and its portrayal of a generation that was willing to question their recent past and come to terms with its contradictions.

William Hope has argued that, in the context of the 1970s, *Ecce Bombo* contributed towards setting up a pattern whereby Italian cinema turned its gaze inwards, dissecting individual trajectories and personal points of view on social reality.[13] In *Ecce Bombo*, this subjective perspective is first of all established upon the central role in the story of the protagonist Michele, played by Moretti himself. Appearing in almost all of the scenes of the film, Michele is the main focaliser of the story and the catalyst of the political and existential problems explored by the film.[14] *Ecce Bombo* revolves around three major narrative threads: Michele's difficult relationship with his family; his problems with women; and the generational anxieties experienced by Michele and his friends. Michele appears in the film as the standard-bearer of the post-1968 generation.[15]

In speaking in the first person, *Ecce Bombo* is a film that oscillates between the singular and the plural, between an 'I' and a 'we'. The subjective perspective articulated by the film is, of course, distinctly male. Significantly, part of the exploration of the anxieties experienced by Michele and his friends is staged within the context of men-only consciousness-raising meetings (Fig. 6.1). In

Figure 6.1 *Ecce Bombo,* one of the men-only consciousness-raising meetings.

this context, the problems that these young men have to tackle do not simply revolve around their disillusionment with the revolutionary aspirations of 1968 but also have much to do with the shifting nature of their relationship to women. Notably, when Michele and his friend Mirko first consider the opportunity to undergo consciousness-raising, the problems that they seem to experience with women are central to their discussion. In an interview, Moretti pointed out that the depiction of these meetings was inspired by his personal experience of consciousness-raising with a group of men in the mid-1970s.[16] In providing a bridge between unarticulated personal experiences and collective male solidarity, consciousness-raising functions in the film as an occasion for the male protagonists to come to terms with their anxieties and become aware of their limits. The influence of a distinctive feminist rhetoric in the film becomes evident, for instance, through one of Michele's friends, Goffredo, the character who most openly invites the other men of the group to interrogate their masculinity and examine the power asymmetries involved in their relations with women. During one of the consciousness-raising meetings, Goffredo admits his difficulties in thinking of women as anything other than sexual objects. His confession is quickly followed by that of Michele and his friends, who talk about their similar difficulties in relating to women on equal terms.

Ecce Bombo directly alludes to one of the central questions tackled by the Italian feminist movement in the 1970s. The discovery that the political oppression of women had direct ramifications in their private lives – as the campaigns in support of the legalisation of abortion and divorce, and against domestic violence demonstrated – led Italian feminists to consider that women's emancipation could not be achieved simply through legal battles and conventional politics.[17] Their struggle had also to deal with an understanding of the way female oppression was perpetuated in the realm of the erotic. In an essay entitled 'La donna clitoridea e la donna vaginale' (1971), Carla Lonzi argued that women's oppression stemmed partly from the culturally hegemonic imposition of men's pleasure on women's bodies. Lonzi emphasized women's need to rediscover their sexuality through a more intimate knowledge of their own bodies. In this sense, she argued for a re-appropriation of women's physiological centre of pleasure, the clitoris, as a fundamental step towards their liberation.[18] Lonzi's radical position is not representative of all the Italian feminist movement but undoubtedly exemplifies an increasing awareness amongst Italian women that their liberation could not take place in the public arena without a shift in their private relations with men.

In its engagement with the sexual politics of the 1970s, *Ecce Bombo* poses the problematic question of a male subject that attempts to endorse the lessons of feminism. Precisely because one of the objectives of feminism has been the possibility for women to speak from the position of subjects of language, Stephen Heath has argued that men's relation to feminism is an impossible one:

> [T]his is a matter for women, [. . .] it is their voices and actions that must determine the change and redefinition. Their voices and actions, not ours: no matter how 'sincere', 'sympathetic' or whatever, we are always also in a male position which brings with it all the implications of domination and appropriation.[19]

Men's position as subjects in relation to feminism, Heath seems to suggest, inevitably resonates with the suspect exclusion of women speaking with their own voices. As Rosi Braidotti, has argued, '[i]t is on the woman's body – on her absence, her disqualification – that phallocentric discourse rests.'[20] *Ecce Bombo* takes on this problematic question by revealing an awareness of the risks for men of speaking as subjects of feminism. At one point, Goffredo makes a call to a radio phone-in show to talk about his bad conscience as a man and about his sexual attitudes to women. With an overly solicitous voice, one of the two female radio presenters tells Goffredo how interesting they are finding his story. The other presenter looks bored and unexcited. As Goffredo carries on with his confession, the radio presenter interrupts him to say that there is a more urgent call on the other line and hangs up. It is only an excuse to cut short Goffredo's call. The other 'urgent' call is that of an unemployed actor reciting some badly written poems. In another instance, Michele comes back to find his mother drunk, crying about her misfortunes as a frustrated housewife who has sacrificed her career to bring up her children. The scene takes place without any melodramatic overtones, with the actress playing the mother speaking in a Brechtian quotational mode. After her drunken outburst, the camera cuts to Michele. As he enters the room, he makes no reference to his mother's monologue and reproaches her for being drunk. Michele tells her that he has attended one of the consciousness-raising meetings. Challenged to explain more clearly what these meetings are about, Michele fails to give a coherent answer. The irony is that, in unsuccessfully sharing with his mother the meanings of a practice that should establish his affiliations with feminism, Michele is actually revealing his distance from his mother's predicament and hence from the pro-feminist sensibility that he so unconvincingly flaunts. In another scene, Michele and his girlfriend Silvia are fighting on the shore of a lake. Having learnt that Silvia has had a one-night stand with a married man, Michele becomes furious. Taking a putative feminist standpoint, he accuses her of failing to see her own sexual objectification by a chauvinist man, who will probably boast about this affair to his friends. Silvia's response is unconcerned. She asserts that she has had the affair because she wanted it. Whilst establishing an affirmative relation to the concerns of feminism, these three scenes dismiss presumptuous proclamations made by men who believe they speak the language of feminism. Here, the implied male subject mocks himself and the position of authority from which he is relating to the object of his concerns, feminism. The object remains external, slippery, non-cooptable.

Yet, it is also the central subject position within the film, Michele, that appears slippery. Michele's statements are often incoherent. Talking on the phone to a friend, he initially says that he will go to a party, only to contradict himself immediately and say that he will not. In another scene, sitting in a café with Silvia, he asks her to leave because he does not want her to meet his friends, who are about to arrive. A second later, Michele asks her to stay, only to change his mind again eventually. Throughout the film, it is often very difficult to tell when Michele is being serious and when he is joking. His statements are at times incoherent, and at others totally out of context. Sentences are left incomplete, their meaning hidden behind the ambiguity of his silences or behind his unreadable facial expression. In a film in which the protagonist hardly invites the spectators to a 'literal reading' of his statements, the prevailing attitude displayed by *Ecce Bombo* seems to be one of irony.

The ironic subject rarely means exactly what he/she is saying, his/her statements often revealing an internal contradiction between explicit and implicit meanings. Irony is a rhetorical mode based on the disjunction between surface and content. It normally allows a person to say one thing and imply something else. In articulating a dynamic relation between different orders of meanings, irony evades dichotomies of sincerity and falsehood. The ironic mode articulated by *Ecce Bombo* seems similar to what Sally L. Kitch describes as 'contrapuntal' irony, a form of irony that 'involves the coexistence of simultaneously contradictory meanings within a given work'.[21] In requiring the reader to consider various meanings at the same time in order to reach a complete understanding of the work, contrapuntal irony works differently from what Wayne Booth calls 'stable irony', where true meaning is the exact contrary to what is explicitly expressed.[22] Whilst the latter form of irony implies a double-edged tension between the literal and the figurative, the former seems to point to a polysemantic mode of articulation.

Pointing out the particularly productive opportunities for self-presentation that irony allows its enunciating subject, David Halperin has suggested that 'being ironic' allows us to complicate and reject the binary trap of 'being for oneself and being for others'.[23] As the implicit subject of irony in *Ecce Bombo*, Nanni Moretti has often expressed his autobiographical connections with the scenarios and preoccupations of his early films. Commenting on his own involvement in the predicament of the post-1968 generation, Moretti has said that 'when one deals with autobiography, a necessary condition to avoid a kind of boring melodrama, is that of being ironic, or rather, given that one is dealing precisely with autobiography, self-ironic.'[24] Moretti's first point is that autobiography is boring. It interests the director because the director is interested in himself, but the spectators are not. The autobiographical material is not intrinsically interesting and becomes interesting only because of the treatment it is given in the film. The second point, the most relevant to this discussion, is that irony functions as a kind of armour that protects the director from too intimate an engagement with the autobiographical material. Saying something ironically implies that the relation between the subject saying something and what is said is not straightforward, the meaning of this 'something' remaining suspended in an undefined area between the 'said' and the 'unsaid'. The polysemantic possibilities implied in the use of irony provide an ideal form to convey the schizophrenic position that Moretti occupies as both the source and the object of the ironic look. As Laura Rascaroli and Ewa Mazierska have argued, 'the filmmaker scrutinizes his own self, which is both the source of the directorial gaze and the object of observation, schizophrenically divided between the observing viewpoint and the observed object.'[25] Moretti's particular use of irony in the film, I would argue, also has the advantage of conveying the kind of twofold relation that the film is trying to establish with the post-1968 legacy, one that is critical of its limits and disappointing outcomes, whilst also maintaining a certain closeness to its wider political project and cultural milieu.

Typical 1968 scenarios, such as communes, experimental theatres and occupied schools, are typical features of Moretti's films at this early stage of his career. Stylistically, *Ecce Bombo* sits in the tradition of 1960s and 1970s leftist counter-cinema.[26] The film avoids a linear narrative progression; scenes are sometimes cut unexpectedly, and intertwined with others whose inclusion in the story is not always logically justified by cause–effect relations. *Ecce Bombo* denies the spectator any easy identification with the story or with the characters. The actors often adopt a quotational style of acting that self-consciously foregrounds the distance between actor and cinematic role. At times, the film exposes the constructedness of the actors' performances through the juxtaposed recital of dialogues apparently unrelated to the main narrative thread. Moretti's cinematic technique at this stage of his career also included extremely long takes without any dialogue. Such breaks in the story inevitably drop the tempo of the film, therefore disrupting the cohesion as well as the coherence of the narrative.[27] These stylistic features highlight Moretti's experimental approach at this point in his career, whilst also suggesting his familiarity with concurrent debates about the political uses of the cinematic medium. In Italy, such debates flourished in the early 1960s but reached their peak in 1968, especially in journals such as *Ombre Rosse* and *Cinemasessanta*. Influenced by the concurrent heated debates in the eminent French journal *Cahiers du cinéma*, a number of Italian film critics started looking at cinema as one of the social technologies serving the interests and demands of the dominant capitalistic order. Their objective quickly became to identify and promote those films that attacked capitalist ideology.[28] In Italy, films such as *Sotto il segno dello scorpione* (1969) and *I dannati della terra* (1967) were praised by the doyen of Italian film criticism of the time, Guido Aristarco. Aristarco argued that these films actively foregrounded the formation of class-consciousness in the masses and, in the light of their formal challenges, constituted quintessential examples of a search for a new revolutionary cinematic language.[29] These debates over the political value of counter-cinema concentrated, in fact, on the idea that a film ought to aspire to be revolutionary not only through content, but also primarily through its form.[30] It was necessary to dismember and reconstitute the coherence of filmic images and implicitly review the meanings attached to those images. The inherent assumption was that a film that aspired to criticise a social and economic system by using the language of that system merely contributed to reproducing, rather than undermining, that system.

The use of irony in *Ecce Bombo* serves two other important purposes, which are, I would argue, interconnected. The first purpose is the attempt to find a point of productive negotiation between the legacy of 1968 (with its distinctive political and cinematic debates) and the lessons of feminism, a point whereby the failure of the leftist revolutionary experience of these young people may be turned into the benchmark for the envisioning of a different future. The second purpose is the attempt to find a viable subjective perspective for the articulation of the political and personal predicament explored by the film.

Whilst being a product of the intellectual, cultural and cinematic climate that accompanied the unrest of 1968, *Ecce Bombo* nevertheless refuses to celebrate 1968. Halfway through the film, the protagonist Michele and his friends go to visit a commune. The commune is presented as a constraining space regulated by a tedious list of duties. Everybody sits still, in silence and in the semi-dark, whilst a light illuminates a table behind which the leader is speaking. The leader monotonously exposes what the major concerns and objectives of their life together should be. At one point, the camera cuts to Michele and his friend Vito. The leader asserts that the main challenge of their experience in the commune will be how to turn their bourgeois crisis into class struggle. It all sounds rather pretentious, a line almost unthinkingly taken straight from the Marxist rhetoric that was so popular within the worker and student movement during the 1970s. Exasperated, Michele and Vito lean their heads back. Their response suggests boredom in relation to a kind of rhetoric that they seem to have heard several times before. The scene epitomises the ironic position from which the film develops its critique of 1968. It is a position that seems to maintain its allegiances with this revolutionary experience of social protest. The critical perspective of the film with regard to 1968 does not coincide here with a denial of the ideals on which the struggle of the worker and student movements was based. The film instead seems to criticise the emptying out of a political rhetoric that appears to be no longer attached to any lived experience of oppression or to any sincere sense of social resistance.

In an essay emblematically entitled *Costruzione della ragione e invito all'ironia* ('Construction of Reason and Invitation to being Ironic') and published in the mid-1960s in the film journal *Cinema Nuovo*, Paolo and Vittorio Taviani explore the function of irony in political filmmaking:

> We must endavour to retrieve irony as a crucial tool that will enable us to stem the tide of all those preoccupations which beset us in our everyday life, so as not to be overwhelmed by this tide but to master it. Only in this way will we be able to turn this tide into productive energy for our objectives. This means to want to be so much inside one thing so that we may be able to get out of it and control it in its totality. [. . .] Irony, as a kind of political passion that frees itself through a form of detachment, through the denial of the fragment. This must be an attitude that distances itself from the fervour of the barricades and from any autobiographical outburst.[31]

In this essay, the Taviani brothers argue that irony should become a primary tool for the politically engaged filmmaker. Their essay constitutes an invitation to return to a new cinema of objectivity. The Tavianis seem to suggest that this objectivity can be acquired only if leftist filmmakers achieve a fine balance between their Marxist revolutionary ideals and their subjective voice. The essay refers to the spheres of autobiography and the subjective in terms of fragmentation, as a 'diversion' from a more objective outlook on politics and on reality. It is a kind of approach to cinematic expression that inevitably qualifies the 'I' in terms of self-centredness and selfish individualism. Significantly, in making *Sotto il segno dello scorpione*, a film that has largely been seen as an allegory for 1968, the Tavianis conceive a story focused on a collective protagonist, the mass. The film is a kind of manifesto of the brothers' disregard at this stage of their career for the autobiographical and for subjectivity. In the same period, another Italian director, Marco Bellocchio, conveys a similar disregard for subjectivity. Talking about his involvement in the worker and student movements, Bellocchio recalls: 'I was on the front line. I decided to make only propaganda cinema, at the service of the people.'[32] Bellocchio is here establishing a hierarchy of priorities for the politically engaged director: the individual artist must work for the people; he/she must put on hold any individualistic quest and instead show total commitment to the struggle of the masses.[33]

In *Ecce Bombo* the use of irony implies a distinctive act of breaking with the militant rhetoric invoked by Bellocchio and the Tavianis, and particularly its collectivist message. In the film, the ironic register is not conducive to the retrieval of a more objective standpoint from which to look at 1968 and its legacy, but is tightly linked to the realm of subjectivity and, particularly, to Moretti's autobiographical world. It is, in fact, co-extensive with a vision of politics that rejects the assimilation of the individual into the concerns of the collectivity and its larger interests. In persistently satirising the superficial modalities of socialisation that the post-1968 generation seems to have inherited, *Ecce Bombo* targets the denial of individual specificity and personal desires of this collectivist legacy as implicitly castrating and self-defeatist. To qualify this point, it is worth pausing to consider further the social and political context in which the film was made.

THE LACK OF A SCRIPT

Made almost ten years after 1968, *Ecce Bombo* is profoundly informed by the cultural and political transformations leading to the rise of what historians call 'the 1977 movement'. Often referred to as 'the generation of the year 9' (a mock version of the Jacobin calendar with reference to 1968), this movement emerged in reaction to what was felt to be the sclerotic radicalism and orthodoxy of 1968. The counter-culture of 1977 celebrated the emergence of a new urban youth culture and adopted more creative forms of protest and socialisation. According to Robert Lumley, the 1977 movement had a significant impact specifically on men, partly as a result of the parallel rise of the sexual liberation movements.[34] It was strongly influenced by two magazines, *Erba Voglio* and *Re Nudo*, which were extremely open to the debates within feminism and the gay liberation movement. *Re Nudo*, in particular, addressed readerships including young men living in the big cities and often discussed issues around sexual morality and attitudes toward nudity. It was in this milieu that a new generation of young men began to think more critically about the contradictions that underpinned their involvement in the social protests of these years. The major challenge for these men was to come to terms with the distance that separated their egalitarian slogans from their actual lived experience as men in a male-dominated society.[35] Through consciousness-raising and frequent contacts with the feminist and gay movements, men were challenged to confront the limits and contradictions of their leftist ideals in the sphere of gender relations.

Undeniably influenced by the 1977 movement, *Ecce Bombo* deals with the problem of envisaging personal and social change from a perspective that is both gendered (male) and historically specific. Michele is repeatedly shown challenging his father and seeking any opportunity to quarrel with him. A significant example is the scene in which Michele enters his father's study room. The scene is shot with the camera at an oblique angle behind the father sitting at his desk. Michele enters the shot from the left, facing his father. Like many scenes in the film, it consists of only one shot, with the frame being still throughout. The camera registers the immobility of Michele's father on his chair in stark contrast with Michele's increasingly erratic movements around the room. Michele challenges his father's passivity and attempts to provoke him. In response to his father's powerless immobility, Michele's anger escalates. He starts messing up his father's papers and finally empties a bin on his desk. Throughout the film, Michele's father appears confused and helpless in facing Michele's resentment and responds by withdrawing from his family. The father seems to be an emotionally inarticulate man, unprepared to confront his son's resentment. During two arguments at the dinner table, he prefers to run away and sit alone in the living room. On one occasion, he even covers himself with a blanket.

Michele's resentment often seems to be a response to his father's outdated attitudes. In trying to prevent his daughter Valentina from joining a student protest at her school, the father attempts to discourage her by pointing out that this protest would be illegal. Leaning against the wall as he listens to his father's words, Michele drops his head back in frustration. The father, this scene seems to suggest, is clearly out of touch with the confrontational spirit of the student protests. Michele's challenge to paternal authority is also a symptom of a conflict between two masculinities separated by the watershed of feminism. At one point, Michele and his father watch TV together. The latter says that he finds one of the female dancers on TV attractive and invites his son to share his tastes in women with him. They are both sitting facing the camera, the view of the female dancers on TV denied to us. Michele, aghast, ignores him, thus seemingly making explicit his rejection of this kind of old-fashioned male camaraderie and the kind of erotic objectification of women that it implies. This episode echoes the first scene showing the family having lunch together, in which the father voices his amazement at seeing two men kissing outside a school. On that occasion, Michele's reaction had been one of embarrassment and annoyance, immediately followed by the mother's decision to change the topic of conversation. Despite never appearing as a strikingly authoritarian figure, the father seems to be associated with an old-style attitude to the shifting sexual mores of the time.

The film presents Michele's resentment against his father in distinctive ironic terms. Whilst being the main target of Michele's contempt, the father is also a permissive parental figure, hardly imposing any authority on his children. Michele's rage against him may appear at times not only unjustified, but also ludicrous. On closer scrutiny, though, it is clear that the father's flaws reflect some of Michele's own shortcomings. Like his father, Michele reveals a certain emotional inarticulacy. This is clear, for example, when he is invited to voice his personal anxieties in front of the other men in the consciousness-raising group after Mirko's inaugural speech. Michele stubbornly refuses to speak. Silence, however, is not the only way in which Michele avoids confrontation with his insecurities and anxieties. On two other occasions, he is encouraged by Mirko and Goffredo to speak about his affair with a woman called Flaminia during their consciousness-raising meetings. Both times, Michele ignores their requests by diverting the focus of the conversation on to other issues. Michele's unease is not simply a result of his difficulties in talking about his emotions and insecurities. Despite his self-professed liberalism, he appears, like his father, to be rather uncomfortable in embracing the new spirit of sexual freedom of the 1970s. Initially defending his sister from his parents' protective attitude, Michele ends up being rather possessive towards her. He lectures her paternalistically about the importance of moderation in the enjoyment of one's freedoms and screams in horror when Valentina tells him about her sexual experiences.

The film suggests that, after all, Michele may not be that different from the paternal figure that he contests. Whilst the father is the figure in the film that crystallises the image of the old male code that Michele is attempting to supersede, Michele's resentment towards him seems to externalise the frustrating perception that this young man may be inescapably connected with this past, and its old gender codes and norms. One scene that makes this condition explicit shows Valentina's friends at the family flat, discussing a plan for the occupation of their school. The students are divided and fight against each other about how to conduct the protest. As the camera pans right, we see Michele lingering on the threshold and listening to them in silence. The camera tracks backwards along the corridor, moving away from Michele, and then stops to show his father, next to another door, who looks at his son in silence (Fig. 6.2). Father and son are stuck along an imaginary line, their immobility being an expression of their connection and closeness. Michele is looking

Figure 6.2   *Ecce Bombo*, Michele and his father.

ahead, at what this younger generation of secondary-school students may teach him. He is looking for models, but it is a frustrating quest that leads only to a further sense of confusion. The backward movement of the camera seems to articulate precisely the hopelessness of this quest. Michele's subject position is split here. Despite the symbolic gesture of looking ahead – to the future – Michele appears instead to be inevitably attached to his past.

And yet, *Ecce Bombo* seems to do more than simply point to a predicament that cannot possibly be resolved. Much of the irony within the film stems from the fact that each critique articulated by Michele eventually rebounds on him. At one point, we see Michele attacking Silvia for her desire to be always surrounded by other people, except that throughout the film it is precisely Michele who seems unable to be on his own. The same happens when Michele satirises the widespread practice of product placement in the Italian cinema of the 1960s and 1970s. To make his point, he mimics the act of showing a packet of cigarettes to the camera. The effect, of course, is that, by doing so, he is contributing to reinforcing precisely the practice that he contests. The point seems to be that, in addressing an object critically, the subject is always already implicated in the act of critiquing and can hardly claim grounds of moral superiority.

MEN AND CHANGE

Michele's major predicament in the film is how to negotiate a new conduct without a script of ready-made slogans and norms. Throughout the film, Michele shows considerable irritation with clichés and commonplaces. In his contacts with women, he tentatively tries to establish meaningful relations by seeking a new language that may be adequate. With Flaminia, he repeats the same confession about his chronic jealousy that he has made after much resistance to his friends. In all these instances, he has to appreciate the failure of his attempts; his new scripts appear to be inadequate.

It has been argued that one of the central problems for Michele in the film is that of identity.[36] The problem primarily concerns the difficult negotiation between subjectivity and collective belonging. Throughout the film, Michele and his male friends compulsively seek each other's company. Goffredo confesses that he often goes to his university simply to escape his solitude and to have people around him. Similarly, Michele recklessly divides his time between his friends and his quest for lasting relationships with women. When his family leaves for the summer holidays, rather than enjoying his independence, Michele frantically checks his telephone book for people to meet. In the second half of the film, Michele wanders around a park where a youth music festival is being held. A placard reads that this is the festival of happiness, an allusion to the outdoor festivals celebrating youth counter-culture that took place in the late 1970s in the major Italian cities (Fig. 6.3). Robert Lumley has pointed out that, in the context of the 1977 movement, such festivals were meant to celebrate alternative forms of sociability. Slogans such as 'let's take control of our lives' and 'being together' symbolised a collective wish to oppose bourgeois civilisation and its alienating dynamics.[37]

Showing some youths crying and others asleep, *Ecce Bombo* satirises a generation that has partly preferred to hide behind facile slogans and has avoided a truly revolutionary process of change in their interpersonal relations. At one point, Michele and his friends make an anonymous call to a woman that they wish to court. Olga, a young woman who is staying at Mirko's, enters the

Figure 6.3 *Ecce Bombo*, Michele at the music festival.

room halfway through the telephone call and rebukes them for underestimating the distress that their anonymous call may cause the other woman. 'Go and speak to her,' she encourages them.[38] Olga invites Michele and his friends to reject an experience of masculinity that alienates them from their true emotions and their subjectivity. She seems to ask these young men to face, without the armour provided by their camaraderie, a reflection on the true stakes of a human relation based on empathy and mutual respect. In these terms, the film seems to underscore the collective dimension under which the hegemonic model of masculinity is lived by men in contemporary Western societies, as discussed by Australian sociologist R. W. Connell.[39] The group is the bearer of masculinity, and the young male protagonists of the film enjoy the privileges that this collective performance grants them. The sequence that I have just analysed evinces the homosocial complicity that is at the basis of such a performance. Furthermore, it conveys the sense of vulnerability that suddenly confronts the male protagonists as Olga invites them to break the shield that their camaraderie grants them.

In the film, the protagonist identifies with and lives through his group of friends. Michele is stuck between a collective performance of male identity that he finds unsatisfactory and an alternative path that he finds hard even to imagine. It is a self-dislocating neurotic experience that seems to represent the problematic position of the post-1968 male subject in having to reject a masculinity that appears inadequate and self-destructive. The experience concerns the difficulty of recreating a new identity without models and examples from the past to follow. *Ecce Bombo* does not show what this alternative model of masculinity might look like, but surely defines some of the terms under which it could emerge.

The figure of Olga plays a fundamental role in this sense. She first appears in Mirko's flat. We learn that she is a friend of Mirko's from Naples, but we are not quite sure why she is there. Her melancholic expression betrays, from her very first appearance, a sort of malaise. When providing some information about her, Mirko vaguely asserts that she is unwell and that she might be schizophrenic. *Ecce Bombo* positions Olga as the figure who most dramatically reflects the confrontation with the experience of failure and vulnerability from which Michele and his friends relentlessly attempt to escape. Olga seems to live her solitude as an individual act of confrontation with her precariousness as a post-1968 subject. But, instead of indulging in her solitude, she seems to search for viable channels of socialisation. At one point, she telephones a number of friends just to talk with them and open her heart. The response she receives is one of embarrassment and awkwardness. One of her friends, after hanging up, wonders whether she has gone mad. The film shows that her search is radically different from the idea of 'being together' that is satirised by the film, and corresponds to a more truthful quest for human warmth, emotional support and solidarity. During the last consciousness-raising meeting, Cesare suggests to the other men that they visit Olga, after explaining how unwell she has been recently. Following this suggestion, the camera registers the increasing enthusiasm that such an idea ignites among Michele's friends, the members of a commune and a group of young people sitting outside a café. Apparently prompted by their shared wish to support Olga through her hard times, the young characters of the film are seen driving in their cars across Rome to reach her house. To the accompaniment of a light-hearted soundtrack that marks the cheerfulness of this collective enterprise, the film follows the journeys of the different characters and their unexpected stops on the way. Goffredo and Mirko decide to make a stop at an open ballroom, where a number of couples begin to dance to the tunes of a 1960s ballad. In observing the couples dancing in the square, Goffredo remarks to Mirko, 'Very Fellini, isn't it?'[40] Far from simply being one of the many ironic cinematic references Moretti introduces in his early films, this allusion calls into question the implications lying behind the atmosphere of joviality and togetherness that distracts the characters on their journey to visit Olga.

In this final resolution, I would argue, the film implicitly establishes its adversarial relationship to Fellini's social vision and his over-romantic indulgence in scenes of camaraderie amongst the male protagonists of *I vitelloni* (1953), the film that has been most closely compared to *Ecce Bombo*.[41] Like *Ecce Bombo*, *I vitelloni* was a generational film recounting the collective experience of restlessness and discontentment of five male protagonists in their late twenties. The affinities with *I vitelloni* are evident in the very title of Moretti's film – *Ecce Bombo* – inspired by the cry of a madman pushing a handcart along the beach as the protagonists wait for the sunrise. The '*Ecce Bombo* loony' is clearly an allusion to the character of Giudizio in *I vitelloni*, to his mad crying, his handcart and his hut on the beach. The initial sequences showing Michele and his friends sitting outside a café, as the camera records the atmosphere of utter stillness and malaise pervading their lives, appear to be similarly inspired by Fellini's sequence depicting the young protagonists sitting outside the town café, just before Fausto's return from Rome. Most importantly, there is also an Olga in *I vitelloni*: Alberto's sister, whom the young men condemn, but who is the one who has been earning money to pay for her brother's life of leisure.

I vitelloni offered the portrayal of a generation of young men stuck with the frustrations and discontentment of provincial life. Fellini's vision was essentially nostalgic, and underscored, in romantic terms, the camaraderie of the protagonists as they got up to various kinds of mischief on the streets of Rimini. By alluding ironically to this romantic vision in the final 'Fellinian' sequences in which Michele's friends fail to reach Olga's, *Ecce Bombo* implicitly sheds light on the individualistic ethos and the apolitical solipsism lying behind Fellini's vision. One could suggest that Fellini offered no solution to the crisis of his characters other than the possibility of leaving for the big city, as exemplified by Moraldo's final escape.[42] In echoing Fellinian scenes of jovial togetherness, *Ecce Bombo* connects the failure of the young protagonists to keep Olga company with the model of social responsibility that is implicit in such a vision. By contrasting the initial enthusiasm of the young protagonists for providing Olga with some company with their eventual failure to do so, *Ecce Bombo* questions an experience of socialisation based on self-centredness and superficial camaraderie. These shortcomings are exposed and questioned by Michele's re-appearance in the final sequence. Michele had initially declined to visit Olga. 'I'm afraid. I can't be next to those who are suffering,' he had claimed.[43] In the final scene, Michele unexpectedly turns up alone at Olga's. A close-up focuses on her gloomy face. The following shot is another close-up of Michele, who appears confused and upset. Standing in silence in front of Olga, Michele slowly turns his eyes towards her. In this silent confrontation with Olga and her experience of sorrow and isolation, Michele faces the unknow-ingness of what it may mean to be a new man and to establish a new kind of relationship to another human being. By showing how easy is for Michele's friends not to follow through on their initial plan to visit Olga, the film reveals the gap that separates a collective experience of social transformation – with its shouted slogans and ideals – from the real costs that such a quest for change implies at an individual level.

One of the central objectives of feminist criticism and women's counter-cinema has been the disruption of the fabric of man-made cinema through an engagement with the particular discourses and practices that may effect self-empowering representations of women. Teresa De Lauretis argues that such a project must address the question of 'who is speaking in a text'. If we accept that the subject of enunciation in cinema is generally male, De Lauretis suggests, one of the projects of feminism in films ought to be an investigation of what 'speaking as a woman' means. De Lauretis argues that the task of women's cinema may be the 'construction of another frame of reference, one in which the measure of desire is no longer just the male subject'.[44] Seen in these terms, *Ecce Bombo*, despite its complex engagement with feminist sexual politics, shows the clear limits of a perspective that is strictly concerned with a male subject position. The subject that is speaking, as De Lauretis would put it, is unequivocally male here. Yet, *Ecce Bombo* arguably provides a self-conscious reflection on the specificity and limits of its gendered voice. In its critical outlook on the orthodoxies and idiosyncrasies of the post-1968 genera-tion, the film opens up a space for critically confronting the master narrative of political *engagement* in Italian cinema and society, along with its collectivist rhetoric and its partial silences about questions pertaining to sexuality and gender relations.

NOTES

1. INTRODUCTION

1. For an examination of the complexities of change within masculinity, see L. Segal, *Slow Motion* (London: Virago Press, 1990).
2. P. Powrie, A. Davies and B. Babington (eds), *The Trouble with Men* (London: Wallflower Press, 2005), p. 13.
3. The period considered is 1968–80 – otherwise called 'the long 1970s'. For a discussion of the historical continuities of these twelve years, see P. Ginsborg, *A History of Contemporary Italy 1943–1980* (London: Penguin, 1990), pp. 298–405.
4. Quoted in F. Faldini and G. Fofi (eds), *Il cinema italiano d'oggi 1970–1984 raccontato dai suoi protagonisti* (Milan: Mondadori, 1984), p. 260.
5. S. Segre (ed.), *L'antimaschio* (Milan: Gammalibri, 1977), p. 9.
6. P. Facchi, 'Non rassegnarsi', *La via femminile*, 2, 1969, p. 3.
7. I do not contend that masculinity is the exclusive property of men. This book, however, focuses on the relation between men and masculinity. For a discussion of masculinity without men, see J. Halberstam, *Female Masculinity* (Durham, NC: Duke University Press, 1998).
8. L. Mulvey, 'Visual Pleasure and Narrative Cinema', *Screen*, 16:3, 1975, pp. 6–18; S. Neale, 'Masculinity as Spectacle', *Screen*, 25:6, 1983, pp. 2–17.
9. See, for example, S. Cohen and I. Rae Hark (eds), *Screening the Male* (New York: Routledge, 1993); P. Lehman, *Running Scared* (Detroit: Wayne State University Press, 2007); D. Peberdy, *Masculinity and Film Performance: Male Angst in Contemporary American Cinema* (Basingstoke: Palgrave, 2013); R. Morag, *Defeated Masculinity* (Brussels: Peter Lang, 2009).
10. P. Powrie, A. Davies and B. Babington (eds), *The Trouble with Men*; P. Kirkham and J. Thumin (eds), *You Tarzan. Masculinity, Movies and Men* (London: Lawrence & Wishart, 1993); P. Kirkham and J. Thumin (eds), *Me Jane. Masculinity, Movies and Women* (London: Lawrence & Wishart, 1995).

11. P. Cook, 'Masculinity in Crisis', *Screen*, 22:3/4, 1982, pp. 39–46.
12. See, for example, B. Bracco, 'Belli e fragili. Mascolinità e seduzione nel cinema italiano del secondo dopoguerra', in E. Dell'Agnese and E. Ruspini (eds), *Mascolinità all'italiana* (Milan: UTET, 2007), pp. 65–78.
13. R. Ben-Ghiat, 'Unmasking the Fascist Man: Masculinity, Film and the Transition from Dictatorship', *Journal of Modern Italian Studies*, 10:3, 2005, pp. 336–65.
14. J. Fisher, 'On the Ruins of Masculinity: The Figure of the Child in Italian Neorealism and the German Rubble-Film', in L. E. Ruberto and K. M. Wilson (eds), *Italian Neorealism and Global Cinema* (Detroit: Wayne State University Press, 2007), pp. 25–53.
15. J. Reich, *Beyond the Latin Lover* (Bloomington: Indiana University Press, 2004).
16. Ibid., p. 9.
17. Ibid., p. 135.
18. Ibid., pp. 135–6.
19. For a similar approach to Reich, see also B. Bracco, 'Belli e fragili. Mascolinità e seduzione nel cinema italiano del secondo dopoguerra'.
20. '[U]na palude stagnante dove pigri nocchieri seduti su barche ammuffite di muschio palustre attendono, senza neppure troppa convinzione, che irrompa una corrente a smuovere le acque ormai limacciose e mefitiche': L. Micciché, *Cinema italiano degli anni '70* (Venice: Marsilio, 1980), p. 18. For other accounts of the crisis in Italian cinema during the 1970s, see B. Torri, 'I mali di sempre e l'esigenza del nuovo', *Cinemasessanta*, 75/6, 1970, pp. 67–84; F. De Bernardinis, '1970–1976: appunti per una mutazione', in F. De Bernardinis (ed.), *Storia del cinema italiano. Volume XII – 1970/1976* (Venice: Marsilio, 2009), pp. 3–26; V. Zagarrio, 'Dopo la morte dei padri. Dagli anni della crisi agli albori della rinascita', in V. Zagarrio (ed.), *Storia del cinema italiano. Volume XIII – 1977/1985* (Venice: Marsilio, 2005), pp. 3–39; M. Gieri, *Contemporary Italian Filmmaking: Strategies of Subversion, Pirandello, Fellini, Scola and the Directors of the New Generation* (Toronto: University of Toronto Press, 1995), p. 200; M. Liehm, *Passion and Defiance: Film in Italy from 1942 to the Present* (London: University of California Press, 1984), p. 249.
21. '[G]li anni settanta si sviluppano all'insegna della chiusura e della perdita: all'orizzonte si materializza, in maniera sempre più tangibile, la «morte del cinema»': G. P. Brunetta, *Storia del cinema italiano vol. 4* (Rome: Editori Riuniti, 1992), p. 427.
22. The year in which producer Dino De Laurentis moved his business to the United States and Pasolini was murdered, 1975, has been seen as the true turning point for the Italian film industry. After the commercial and artistic achievements of the previous three decades, this is considered the year in which the industry went into free fall. See N. Hasted, 'Maestros and Mobsters', *Sight & Sound*, 20:5, 2010, p. 24.
23. F. Casetti, 'Gli anni settanta e la «crisi» del cinema', in M. Monicelli (ed.), *Cinema italiano, ma cos'è questa crisi?* (Bari: Laterza, 1979), pp. 28–44; B. Torri, 'Industria, mercato, politica', in L. Micciché (ed.), *Il cinema del riflusso* (Venice: Marsilio, 1997), pp. 16–26.
24. B. Corsi, *Con qualche dollaro in più* (Rome: Editori Riuniti, 2001), p. 124.
25. Ibid., p. 125.
26. F. Casetti, 'Gli anni settanta e la «crisi» del cinema italiano', p. 29.
27. B. Corsi, *Con qualche dollaro in più*, pp. 108–9.
28. F. De Bernardinis, '1970–1976: appunti per una mutazione', pp. 15–19.
29. This is an argument that is partly supported by evidence showing a decrease in the production of Spaghetti westerns during the early 1970s – the *filone* that, throughout the 1960s, had contributed most to the financial stability of the industry – and

a simultaneous increase in the production of erotic comedies. These comedies have been seen as the most financially profitable *filone* of the 1970s. Monica Repetto, 'Ciao mamma ovvero porno soffice ed erotismo da ridere', in L. Micciché (ed.), *Il cinema del riflusso*, pp. 318–19.

30. G. Michele, *La commedia erotica all'italiana* (Rome: Gremese Editore, 2000). To my knowledge, the only studies of the genre in English are both by Tamao Nakahara: T. Nakahara, 'Moving Masculinity: Incest Narratives in Italian Sex Comedies', in L. Bayman and S. Rigoletto (eds), *Popular Italian Cinema* (Basingstoke: Palgrave Macmillan, 2013), pp. 98–116; T. Nakahara, *Bawdy Tales and Veils: The Exploitation of Sex in Post-War Italian Cinema (1949–1979)*, PhD dissertation, University of California, Berkeley, 2005.

31. See especially S. Gundle, 'From Neorealism to Luci Rosse: Cinema, Politics, Society, 1945–85', in Z. Baranski and R. Lumley (eds), *Culture and Conflict in Postwar Italy* (Basingstoke: Palgrave Macmillan, 1990), pp. 218–20.

32. S. Gundle, *Bellissima* (London: Yale University Press, 2007), p. 194; G. P. Brunetta, *Storia del cinema italiano vol. 4*, p. 430.

33. F. S. Gerard, T. J. Kline and B. Sklarew (eds), *Bernardo Bertolucci. Interviews* (Jackson: University Press of Mississippi, 2000), p. 67.

34. F. De Bernardinis, '1970–1976: appunti per una mutazione', p. 15. Exactly the same point is made by Attilio Coco: A. Coco, 'Autori senza l'urgenza del presente', in F. De Bernardinis (ed.), *Storia del cinema italiano. Volume XII 1970/1976*, p. 349.

35. M. Marcus, *Italian Film in the Light of Neorealism* (Princeton: Princeton University Press, 1986), p. 23.

36. C. Lonzi, 'Let's spit on Hegel', in P. Bono and S. Kemp (eds), *Italian Feminist Thought* (Cambridge: Basil Blackwell, 1991), p. 41.

37. David Forgacs points out that the models of popular cultural activities promoted by the Italian Communist Party were essentially public, collective and largely male: D. Forgacs, 'The Communist Party and Culture', in Z. Baranski and R. Lumley (eds), *Culture and Conflict in Postwar Italy* (Basingstoke: Macmillan, 1990), p. 104. For an in-depth analysis of the cultural policies of the Italian Communist Party during the post-war period, see also S. Gundle, *Between Hollywood and Moscow: The Italian Communist Party and the Challenge of Mass Culture* (Durham, NC: Duke University Press, 2000).

38. D. Forgacs, 'Fascism and Anti-Fascism Reviewed: Generations, History and Film in Italy', in H. Peitsch, C. Burdett and C. Gorrara (eds), *European Memories of the Second World War* (Oxford: Berghahn, 1999), p. 195.

39. Ibid.

2. MALE CRISIS: BETWEEN APOCALYPSE AND NOSTALGIA

1. Interspersed in this scene are shots of children jumping up and down in the train compartment.

2. The script confirms that the woman occupies the viewing subject position and Snaporaz's role as the object of her look: 'The pretty lady was staring *at him* with a seemingly ironic smile' (La bella signora lo stava fissando con un sorrisetto forse ironico).' In this first scene from the script, no mention is ever made of Snaporaz holding the gaze. *La città delle donne* (Milan: Garzanti, 1980), p. 7.

3. In non-Italian versions of the film, this character is called Gérard.

4. L. Mulvey, 'Visual Pleasure and Narrative Cinema', *Screen*, 16:3, 1975, pp. 6–18; M. A. Doane, 'Film and the Masquerade: Theorising the Female Spectator', *Screen*, 23:3/4, 1982, pp. 74–88.

5. Ibid.
6. P. Middleton, *The Inward Gaze: Masculinity and Subjectivity in Modern Culture* (London: Routledge, 1992), p. 7.
7. See, in particular, L. Mulvey, 'Visual Pleasure and Narrative Cinema'.
8. J. Butler, *Gender Trouble* (London: Routledge, 1990), pp. xxvii–xxviii.
9. 'In fondo, siamo negli anni settanta!'
10. J. Reich, *Beyond the Latin Lover* (Bloomington: Indiana University Press, 2004), pp. 105–39.
11. S. Neale and F. Krutnik, *Popular Film and Television Comedy* (London: Routledge, 1990), pp. 133–73.
12. K. Rowe, 'Melodrama and Men in Post-Classical Romantic Comedy', in P. Kirkham and J. Thumin (eds), *Me Jane. Masculinity, Movies and Women* (London: Lawrence & Wishart, 1995), p. 186.
13. Ibid., p. 187.
14. F. Walsh, *Male Trouble: Masculinity and the Performance of Crisis* (Basingstoke: Palgrave, 2010), pp. 1–2.
15. S. Hall, 'The Rediscovery of "Ideology": Return of the Repressed in Media Studies', in T. Bennett et al. (eds), *Culture, Society and the Media* (London: Methuen, 1982), p. 60.
16. S. Hall, 'The Work of Representation', in S. Hall (ed.), *Representation: Cultural Representations and Signifying Practices* (London: Sage, 1997), p. 42.
17. T. De Lauretis, *Alice Doesn't* (Basingstoke: Macmillan, 1984).
18. M. Foucault, 'The Subject and Power', *Critical Inquiry*, 8:4, 1982, pp. 777–95.
19. In *The Seed of Man* (*Il seme dell'uomo*: 1969), the totem is the carcass of a whale, whereas in *The Future is Female* (*Il futuro è donna*: 1984) it is a gigantic Mazinga robot.
20. J. Orr, *Cinema and Modernity* (Cambridge: Polity, 1993), pp. 15–34; see also I. Christie, 'Celluloid Apocalypse', in F. Carey (ed.), *The Apocalypse* (London: British Museum Press, 1999), pp. 321–40.
21. G. Nowell-Smith, 'Minnelli and Melodrama', in M. Landy (ed.), *Imitations of Life* (Detroit: Wayne State University Press, 1991), pp. 268–74.
22. See S. Thornham (ed.), *Feminist Film Theory: A Reader* (Edinburgh: Edinburgh University Press, 1999).
23. L. Mulvey, 'Visual Pleasure and Narrative Cinema'.
24. Ibid., p. 21.
25. 'Cos'altro vuoi che faccia?'
26. A. Migliarini, *Marco Ferreri: la distruzione dell'uomo storico* (Pisa: ETS, 1984), p. 58.
27. 'Chi sei tu? Gesù bambino?'
28. J. Mitchell, *Psychoanalysis and Feminism* (London: Penguin, 1974), p. 110.
29. 'Che idea stupida quella di non chiavare. Adesso ce l'ho duro come un bastone.'
30. 'Scimmia uccisa . . . mangiata . . . dai topi.'
31. 'Guardati. Questo è ciò che tu eri.'
32. 'Non c'è nulla da capire. Bisogna solo obbedire.'
33. T. Nakahara, 'Moving Masculinity: Incest Narratives in Italian Sex Comedies', in L. Bayman and S. Rigoletto (eds), *Popular Italian Cinema* (Basingstoke: Palgrave, 2013), pp. 98–116.
34. F. Colombo (ed.), 'Gli anni delle cose. Media e società italiana negli anni settanta', *Comunicazioni sociali*, 1, 2001, p. 82.
35. F. Fellini, 'Preface to Satyricon', in P. Bondanella (ed.), *Federico Fellini: Essays in Criticism* (London: Oxford University Press, 1978), pp. 16–19.
36. Fellini considered Casanova a quintessential icon of Italian masculinity: 'He is

really Italian, The Italian: the indefiniteness, the indifference, the commonplaces, the conventional ways, the facade, the attitude': A. Tassone, 'Casanova: An Interview with Aldo Tassone', in P. Bondanella (ed.), Essays in Criticism: Federico Fellini (Oxford: Oxford University Press, 1978), p. 29.

37. G. Marrone, 'Memory in Fellini's City of Women', in P. Bondanella and C. Degli Espositi (eds), Perspectives on Fellini (Oxford: Macmillan, 1993), pp. 54–67.

38. M. Buffa, 'Grado zero della trasparenza', Film critica, 304, 1980, p. 156; R. Escobar, 'La città delle donne', Cineforum, 195, 1980, p. 385.

39. G. Bachman, 'Federico Fellini: the Cinema Seen as a Woman', Film Quarterly, 34:2, 1980–1, p. 9.

40. 'Io non scappo. Raggiungo.'

41. 'Capisco i problemi del femminismo, ma c'è bisogno di essere così arrabbiate?'

42. M. J. Lederman, 'Dreams and Visions in Fellini's City of Women', Journal of Popular Film and Television, 9:3, 1981, p. 114.

43. Ibid., p. 114.

44. 'Ancora Marcello? Prego Maestro.'

45. 'Ancora una volta siamo state tradite.'

46. 'Gli occhi di questo uomo sono gli occhi di sempre che deformano tutto nello specchio della derisione e della beffa. Il mascalzone è sempre lo stesso. Noi donne siamo solo dei pretesti per permettergli di raccontare ancora una volta il suo bestiario, il suo circo.'

47. P. Bondanella, The Cinema of Federico Fellini, pp. 291–7.

48. D. Lowenthal, The Past is a Foreign Country (Cambridge: Cambridge University Press, 1985), p. 4.

49. M. Klein, 'Mourning and its Relation to Manic-depressive States', International Journal of Psychoanalysis, 21, 1941, pp. 125–53.

50. This sequence reprises Guido's flashback to his childhood in 8½, when he is pampered after taking a bath in a tank full of wine with the other children and taken to bed.

51. P. Bondanella, The Cinema of Federico Fellini, p. 322.

52. J. Reich, Beyond the Latin Lover, p. 92.

53. P. Bondanella, The Cinema of Federico Fellini, p. 296.

54. '[Q]uanta libertà, quanta autenticità, quanto amore, quanta vita ci è stata tolta.'

55. 'Lo sai di cosa è fatta la mia giornata?'

56. 'Invecchiare con te? Per farti da infermiera . . . Scordatelo!'

57. Quoted in G. Marrone, 'Memory in Fellini's City of Women', p. 58.

58. P. Cook, Screening the Past (London: Routledge, 2005), pp. xi–xx.

3. CONTESTING NATIONAL MEMORY: MALE DILEMMAS AND OEDIPAL SCENARIOS

1. See, in particular, A. Britton, 'Bernardo Bertolucci: Thinking about the Father', Movie, 73, 1977, pp. 9–22; R. P. Kolker, Bernardo Bertolucci (New York: Oxford University Press, 1985), pp. 181–241; L. Caldwell, 'Is the Political Personal? Fathers and Sons in Bertolucci's Tragedia di un uomo ridicolo and Amelio's Colpire al cuore', in A. Cento Bullo and A. Giorgio (eds), Speaking Out and Silencing: Culture, Society and Politics in Italy in the 1970s (Leeds: Legenda, 2006), pp. 51–61.

2. Questioned as to why he decided to make films, Bernardo Bertolucci often answered very simply: 'Mio padre'.

3. In his first film, The Grim Reaper (La commare secca: 1962), Bertolucci was strongly influenced by Pasolini, who had written the script for the film and had helped him

become a film director. From *Before the Revolution* (*Prima della rivoluzione*: 1964) onwards, Godard's films became a source of inspiration for the young Bertolucci, who tried to assimilate his experimental style and radical politics into *Partner* (1968) and *Before the Revolution*. He eventually moved away from Godard's cinema towards more conventional narratives, particularly with *The Conformist*. This act of separation was marked by a symbolic parricide. *The Conformist* was, according to Bertolucci, a story about Godard and himself, which he projected on to the Oedipal bond between Professor Quadri and Marcello, the protagonist of the film. Significantly, in the film, Quadri's telephone number corresponds to the real number of Godard's Parisian flat. For a discussion of Bertolucci's conflictual relationship with his father figures, see Y. Loshitzky, *The Radical Faces of Godard and Bertolucci* (Detroit: Wayne State University Press, 1995), pp. 13–22. In a recent article, Stefano Baschiera has challenged the ideas that *The Grim Reaper* was too Pasolinian and that *Before the Revolution* should be considered Bertolucci's true first film: S. Baschiera, 'Bertolucci's *The Grim Reaper*: Rome as a New Wave city?', in R. Wrigley (ed.), *Cinematic Rome* (Leicester: Troubador, 2009), pp. 85–96.

4. Zagarrio's comment is supported by the striking appearance of a number of stories of filial rebellion against paternal figures – *Ecce Bombo* (1977), *Padre padrone* (1977) and *La fine del gioco* (1970) – and a series of films in which the oppressive father to be killed is the Church, the State or the Army – *Victory March* (*Marcia trionfale*: 1976), *In the Name of the Father* (*Nel nome del padre*: 1972), *Investigation of a Citizen Above Suspicion* (*Indagine su un cittadino al di sopra di ogni sospetto*: 1970): V. Zagarrio, 'Bertolucci: padri-padroni e padri-padrini', in L. Micciché (ed.), *Il cinema del riflusso. Film e cineasti italiani degli anni '70* (Venice: Marsilio Editori, 1997), p. 146.

5. P. Ginsborg, *A History of Contemporary Italy 1943–1980* (London: Penguin, 1990), p. 305.

6. M. Goldin, 'Bertolucci on *The Conformist*. An interview with Marilyn Goldin', *Sight & Sound*, 41:1, 1971, p. 66.

7. D. Forgacs, 'Fascism and Anti-fascism Reviewed: Generations, History and Film in Italy after 1968', in H. Peitsch, C. Burdett and C. Gorrara (eds), *European Memories of the Second World War* (Oxford: Berghahn, 1999), p. 187.

8. Ibid.

9. P. P. Pasolini, *Lettere luterane. Il progresso come falso progresso* (Turin: Einaudi, 1976), pp. 5–14.

10. V. Riva, '*Amarcord*: The Fascism with Us: An Interview with Valerio Riva', in P. Bondanella (ed.), *Federico Fellini: Essays in Criticism* (New York: Oxford University Press, 1988), p. 20.

11. Catherine O'Rawe has discussed the frequent appearance in contemporary Italian cinema of stories showing masculine conflicts in the family as metaphors for the lacerations in Italy's body politic: 'Future Perfect: The Child and Politics in Recent Italian Cinema', paper given at the conference 'Re-envisioning the Child in Italian Film', University of Exeter, July 2008.

12. A. Miceli, 'Last Tango in Paris: Death, Eroticism, and the Female Oedipus', *The Italianist*, 21/2, 2001/2, p. 126.

13. Emphasis added: D. Forgacs, 'Fascism and Anti-fascism Reviewed: Generations, History and Film in Italy after 1968', p. 187.

14. Both the father and the son are called Athos Magnani. To distinguish them, I will refer to the former as Athos Magnani and to the latter as Athos.

15. For a much more detailed analysis of De Sica's visual style in *Bicycle Thieves*, see C. Wagstaff, *Italian Neorealist Cinema* (Toronto: University of Toronto Press, 2007), pp. 291–406.

16. R. P. Kolker, *Bernardo Bertolucci*, p. 108.
17. R. Ben-Ghiat, 'Liberation: Film and the Flight from the Italian Past: 1945–1950', in R. Bosworth and P. Dogliani (eds), *Italian Fascism: History, Memory and Representation* (New York: St Martin's Press, 1999), p. 84.
18. This condoning attitude towards Italian fascism not only was typical of Neorealism, but also appeared in comedies of the post-war period, such as Luigi Comencini's *Everybody Go Home (Tutti a casa*: 1960), where the fascists are shown as naïve and thoughtless participants in a war whose meanings and consequences they often ignored.
19. This is also clear when Athos asks the owner of the hotel whether he knows Draifa, his father's mistress. The man is hesitant, like a child who has been instructed not to reveal a secret, a reaction that suggests the potentially disruptive role that this woman plays in relation to the official narrative surrounding the cult of Athos Magnani.
20. When Gaibazzi meets Athos on his way back from Beccaccia's estate, he introduces himself as his father's friend; he then reproaches him for not recognising him. The story strongly suggests that Athos could not have met him before because this is the first time he visits Tara. Hence, by asking him why he does not recognise him, Gaibazzi blurs the identities of son and father.
21. L. Caldwell, 'Relations between Men: Bernardo Bertolucci's *The Spider's Stratagem*', in P. Kirkham and J. Thumin (eds), *Me Jane. Masculinity, Movies and Women* (London: Lawrence & Wishart, 1995), p. 59.
22. R. P. Kolker, *Bernardo Bertolucci*, p. 124. On a similar note, Penelope Houston points out that in *Spider's Stratagem* the son can only emerge into the father, forever stuck in this symbolic point of origin from which his own present descends: P. Houston, 'The Spider's Stratagem', *Sight & Sound*, 46:1, 1976, p. 56.
23. This interpretation is informed by the logic of inevitability pervading the Oedipus myth. Here, Laius is punished for his attempt to outwit the gods and defy the prophecy of the Delphic oracle, according to which his future child will commit parricide and marry his mother. The myth reveals the inevitability of the gods' logic by which the sin of the father is eventually visited upon his sons and grandchildren. Oedipus is cursed and so is his progeny.
24. 'Un traditore!?!?'
25. This material was added to the film after its first showing on Italian TV. Bertolucci felt that the flashbacks would help his audience to understand the story better.
26. 'C'è una frase che ... Un uomo è fatto di tutti gli uomini. Li vale tutti e tutti valgono lui.'
27. A. Moravia, *Il conformista* (Milan: Bompiani, 2002), p. 28.
28. F. Casetti, *Bertolucci* (Florence: La Nuova Italia, 1976), p. 5.
29. On its release, this scene had originally been removed. I thank Danielle Hipkins for directing my attention to it during a private conversation.
30. 'Belle parole. Lei se ne è andato ed io sono diventato un fascista.'
31. B. Anderson, *Imagined Communities: Reflections on the Origin and Spread of Nationalism* (London: Verso, 2006).
32. J. Butler, *Gender Trouble* (London: Routledge, 1990); J. Butler, *Bodies that Matter* (London: Routledge, 1993).
33. J. Butler, *Gender Trouble*, pp. 141–8.
34. A. Dalle Vacche, *The Body in the Mirror* (Princeton: Princeton University Press, 1992), pp. 57–92.
35. D. Ranvaud and E. Ungari (eds), *Bertolucci by Bertolucci* (London: Plexus, 1982), p. 72.
36. C. Wagstaff, 'Forty-seven Shots of Bertolucci's *Il conformista*', *The Italianist*, 2, 1982, p. 81.

37. Ibid.
38. Moravia, *Il conformista*, p. 31.
39. Ibid., p. 90.
40. Dalle Vacche, *The Body in the Mirror*, p. 70.
41. J. Kline, *Bertolucci's Dream Loom* (Amherst: University of Massachusetts Press, 1987), p. 123.
42. L. Mulvey, *Visual and Other Pleasures* (Basingstoke: Macmillan, 1989), pp. 174–5.

4. UNDOING GENRE, UNDOING MASCULINITY

1. W. Reich, *The Mass Psychology of Fascism* (Harmondsworth: Penguin, 1975).
2. 'Sei come un bambino.'
3. Significantly, *Investigation* was released in the same year as Dario Fo's play, *Morte accidentale di un anarchico*, in the aftermath of the police killing of the anarchist Giuseppe Pinelli. Pinelli had been arrested and held by the police as a scapegoat for the far-right terrorist bombing of Piazza Fontana in Milan in 1969. The play revolves around the absurd official account of Pinelli's death given by the police. According to this official version, Pinelli, who fell from the fourth-floor window of a police station during the interrogation, had committed suicide in despair at having been found out for his crime. It soon became clear, however, that Pinelli's death had been a case of outright murder committed by the interrogators. Dario Fo's play was a sharp satire not only on the authoritarianism of the police in relation to this murder, but also, more generally, on the corruption of State institutions. In the same year as *Investigation*, Elio Petri also directed, together with Nello Risi, a documentary entitled *Ipotesi su Giuseppe Pinelli* (1970), which satirised the police and the three different versions that were given of the circumstances of Pinelli's 'suicide'.
4. See, for example, Petri's interview with Joan Mellen: J. Mellen, '"Cinema is not for the Elite but for the Masses". An Interview with Elio Petri', *Cineaste*, 7:1, 1973, p. 10.
5. For the box-office data, see the appendices in F. Colombo (ed.), 'Gli anni delle cose. Media e società italiana negli anni settanta', *Comunicazioni sociali*, 1, 2001, p. 81.
6. P. Bondanella, *Italian Cinema: From Neorealism to the Present* (New York: Continuum, 1990), p. 336.
7. M. Marcus, *Italian Film in the Light of Neorealism* (Princeton: Princeton University Press, 1986), p. 266.
8. Krutnik's study concentrates mainly on the Hollywood *film noir* of the 1940s but is nevertheless relevant for a wider conceptualisation of the crime genre. F. Krutnik, *In a Lonely Street. Film Noir, Genre, Masculinity* (London: Routledge, 1991), pp. 86–8. See also P. Gates, *Detecting Men: Masculinity and the Hollywood Detective Film* (New York: State University of New York Press, 2006).
9. See, for example, C. Brundson, 'A Subject for the Seventies', *Screen*, 23:3/4, 1982; B. Creed, 'The Position of Women in Hollywood Melodramas', *Australian Journal of Screen Theory*, 4, 1977, pp. 67–88; M. Haskell, *From Reverence to Rape* (London: Penguin, 1979); E. A. Kaplan (ed.), *Women in Film Noir* (London: BFI, 1998); L. Williams, 'When the Woman Looks', in M. A. Doane et al. (eds), *Revision: Essays in Feminist Film Criticism* (Los Angeles: American Film Institute, 1984), pp. 83–99; S. Neale, *Genre* (London: BFI, 1980).
10. M. Günsberg, *Italian Cinema: Genre and Gender* (Basingstoke: Palgrave, 2005), pp. 1–18.
11. The films under focus in this chapter may be said to belong to one of the categories of political cinema described by Jean-Louis Comolli and Jean Narboni in their

famous essay, 'Cinema/Ideology/Criticism' in *Cahiers du cinéma*. Comolli and Narboni refer to films that 'seem at first sight to belong firmly within the ideology and to be completely under its sway, but which turn out to be so only in an ambiguous manner. For though they start from a non-progressive standpoint, ranging from the frankly reactionary through the conciliatory to the mildly critical, they have been worked upon, and work, in such a real way that there is a noticeable gap, a dislocation, between the starting point and the finished product' (J. Comolli and J. Narboni, 'Cinema/Ideology/Criticism', in J. Hillier (ed.), *Cahiers du Cinéma 1969–1972: The Politics of Representation* (London: BFI, 1986), p. 62).

12. K. Rowe, 'Melodrama and Men in Post-Classical Romantic Comedy', in P. Kirkham and J. Thumin (eds), *Me Jane. Masculinity, Movies and Women* (London: Lawrence & Wishart, 1995), p. 185.

13. H. Bergson, *Laughter. An Essay on the Meaning of the Comic* (London: Macmillan, 1911), p. 3.

14. P. McIsaac and G. Blumenfeld, '"You Cannot Make the Revolution on Film." An Interview with Lina Wertmüller', *Cineaste*, 7:2, 1974, p. 7.

15. L. Micciché, *Cinema italiano degli anni '70* (Venice: Marsilio, 1980), p. 212.

16. T. Gunning, 'Mechanism of Laughter: Devices of Slapstick', in T. Paulus and R. King (eds), *Slapstick Comedy* (New York: Routledge, 2010), p. 139.

17. K. Rowe, *The Unruly Woman: Gender and the Genres of Laughter* (Austin: University of Texas Press, 1995).

18. C. Uva and M. Picchi, *Destra e sinistra nel cinema italiano* (Rome: Edizioni Interculturali, 2006), p. 169.

19. Quoted in E. Ferlita and J. R. May, *The Parables of Lina Wertmüller* (Toronto: Paulinist Press, 1977), p. 26.

20. J. Mellen, 'On Lina Wertmüller', in A. A. Berger (ed.), *Film in Society* (New Brunswick, NJ: Transaction, 1980), p. 99.

21. R. W. Connell, *Masculinities* (Cambridge: Polity, 1995), p. 71.

22. M. Russo, 'Female Grotesques: Carnival and Theory', in T. De Lauretis (ed.), *Feminist Studies. Critical Studies* (Bloomington: Indiana University Press, 1986), p. 219.

23. M. A. Doane, 'Film and the Masquerade: Theorising the Female Spectator', *Screen*, 23:3–4, 1982, pp. 74–88.

24. S. Neale and F. Krutnik, *Popular Film and Television Comedy* (London: Routledge, 1990), pp. 149–55.

25. V. Russo, *The Celluloid Closet* (Cambridge, MA: Harper & Row, 1985).

26. O. Klapp, *Heroes, Villains and Fools* (Englewood Cliffs: Prentice-Hall, 1962).

27. V. Patanè, 'Breve storia del cinema omosessuale', afterword to V. Russo, *Lo schermo velato. L'omosessualità nel cinema* (Milan: Baldini Castaldi, 1991), p. 454.

28. 'Scusi, lei è normale?'

29. '[U]n film civile, onesto, efficace nel prendere di petto il tema dell'omosessualità': M. Morandini, 'Pozzetto operaio nei pasticci', *Il giorno*, 31 October 1979, p. 10.

30. Examples of negative reviews are: A. Farassino, 'Tanto diverso da essere normale', *La repubblica*, 2 November 1979, p. 10; P. Tarallo, 'La patata bollente', *Lambda*, 10, 1979, p. 1.

31. Private recording from Italian TV channel La7. The interview with Vanzina was broadcast during the programme 'I ricordi del cuore' in 2007. The exact date of this broadcast is unknown.

32. In the 1960s, Pasolini had already noted the hypocrisy of the Italian Left in this respect: 'Il problema sessuale non è evidentemente un problema morale: ma, poiché

la piccola borghesia cattolica è abituata, ipocritamente, a considerarlo tale, tale lo considera anche il dirigente medio comunista, come, direi, per inerzia. Infatti, la questione non è mai stata impostata a chiare lettere: dato che si tratta di una questione secondaria. Ci sono questioni più importanti da risolvere . . .' (Quoted in F. Giovannini, *Comunisti e Diversi. Il PCI e la questione omosessuale* (Bari: Dedalo, 1980), pp. 5–6).

33. Ibid., p. 7.
34. In presenting the triangle on which the film was based, one poster advertising *La patata bollente* ironically alludes to the homosexual character as *'l'altro con il vizietto'* ('the other one with the bad habit'). *Il vizietto* was the Italian title of *La Cage aux folles*. See also L. P., 'La patata bollente', *L'Unità*, 6 November 1979, p. 23; M. Morandini, 'Pozzetto operaio nei pasticci', *Il Giorno*, 31 October 1979, p. 13; A. Farassino, 'Tanto diverso da essere normale', *La Repubblica*, 2 November 1979, p. 10; P. Tarallo, 'La patata bollente', *Lambda*, 10, 1979, p. 10; 'La patata bollente', *Variety*, 20 February 1980, p. 23.
35. Claudio's invisibility is also functional for the comic purpose of the story. It is initially linked to a total withdrawal of knowledge. When Claudio first calls his boyfriend, this knowledge comes to be partially revealed, so that there is a discrepancy between what the audience now know and Gandhi's ignorance. This discrepancy serves to render Gandhi's gaffes laughable as he makes repeated offensive references to homosexuals, unaware that Claudio is one of them. Here, the laughter stems from the fact that we know something new about Claudio whereas he does not.
36. F. Krutnik, 'A Spanner in the Works? Genre, Narrative and the Hollywood Comedian', in K. Karnick and H. Jenkin (eds), *Classical Hollywood Comedy* (London: Routledge, 1995), p. 29.
37. The character of Gabriele was built upon the real fugure of the EIAR radio announcer, Nunzio Filogamo (see also note 47).
38. Interview with Ettore Scola: *Una giornata particolare* (DVD, 2002, extras).
39. Ibid. Pasolini was expelled from the Communist Party in 1949 after being reported to the police for having engaged in sexual activity with three young boys in Friuli.
40. Interview with Ettore Scola: *Una giornata particolare* (DVD, 2002, extras).
41. Before *Una giornata particolare*, Loren and Mastroianni had also played together in *Too Bad She's Bad* (*Peccato che sia una canaglia*: 1955), *Sunflower* (*I girasoli*: 1970), *The Priest's Wife* (*La moglie del prete*: 1970) and *Sex Pot* (*La pupa del gangster*: 1975).
42. T. Kezich and A. Levantesi (eds), *Una giornata particolare. Incontrarsi e dirsi addio nella Roma del '38* (Turin: Lindao, 2003), p. 150.
43. J. Reich, *Beyond the Latin Lover* (Bloomington: Indiana University Press, 2004), p. 134.
44. Anon., '*Una giornata particolare*', *Cineforum*, 169, Nov. 1977, p. 705.
45. D. Bordwell, 'Classical Hollywood Cinema: Narrational Principles and Procedures', in P. Rosen (ed.), *Narrative, Apparatus, Ideology* (New York: Columbia University Press, 1986), p. 19.
46. For detailed studies of the cult of virility during the fascist regime, see G. Mosse, *The Image of Man* (Oxford: Oxford University Press, 1996), pp. 155–80; B. Spackman, *Fascist Virilities* (London: University of Minnesota Press, 1996).
47. EIAR is the acronym for Ente Italiano Audizioni Radiofoniche, the State radio station founded in 1927, whose name was eventually changed to Radiotelevisione Italiana (RAI) after the fall of fascism; 'non era come prescrive il regolamento EIAR: solenne, marziale e vibrante di romano orgoglio'.
48. K. Glitre, *Hollywood Romantic Comedy* (Manchester: Manchester University

Press, 2006), p. 15.

49. See K. Glitre, *Hollywood Romantic Comedy*.
50. For an account of the politics of alliance between gay militants and feminists in the 1970s, see M. Cristallo, *Uscir fuori* (Milan: Teti, 1989) and G. Rossi Barilli, *Il movimento gay in Italia* (Milan: Feltrinelli, 1999).
51. V. Russo, *The Celluloid Closet* (London: Harper & Row, 1987).

5. PIER PAOLO PASOLINI'S EROTIC IMAGERY AND THE SIGNIFICANCE OF THE MALE BODY

1. J. D. Rhodes, 'Watchable Bodies: Salò's Young Non-actors', *Screen*, 53:4, 2012, p. 453.
2. Ibid., p. 455.
3. Ibid.
4. Ibid., p. 458.
5. 'First of all you are, and must be, very pretty. Not perhaps in the conventional sense. In build you can be very small and indeed even a little skinny; your features already show the marks which with the years will inevitably turn your face into a mask. But your eyes must be black and shining; your mouth a little wide; your face fairly regular; your hair must be short at the neck and behind the ears; whereas on your brow I have no difficulty in granting you a fine quiff, high, warlike and perhaps a little exaggerated and ridiculous. I would not mind if you were a bit of a sportsman and solid in legs' (P. P. Pasolini, *Lutheran Letters*, trans. S. Hood (New York: Carcanet, 1987), p. 18).
6. J. D. Rhodes, 'Watchable Bodies: Salò's Young Non-actors', p. 458.
7. Borrowing from Jonathan Dollimore's work on perversion, I understand 'perverse reading' to be a kind of reading that aims to retrieve something that has been repressed or expunged from the standard interpretative framework of a text: J. Dollimore, 'The Cultural Politics of Perversion: Augustine, Shakespeare, Freud, Foucault', *Textual Practice*, 4:2, 1990, pp. 179–96.
8. J. Boone, 'Rubbing Aladdin's Lamp', in M. Dorenkamp and R. Henke (eds), *Negotiating Gay and Lesbian Subjects* (London: Routledge, 1995), p. 155.
9. J. D. Rhodes, 'Watchable Bodies: Salò's Young Non-actors', p. 458.
10. B. George, 'Sacred Scandal. The Cinema of Pasolini', *Metro*, 95, 1993, p. 96.
11. R. Gordon, *Pasolini. Forms of Subjectivity* (Oxford: Clarendon Press, 1996), p. 255.
12. Ibid., p. 196.
13. See, for example, J. Boone, 'Rubbing Aladdin's Lamp'.
14. This is not to say that a female spectatorial position is persistently denied or rendered implausible in Pasolini's films. Yet, it seems to me that, to be plausible, such a position would often need to rely on a fantasy of homoerotic masculinisation.
15. R. Gordon, *Pasolini. Forms of Subjectivity*, p. 208.
16. G. Nowell-Smith, 'Pasolini's Originality', in P. Willemen (ed.), *Pier Paolo Pasolini* (London: BFI, 1977), p. 18.
17. L. Mulvey, 'Visual Pleasure and Narrative Cinema, *Screen*, 16:3, 1975, p. 9.
18. Ibid., p. 6.
19. P. Rumble, *Allegories of Contamination: Pier Paolo Pasolini's Trilogy of Life* (Toronto: University of Toronto Press, 1996), p. 139.
20. '[E]ra la prima volta che un nudo maschile integrale, quello del protagonista Terence Stamp, appariva sullo schermo': E. Siciliano, *Vita di Pasolini* (Milan: Rizzi Editore, 1978), p. 414.
21. 'Non c'è limite alla libertà di espressione e di rappresentazione. Non ci può essere limite. [. . .] Al fondo della mia rappresentazione [. . .] c'è l'esigenza della totale

rappresentabilità del reale, intesa come conquista civile': P. P. Pasolini, 'Libertà e sesso secondo Pasolini', *Il corriere della sera*, 4 February 1973, p. 3.

22. P. P. Pasolini, *Heretical Empiricism*, trans. B. Lawtan and L. K. Barnett (Washington, DC: New Academia Publishing, 2005).

23. N. Greene, *Pier Paolo Pasolini: Cinema as Heresy* (Princeton: Princeton University Press, 1990), p. 101.

24. C. Corradi, 'Pier Paolo Pasolini presenta *Il fiore delle mille e una notte*', *TV Sorrisi e Canzoni*, 20 January 1974, pp. 58–60.

25. 'Anche il sesso nella sua estrema e indifesa nudità – che è parte immensa della vita reale – ha diritto di essere espresso e di essere rappresentato': P. P. Pasolini, 'Libertà e sesso secondo Pasolini', *Il corriere della sera*, 4 February 1973, p. 3.

26. P. P. Pasolini, *Heretical Empiricism*.

27. Extract from an interview on BBC Television (audiovisual material from the Archivio Pasolini at Cineteca di Bologna; date of recording unknown).

28. M. Marcus, *Italian Film in the Light of Neorealism*, p. 251; Robert Gordon's commentary in the DVD extras of the recent BFI release of *Teorema* (2007).

29. L. Williams, *Screening Sex* (Durham, NC: Duke University Press, 2008), p. 3.

30. S. Neale, 'Masculinity as Spectacle', in *Screen* (eds), *The Sexual Subject* (London: Routledge, 1992), p. 285.

31. For a brief discussion of the theorematic structure of the film, see A. Restivo, *The Cinema of Economic Miracles: Visuality and Modernization in the Italian Art Film* (Durham, NC: Duke University Press, 2002), p. 86.

32. L. Mulvey, 'Visual Pleasure and Narrative Cinema', p. 8.

33. The hyperbolic visibility of the desiring gaze has been extensively discussed by Steve Shaviro in his study of *Querelle* (1982): S. Shaviro, *The Cinematic Body* (Minneapolis: University of Minnesota Press, 1993), pp. 159–200.

34. A. Restivo, *The Cinema of Economic Miracles*, p. 87.

35. For a discussion of direct address in the cinema, see T. Brown, *Breaking the Fourth Wall* (Edinburgh: Edinburgh University Press, 2012).

36. P. Willemen, *Looks and Frictions. Essays in Cultural Studies and Film Theory* (London: BFI, 1994), p. 107.

37. R. Gordon, *Pasolini. Forms of Subjectivity*, p. 258.

38. P. P. Pasolini, 'Libertà e sesso secondo Pasolini', p. 3.

39. P. P. Pasolini, 'Il sesso come metafora del potere', *Il corriere della sera*, 25 March 1975, p. 15.

40. P. P. Pasolini, *Il caos* (Milan: Mondadori, 1988), p. 76.

41. P. G. Marino, *Pier Paolo Pasolini, La trilogia della vita: analisi di un momento gaio*, Tesi di Laurea, 1991/2, Facoltà di Lettere e Filosofia, Università La Sapienza, Rome, p. 153.

42. '[P]rotagonista dei miei film è la corporalità popolare': P. P. Pasolini, 'Tetis', in V. Boarini (ed.), *Erotismo Eversione Merce* (Bologna: Cappelli, 1973), p. 10.

43. D. Maraini, 'Ma la donna non è una slot machine. Colloquio con Pier Paolo Pasolini', *L'espresso*, 22 October 1972, p. 50; P. Pasolini, 'La vera pornografia la fa la TV italiana', *La notte*, 4 May 1973, p. 13.

44. G. Michele, *La commedia erotica italiana* (Rome: Gremese, 2000).

45. N. Greene, *Pier Paolo Pasolini: Cinema as Heresy*, p. 81.

46. Ibid., p. 183.

47. [L]'ideologia c'era, eccome, ed era proprio lì, nel cazzo enorme sullo schermo, sopra le loro teste che non volevano capire': P. P. Pasolini, 'Tetis', p. 101.

48. J. R. MacBeane, 'Between Kitsch and Fascism. Notes on Fassbinder, Pasolini, (Homo)sexual Politics, the Exotic, the Erotic & Other Consuming Passions', *Cineaste*, 13:4, 1984, p. 14.

49. J. Boone, 'Rubbing Aladdin's Lamp', p. 164.
50. T. Yingling, 'How the Eye is Caste: Robert Mapplethorpe and the Limits of Controversy', *Discourse*, 12:2, 1990, p. 8.
51. P. J. Smith, *Desire Unlimited. The Cinema of Pedro Almodóvar* (London: Verso, 2000), p. 26.
52. For a discussion of the in/visibility of the penis in the media, see P. Lehman, 'Crying over the Melodramatic Penis: Melodrama and Male Nudity in Films of the '90s', in P. Lehman (ed.), *Masculinity. Bodies, Movies, Culture* (New York: Routledge, 2001), pp. 25–41; P. Lehman, *Running Scared* (Detroit: Wayne State University Press, 2007).
53. L. Williams, *Screening Sex*, p. 2.
54. For a discussion of the conditions regulating this invisibility in the media, see P. Lehman, 'Crying over the Melodramatic Penis', pp. 25–41.
55. J. Lacan, *Ecrits: A Selection*, trans. B. Fink (New York: Routledge, 2011), pp. 215–22.
56. J. Butler, *Bodies that Matter* (London: Routledge, 1993), p. 84.
57. Ibid.
58. One could mention Richard Dyer's famous comments on the striking discrepancy between phallic symbols and what penises actually are. Despite the connotations of turgidity and erectness persistently invoked by phallic symbols, Dyer notes that '[m]ale genitals are fragile, squashy, delicate things; even when erect, the penis is spongy, seldom straight, and rounded at the tip': R. Dyer, *The Matter of Images* (New York: London, 1993), p. 90.
59. K. MacKinnon, 'After Mulvey: Male Erotic Objectification', in M. Aaron (ed.), *The Body's Perilous Pleasures* (Edinburgh: Edinburgh University Press, 1999), pp. 13–29; R. Dyer, 'Don't Look Now: The Male Pin Up', in *Screen* (eds), *The Sexual Subject. A Screen Reader in Sexuality* (London: Routledge, 1992), pp. 61–72.
60. K. MacKinnon, 'After Mulvey: Male Erotic Objectification', p. 19.
61. R. Gordon, *Pasolini: Forms of Subjectivity*, p. 191.
62. Ibid., p. 194.
63. P. Pasolini, *Heretical Empiricism*, pp. 167–86.
64. J. Lacan, *Ecrits: A Selection*, pp. 1–7.

6. MALE SUBJECTIVITY AND THE LEGACY OF 1968: NANNI MORETTI'S
ECCE BOMBO

1. L. Bersani and U. Dutoit, *Forms of Being: Cinema, Aesthetics, Subjectivity* (London: BFI, 2004), p. 8.
2. A. Astruc, 'The Birth of a New Avant-Garde: La Caméra-Stylo', in P. Graham and G. Vincendeau (eds), *The French New Wave: Critical Landmarks* (London: BFI, 2009), pp. 31–6.
3. Ibid., p. 34.
4. Ibid.
5. S. De Beauvoir, *The Second Sex*, trans. H. M. Parshley (Harmondsworth: Penguin, 1983), p. 15.
6. Through the entire chapter, the terms '1968' and 'post-1968 social movements' will be used interchangeably to refer to the whole decade of social mobilisation.
7. Quoted in R. Lumely, *States of Emergency* (London: Verso, 1990), p. 2.
8. L. Passerini, *Autobiography of a Generation*, trans. L. Erdberg (London: Wesleyan University Press, 1996).
9. P. Ginsborg, *A History of Contemporary Italy: Society and Politics 1943–1988* (London: Penguin, 1990), p. 306.

10. S. Voli, *Quando il privato diventa politico* (Rome: Edizioni Associate, 2006).
11. '[I]l destino del sessantotto [. . .] è quello di dissolversi dopo aver ridotto uomini e donne a interpreti nella rappresentazione di un copione già scritto: quello in cui tutto è lotta di classe': G. Viale, *Sessantotto. Tra rivoluzione e restaurazione* (Milan: Mazzotta, 1978), p. 14.
12. C. Lonzi, 'Let's Spit on Hegel', in P. Bono and S. Kemp (eds), *Italian Feminist Thought. A Reader* (Oxford: Basil Blackwell, 1991), pp. 40–59.
13. W. Hope, 'Introduction', in W. Hope (ed.), *Italian Cinema: New Directions* (London: Lang, 2005), p. 11. For a discussion of Moretti's use of autobiography and the subjective point of view in *Ecce Bombo*, see also E. Mazierska and L. Rascaroli, *The Cinema of Nanni Moretti* (London: Wallflower Press, 2004), pp. 14–45.
14. Another important catalyst of the generational anxieties explored by the film is Olga; yet, in terms of the story-line, she has only a marginal role and appears in the film rather rarely, compared to Michele.
15. M. Marcus, *After Fellini* (London: Johns Hopkins University Press, 2002), p. 286.
16. Interview with Moretti in M. Giovannini, E. Magrelli and M. Sesti, *Nanni Moretti* (Naples: Edizioni Scientifiche Italiane, 1986), p. 32.
17. During these years, the feminist movement was heavily involved in campaigns and protests that eventually led to the reform of family law (1975) and to the legalisation of divorce (1970) – upheld by popular referendum in 1974 – and of abortion (1978).
18. C. Lonzi, *Sputiamo su Hegel: la donna clitoridea e la donna vaginale* (Milan: Gammalibri, 1982), pp. 76–124.
19. S. Heath, 'Male feminism', in A. Jardine and P. Smith (eds), *Men in Feminism* (New York: Routledge, 1987), p. 1.
20. R. Braidotti, 'Envy: or With My Brains and Your Look', in A. Jardine and P. Smith (eds), *Men in Feminism*, p. 235.
21. S. L. Kitch, 'Feminist Literary Criticism and Irony', *Rocky Mountain Review of Language and Literature*, 41:1/2, 1987, p. 8.
22. W. Booth, *The Rhetoric of Irony* (Chicago: University of Chicago Press, 1974), p. 5.
23. D. Halperin, 'Love's Irony: Six Remarks on Platonic Eros', in S. Bartsch and T. Bartscherer (eds), *Erotikon* (Chicago: University of Chicago Press, 2005), p. 48.
24. 'Quando si fa dell'autobiografia, una condizione necessaria per non sconfinare in una noiosa melo-filodrammatica, è appunto quella di essere ironici, anzi, trattandosi di autobiografia, autoironici': Anon., 'Nanni Moretti. Ironizzare su se stessi', *Cinesessanta*, 126, 1979, p. 37.
25. E. Mazierska and L. Rascaroli, *The Cinema of Nanni Moretti*, p. 93.
26. I am referring in particular to a tendency to use a number of Brechtian devices aimed at drawing the viewer's attention to the film's structure.
27. G. Bonsaver, 'The Egocentric Cassandra of the Left: Representations of Politics in the Films of Nanni Moretti', *The Italianist*, 21/2, 2001/2, pp. 174–5.
28. Arguably, one of the main limits in this identification of cinema as an apparatus serving the perpetuation of the dominant order is the failure to see cinema as part of a larger continuum, at times in contradictory relation with the dominant ideology. Too much emphasis on theory and the totalising condemnation of the cinematic medium often did not allow any recognition of the potential to resist the dominant apparatus of mainstream cinema from within.
29. G. Aristarco, 'Relazione di "Cinema Nuovo" presentata da Guido Aristarco', in V. Camerino (ed.), *Il cinema e il '68: le sfide dell'immaginario* (Modena: Barbieri, 1998), pp. 165–79.

30. C. Tiso, 'Cinema poetico/politico o la politicità del film', in F. Rosati (ed.), '1968–1972. Esperienze di cinema militante', *Bianco Nero*, 7/8, 1973, p. 181.
31. 'Un elemento da recuperare [è] l'ironia [che nasce] dalla necessità di porre un argine alla marea delle cose che quotidianamente ci assale, per non farcene travolgere ma per dominarla, trasformarla in energia al nostro servizio. Significa voler essere tanto dentro alla cosa da uscirne al di fuori per possederla nella sua totalità. [. . .] Ironia come passione che si libera nel distacco, negazione del frammento. Un atteggiamento lontano sia dal furore barricadero che dallo sfogo autobiografico': P. and V. Taviani, 'Costruzione della ragione e invito all'ironia', *Cinema Nuovo*, 161:1, 1963, p. 27.
32. 'Io ero in prima fila. [. . .] Avevo deciso di fare unicamente del cinema di propaganda, al servizio del popolo, e quindi del partito': quoted in M. Ghirelli, *'68 venti anni dopo* (Rome: Editori Riuniti, 1988), pp. 24–5.
33. *Ecce Bombo* is a long way from Bellocchio's political films of the same period. However, in its satire on the self-absorption and self-importance of youth, and in its resort to autobiography as a way of getting into filmmaking in the first place, it has many affinities with Bellocchio's *Fists in the Pockets* (*I pugni in tasca*: 1965).
34. R. Lumley, *States of Emergency* (London: Verso, 1990), p. 298.
35. S. Segre, *L'antimaschio*, p. 9.
36. E. Mazierska and L. Rascaroli, *The Cinema of Nanni Moretti*, p. 25.
37. R. Lumley, *States of Emergency*, p. 297.
38. 'Andateci a parlare.'
39. R. W. Connell, *Masculinities* (Cambridge: Polity, 2005), pp. 196–8.
40. '[F]a molto Fellini, vero?'
41. See, for example, R. Escobar, '"Ecce Bombo" di Nanni Moretti: una via d'uscita dalla crisi', *Cineforum*, 18:7/8, 1978, pp. 430–6.
42. Indeed, both films savagely satirise the solipsism of their protagonists. In *I vitelloni*, Fellini offers a very conservative alternative to the shallowness of his characters, which is epitomised by the work ethic of Fausto's father and the shopkeeper.
43. '[H]o paura, non ci riesco a stare con le persone che stanno male.'
44. T. De Lauretis, *Alice Doesn't* (Basingstoke: Macmillan, 1984), p. 9.

INDEX